THE COMPLETE
BARBECUE
COOKBOOK

family circle®

THE COMPLETE
BARBECUE
COOKBOOK

MURDOCH
BOOKS

Tuna with Caponata, page 135

Pesto, page 211

Salmon and Prawn Kebabs, page 16

Contents

Yakitori Chicken, page 25

You will find the following cookery ratings on the recipes in this book:

A single pot symbol indicates a recipe that is simple and generally straightforward to make—perfect for beginners.

Two symbols indicate the need for just a little more care and a little more time.

Three symbols indicate special recipes that need more investment in time, care and patience—but the results are worth it.

Tomato and Bocconcini Salad, page 169

Tandoori Chicken, page 88

Strawberries with Balsamic Vinegar, page 231

Calamari Rings with Salsa Verde, page 137

Barbecue Basics

Some barbecues can be as formal as a dinner party, others as relaxed as a picnic on the beach. Whatever the case, you will need to be prepared—choose the barbecue that suits you best, light the perfect fire and prepare the food to its maximum advantage.

CHOOSING THE BARBECUE

There is a huge range of barbecues on the market these days; each has its own advantages and your decision will depend on how much room you have available, how many you are cooking for and what style of cooking you prefer.

FUEL-BURNING BARBECUES

Brazier This is the simplest style of fuel-burning barbecue, of which the small, cast-iron hibachi is probably the best known. A brazier consists of a shallow fire-box for burning fuel with a grill on top. Some grills are height-adjustable or can rotate. Braziers are best fitted with a heat-reflecting hood, so that the food is cooked at an even temperature.

Covered kettle barbecue (weber) One of the most popular styles of portable barbecue, the kettle barbecue features a close-fitting lid and air vents at top and bottom which allow for greater versatility and accuracy in cooking. Covered barbecues can function as traditional barbecues, ovens or smokers. Kettle barbecues only burn charcoal or heat beads (wood is not recommended) and are relatively small. The standard diameter is 57 cm so, if barbecuing for large groups, you may need more than one.

Fixed barbecue Many gardens contain some sort of fixture for barbecuing. These are relatively simple constructions, usually made from bricks or cement and featuring two grills—the bottom for building the fire, the top for cooking the food. These grills are not generally height-adjustable, so cooking can only be regulated by adjusting the fire, or moving the food away from or towards the fire. Being fixed, these barbecues cannot, of course, be put out of high winds or moved to shelter in the event of rain. Despite this, fixed barbecues are easy to use and maintain and are best if you intend to cook for large numbers.

GAS OR ELECTRIC BARBECUES

Although often more expensive, these barbecues are very simple to use. They do not require an open flame, only connection to their heat source. In most cases, the gas or electricity heats a tray of reusable volcanic rock. Hickory chips can be placed over the

rock-bed to give a smoky flavour to the food. Sizes vary, the largest being the trolley-style, which usually features a workbench, reflecting hood and bottom shelf for storage. While small portable gas models, which require only the connection of a gas bottle, are easily manoeuvrable, electric models are confined to areas with mains electricity. Make sure you turn the gas off at the bottle when you have finished cooking to avoid any possibility of a gas leak. Most gas or electric barbecues have temperature controls and accuracy is their primary advantage. Electric models can be fitted with rotisseries or spit turners.

THE FIRE

Fuel Although traditional, wood is not an ideal fuel for cooking. It can be difficult to light and burns with a flame. Charcoal or heat beads are preferable. They will create a bed of glowing heat which is perfect for cooking. They are readily available in supermarkets or hardware shops and are sometimes known as barbecue briquettes (these should not be confused with heating briquettes,

which are not suitable for cooking). Charcoal is wood that has already been burnt down and is the most efficient fuel for barbecuing.

Heat beads don't smell, smoke or flare, but they are difficult to ignite, making firelighters essential. Firelighters have been soaked in kerosene and ignite instantly, but they give off kerosene fumes and food should never be cooked on a barbecue while they are still burning. A couple of firelighters are usually sufficient to light about 20 pieces of charcoal or heat beads. Charcoal and heat beads turn white and have an ash-like coating when ready to use. They burn down to a fine powder, so put a tray underneath for the ash.

A 'normal' fire consists of about 50–60 heat beads or pieces of charcoal and will last for several hours. All recipes in this book can be cooked over a normal fire. The temperature of a fire can always be lowered by damping it with a fine spray of water (a trigger-style plastic spray bottle is ideal). Damping produces steam that will keep the food moist. Do remember that steam burns, so keep your hands well away. Do not damp

down a gas barbecue unless it has a metal shield covering the burners.

The best and safest way to increase the heat of a fire is to add more fuel and wait for the fire to develop. Do not fan a fire to increase its heat; this will only produce a flame. Never pour flammable liquids onto a fire.

Smoking Smoking chips or chunks come from hickory wood, mesquite, dried mallee root, red-gum or acacia trees and are available from barbecue specialists and hardware stores. Their smoke provides an extra and unusual flavour to the cooked food. (Some woods, such as pine, cedar or eucalyptus produce acrid smoke and are unsuitable for cooking. Use only wood sold specifically for smoking.)

Smoking is best done on a covered barbecue (see below) but can also be done on an open fire. Scatter smoking wood throughout the coals. Once the wood is burning, damp down with a little water to create more smoke. Smoking wood is available in chips and chunks; chips burn quickly so should be added towards the end of the cooking process. Chunks should last through the cooking process.

INDIRECT COOKING

Indirect cooking on a covered kettle barbecue (weber) roasts or bakes food more slowly than direct cooking. Fragrant wood chips can be added to the coals to give the food flavour.

To prepare for indirect cooking:
1 Remove the lid. Open bottom vent.
2 Put the bottom grill inside the bowl and attach charcoal rails. Heap coals in rails. Put firelighters inside coals.
3 Light fire, leaving lid off. When coals reach fine-ash stage, put a drip-tray or baking dish on bottom grill. Position top grill; add food.

To prepare for smoking:
1 Prepare the barbecue as above.
2 When the coals reach fine-ash stage, add wood chips, fill a drip tray with 1 litre hot water and cover with a lid until fragrant smoke develops.
3 Centre food on top grill and cover.

Heap coals in the charcoal rails and then position two or three firelighters within the coals.

Place a drip tray underneath the top grill when the coals are ready.

Light the fire and leave the lid off to allow the coals to reach fine-ash stage.

For smoking, spoon a generous quantity of smoking wood over the hot coals.

PLANNING YOUR BARBECUE

If you are planning a large get-together with the barbecue as your means of cookery, it is a good idea to design the whole menu to take full advantage of the barbecue—vegetables, kebabs, breads, even desserts can be cooked or, at least, warmed through easily.

Serve at least one salad or vegetable with the cooked food. Most salad dressings and special sauces can be made in advance and stored in a screw-top jar in the fridge.

Light the fire about an hour before you are planning to use it and don't forget to check the fire occasionally; it can easily go out if unattended.

Assemble all necessary utensils and accessories (for example, tongs, forks, knives, plates and basting brushes) before cooking.

Prepare drinks and dips for when guests arrive, but keep them well away from the fire, both for safety reasons and so the cooking area doesn't get crowded.

Keep a spray bottle of water handy for damping down the fire and a hose or water bottle standing by in case of emergencies. (As a general safety rule, do not attempt to barbecue in strong winds.) A torch may be useful if barbecuing at night. Buy plenty of firelighters and charcoal or heat beads, if that is the fuel you are using.

Always extinguish a fire once you have finished cooking on it. If possible, clean out the barbecue as soon as it has cooled down; brush or scrape grills and flatplates and discard ash and embers.

EQUIPMENT

Again, there is a large selection of equipment for the barbecue and it is up to you how much you buy. However, a few essentials for outdoor cooking are a stiff wire brush or scraper for cleaning away cooked-on food from the grill plate; a pair of long-handled tongs for turning food without singeing the hairs on your arms; a metal slice with a serrated edge for turning burgers and onions; two pastry brushes for basting; a heatproof mitt for handling metal skewers and hot pans; and a fire blanket or extinguisher.

You could consider a wire fish frame if you like to cook whole fish on the barbecue, or a meat thermometer for testing if large cuts of meat are cooked through.

MARINATING AND BASTING

Marinating Because most foods are cooked quickly over high heat on the barbecue, marinating can be used to tenderise meats and fish as well as to add extra flavour. The longer foods are left to marinate, the stronger the flavour will be. Marinating overnight is ideal for beef, lamb and chicken. However, the exception to this rule is fish, which should only be marinated for up to 2 hours or the flesh will start to 'cook' itself in the marinade and become soggy.

To tenderise meat, most marinades will include an acid such as vinegar, citrus juice, wine, or fruit high in enzymes, such as papaya or pineapple. If so, the food must always be left to marinate in a non-metallic dish, or the acid in the marinade will react with the metal in the dish and affect the food's flavour.

Foods marinated in buttermilk or yoghurt will form a crispy crust—this kind of marinade is perfect for lamb or chicken.

Once the food is marinated, be sure to drain it thoroughly before cooking (unless stated in the recipe). If you add the meat to a flatplate with its marinade, it will stew in the liquid and become tough.

If the marinade is oil- or vinegar-based, you can save it to use as a baste while the meat is cooking. Some marinades can even be put in a pan, brought to the boil and served as a sauce. However, it is very important to remember that marinades have been in contact with raw meat and chicken and need to be boiled over high heat before serving. Never be tempted to keep a marinade to re-use—it contains raw meat juices.

Basting Basting is very useful if you don't have the time to marinate, but would still like to add a little flavour to the food you are barbecuing. While not all foods need to be marinated before barbecuing, all should be basted during cooking, even if it is just with oil to prevent the food sticking to the barbecue. Basting seals moisture and prevents the food from sticking. Baste with olive oil or a reserved marinade, lightly, on both sides. A pastry brush, or clean, unused paintbrush is ideal for this. Do not use a brush with plastic bristles as the plastic may melt onto the food.

RARE, MEDIUM OR WELL-DONE MEAT?

Pork and chicken must always be cooked through but with beef and lamb this is a matter of personal taste. Test for 'doneness' by gently pressing the meat with tongs or a flat-bladed knife. If in doubt, remove meat from the barbecue and make a small cut to check its colour. These five classic degrees of 'doneness' have very different appearances and textures.

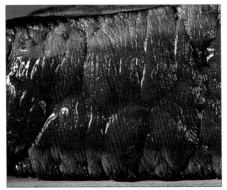

Bleu: Very soft to touch, red-raw inside, outer edge lightly cooked.

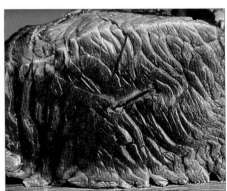

Rare: Soft to touch, red centre, thin edge of cooked meat.

COOKING TECHNIQUES

Once food has been marinated, it is ready to cook. Most recipes in this book call for the food to be cooked over a direct flame. Recipes using indirect cooking on covered kettle barbecues can be found on pages 150–61. See the panel on page 7 for instructions on indirect cooking.

Preparation To use your barbecue efficiently, you are looking for heat rather than flames—always let the flames die down to a bed of red-hot coals before you begin cooking. Once lit, fires should be left to burn for 40–50 minutes before cooking—the heat beads or charcoal will turn white and develop a fine, ash-like coating. (Wood will have a low flame and have begun to char by the time it is ready for cooking.)

Build the fire in the middle of the grate, so that cooked food can be moved to the edge of the grill and kept warm.

To test if the barbecue is ready for cooking, hold the palm of your hand about 10 cm (4 inches) above the grill or plate. If you have to pull it away after 2 seconds, the barbecue is ready.

Direct cooking As with grilling or frying in the kitchen, the less turning or handling of the food the better. Once the fire is ready, lightly brush the grill or flatplate with oil. Place the food over the hottest part of the fire and sear quickly on both sides—this will help the food retain its moisture by sealing the surface. Once seared, move the food to a cooler part of the

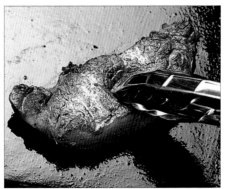
Test meat for 'doneness' by pressing gently with tongs without letting the juices escape.

Fish is ready when the flesh has turned opaque and flakes back easily with a fork.

grill or flatplate to cook for a few more minutes. Barbecuing is a fast-cooking process so even well-done food will not take very long. The barbecue flatplate is also ideal for stir-frying.

Test meat for doneness by firmly pressing it with tongs or the flat edge of a knife. Meat that is ready to serve should 'give' slightly but not resist pressure too easily. At first, you may find it difficult to judge, but try to resist cutting or stabbing the meat—this not only reduces its succulence by releasing the juices, but the juices can also cause the fire to flare.

While beef and lamb can be cooked from rare to well-done, according to your personal taste (see panel below), pork and chicken should never be served rare. If you are in any doubt whether they are cooked through, remove to a separate plate and make a slight cut in the thickest part of the meat. If the juices do not run clear, return to the heat for further cooking.

Test fish for doneness by gently flaking back the flesh in the thickest part with a fork. Cooked flesh should be white and opaque, but still moist.

SAFETY

Barbecues involve open flames, crowds of people and, often, alcohol, so it is a good idea to keep a few safety tips in mind.

Keep a hose or bucket of water close by. A fire extinguisher or fire blanket is more suitable if you intend to use your barbecue regularly. Never light a barbecue with a flammable liquid, instead always use firelighters or light up some twigs and paper.

Keep any children well away from the barbecue and put the matches away as soon as you have finished lighting the barbecue. Listen to the radio reports on hot days—if a total fire ban is in place, you will have to make other plans and not light your barbecue. Make sure you turn off the barbecue or extinguish the fire before you sit down to eat your meal. Remember to turn the gas off at the bottle if you are using one of the gas barbecues. And do not attempt to damp down a gas barbecue with a spray of water unless it has a metal shield covering the burners.

Medium-rare: Springy to touch with moist, pale-red centre.

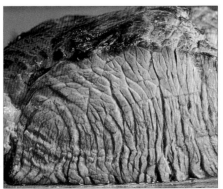
Medium: Firm to touch, pink in centre and crisp, brown edges.

Well-done: Very firm to touch, brown outside and evenly cooked.

Burgers, Skewers & Sausages

BEST-EVER BURGER WITH BARBECUE SAUCE

Preparation time: 20 minutes +
    30 minutes refrigeration
Total cooking time: 25 minutes
Serves 6

750 g (1¹/₂ lb) beef mince
250 g (8 oz) sausage mince
1 small onion, finely chopped
1 tablespoon Worcestershire sauce
2 tablespoons tomato sauce
1 cup (90 g/3 oz) fresh breadcrumbs
1 egg, lightly beaten
2 large onions, extra, thinly sliced
6 wholemeal rolls
6 small lettuce leaves
1 large tomato, sliced

BARBECUE SAUCE
2 teaspoons oil
1 small onion, finely chopped
3 teaspoons brown vinegar
1 tablespoon soft brown sugar
4 tablespoons tomato sauce
2 teaspoons Worcestershire sauce
2 teaspoons soy sauce

1 Place the beef and sausage mince in a large bowl. Add the onion, sauces, breadcrumbs and egg. Mix thoroughly with your hands. Divide the mixture into six equal portions and shape into patties. Refrigerate the patties for at least 30 minutes.
2 Place the patties on a hot, lightly oiled barbecue grill or flatplate. Barbecue over the hottest part of the fire for 8 minutes each side. Meanwhile, fry the extra onions on an oiled flatplate until golden.
3 To make the barbecue sauce, heat the oil in a small pan. Cook the onion for 5 minutes or until soft. Add the vinegar, sugar and sauces and stir until the sauce comes to the boil. Reduce the heat and simmer for 3 minutes. Allow to cool.
4 Split the rolls in half and fill each one with a lettuce leaf, patty, tomato slice and fried onions. Top with a generous quantity of barbecue sauce.

NUTRITION PER SERVE
Protein 45 g; Fat 35 g; Carbohydrate 65 g; Dietary Fibre 9 g; Cholesterol 145 mg; 3160 kJ (755 cal)

Divide the mixture into six portions and shape each into a patty.

Cook the burgers over the hottest part of the fire for 8 minutes on each side.

CHEESEBURGER WITH CAPSICUM SALSA

Preparation time: 25 minutes +
   1 hour standing
Total cooking time: 20 minutes
Serves 6

1 kg (2 lb) beef mince
1 small onion, finely chopped
2 tablespoons chopped fresh parsley
1 teaspoon dried oregano
1 tablespoon tomato paste
70 g (2$^1/_2$ oz) Cheddar cheese
6 bread rolls

CAPSICUM SALSA
2 red capsicums
1 ripe tomato, finely chopped
1 small red onion, finely chopped
1 tablespoon olive oil
2 teaspoons red wine vinegar

1 Mix together the mince, onion, herbs and tomato paste with your hands. Divide into six portions and shape into patties. Cut the cheese into small squares. Make a cavity in the top of each patty with your thumb. Place a piece of cheese in the cavity and smooth the mince over to enclose the cheese completely.

2 To make the salsa, quarter the capsicums, remove the seeds and membranes and cook on a hot, lightly oiled barbecue grill, skin-side-down, until the skin blackens and blisters. Place in a plastic bag and leave to cool. Peel away the skin and dice the flesh. Combine with the tomato, onion, olive oil and vinegar and leave for at least 1 hour to let the flavours develop. Serve at room temperature.

3 Cook the patties on a hot, lightly oiled barbecue grill or flatplate for

4–5 minutes each side, turning once. Serve in rolls with salad leaves and the capsicum salsa.

NUTRITION PER SERVE
Protein 46 g; Fat 28 g; Carbohydrate 47 g; Dietary Fibre 4 g; Cholesterol 117 mg; 2600 kJ (620 cal)

STORAGE: The salsa will keep for a day in the fridge. The burgers can be kept in the fridge for 4 hours before cooking.

VARIATION: Camembert, Brie or any blue cheese can be used to stuff the burgers.

Make an indentation in the burger with your thumb, then press a piece of cheese inside.

Cook the capsicum on a hot barbecue grill until the skin blackens and will peel away easily.

Cook the burgers on a hot grill or flatplate for 4–5 minutes on each side.

BRUNCH BURGER WITH THE WORKS

Preparation time: 40 minutes
Total cooking time: 15 minutes
Serves 6

750 g (1¹/₂ lb) lean beef mince
1 onion, finely chopped
1 egg
¹/₂ cup (40 g/1¹/₄ oz) fresh
    breadcrumbs
2 tablespoons tomato paste
1 tablespoon Worcestershire sauce
2 tablespoons chopped fresh parsley
3 large onions
30 g (1 oz) butter
6 slices Cheddar cheese
6 eggs, extra
6 rashers bacon
6 large hamburger buns, lightly
    toasted
shredded lettuce
2 tomatoes, thinly sliced
6 large slices beetroot, drained
6 pineapple rings, drained
tomato sauce

1 Mix together the mince, onion, egg, breadcrumbs, tomato paste, Worcestershire sauce and parsley with your hands. Season well. Divide into six portions and shape into burgers. Cover and set aside.
2 Slice the onions into thin rings. Heat the butter on a barbecue flatplate. Cook the onions, turning often, until well browned. Move the onions to the outer edge of the flatplate to keep warm. Brush the barbecue grill or flatplate liberally with oil.
3 Cook the burgers for 3–4 minutes each side or until browned and cooked through. Move to the cooler part of the barbecue or transfer to plate and keep warm. Place a slice of cheese on each burger.
4 Heat a small amount of butter in a large frying pan. Fry the eggs and bacon until the eggs are cooked through and the bacon is golden and crisp. Fill the hamburger buns with lettuce, tomato, beetroot and pineapple topped with a burger. Pile the onions, egg, bacon and tomato sauce on top of the burger.

NUTRITION PER SERVE
Protein 35 g; Fat 23 g; Carbohydrate 11 g; Dietary Fibre 2 g; Cholesterol 300 mg; 1610 kJ (385 cal)

Mix together the mince, onion, egg, bread-crumbs, tomato paste, sauce and parsley.

Divide the meat mixture into six portions and shape each one into a burger.

Cook the burgers on a barbecue grill or flatplate for 3–4 minutes on each side.

BEEF KEBABS WITH MINT YOGHURT DRESSING

Preparation time: 30 minutes +
  2 hours marinating
Total cooking time: 10 minutes
Makes 8 kebabs

500 g (1 lb) lean beef fillet, cubed
1/2 cup (125 ml/4 fl oz) olive oil
1/3 cup (80 ml/2³/4 fl oz) lemon juice
1 tablespoon chopped fresh rosemary
1 red onion, cut into wedges
200 g (6¹/2 oz) slender eggplants,
  sliced

MINT YOGHURT DRESSING
1 cup (250 g/8 oz) plain yoghurt
1 clove garlic, crushed
1 small Lebanese cucumber, grated
2 tablespoons chopped fresh mint

1 Leave 8 wooden skewers to soak in cold water to prevent scorching. Put the beef in a non-metallic bowl, combine the olive oil, lemon juice and rosemary and pour over the beef. Cover and refrigerate for 2 hours.
2 To make the mint yoghurt dressing, mix together the yoghurt, garlic, cucumber and mint and season with salt and pepper.

3 Drain the beef and thread onto the skewers, alternating pieces of beef with the onion wedges and slices of eggplant.
4 Cook the kebabs on a hot, lightly oiled barbecue grill or flatplate, turning often, for 5–10 minutes, or until the beef is cooked through and tender. Serve with the dressing.

NUTRITION PER KEBAB
Protein 15 g; Fat 15 g; Carbohydrate 3 g;
Dietary Fibre 1 g; Cholesterol 40 mg;
1010 kJ (240 cal)

Marinate the beef in a non-metallic bowl so that the acidic citrus marinade doesn't react.

Cut the slender eggplants (aubergines) into slices before threading onto the skewers.

Alternate cubes of beef with pieces of eggplant and wedges of onion.

PORK AND TOMATO BURGERS

Preparation time: 20 minutes +
   15 minutes refrigeration
Total cooking time: 15 minutes
Serves 4

350 g (11 oz) pork and veal mince
100 g (3¹/₂ oz) sun-dried tomatoes,
   chopped
3 spring onions, finely chopped
2 tablespoons chopped fresh basil
1 red capsicum, seeded and sliced
1 tablespoon balsamic vinegar

1 Mix together the mince, sun-dried tomato, spring onion and basil. Season well and knead for 2 minutes, or until a little sticky. Form into four burgers and refrigerate for 15 minutes.
2 Mix the capsicum with a little olive oil. Cook on a hot, lightly oiled barbecue grill or flatplate, tossing well and drizzling with the balsamic vinegar, until just softened. Set aside.
3 Wipe the barbecue clean and reheat. Brush the burgers with a little olive oil and cook for 4–5 minutes each side, or until browned and cooked through. Serve with the chargrilled capsicum.

NUTRITION PER SERVE
Protein 20 g; Fat 10 g; Carbohydrate 5 g;
Dietary Fibre 2 g; Cholesterol 45 mg;
840 kJ (200 cal)

Cook the capsicum, tossing well and drizzling with balsamic vinegar, until softened.

Clean the barbecue plate before you reheat it to cook the burgers.

Brush the burgers with a little oil and cook until they are browned.

SALMON AND PRAWN KEBABS WITH CHINESE SPICES

Preparation time: 15 minutes +
  2 hours marinating
Total cooking time: 20 minutes
Serves 6

4 x 200 g (6¹/2 oz) salmon fillets
36 raw prawns, peeled, deveined, tails
  intact
5 cm (2 inch) piece fresh ginger, finely
  shredded
²/3 cup (170 ml/5¹/2 fl oz) Chinese rice
  wine
³/4 cup (185 ml/6 fl oz) kecap manis
¹/2 teaspoon five-spice powder

200 g (6¹/2 oz) fresh egg noodles
600 g (1¹/4 lb) baby bok choy, leaves
  separated

1 Remove the skin and bones from
the salmon and cut it into bite-sized
cubes (you should have about 36).
Thread three cubes of salmon
alternately with three prawns onto
each skewer. Lay the skewers in a
non-metallic dish.
2 Mix together the ginger, rice wine,
kecap manis and five-spice powder.
Pour over the skewers, then cover and
marinate for at least 2 hours. Turn over
a few times to ensure even coating.
3 Drain, reserving the marinade.
Cook the skewers in batches on a hot,
lightly oiled barbecue flatplate or grill

for 4–5 minutes each side, or until they
are cooked through.
4 Meanwhile, place the noodles in a
bowl and cover with boiling water.
Leave for 5 minutes, or until tender,
then drain and keep warm. Place the
reserved marinade in a saucepan and
bring to the boil. Reduce the heat,
simmer and stir in the bok choy
leaves. Cook, covered, for 2 minutes,
or until just wilted.
5 Top the noodles with the bok choy,
then the kebabs. Spoon on the heated
marinade, season and serve.

NUTRITION PER SERVE
Protein 50 g; Fat 15 g; Carbohydrate 24 g;
Dietary Fibre 5 g; Cholesterol 246 mg;
1856 kJ (440 cal)

Mix together the marinade ingredients and pour
over the skewers.

Cook the skewers in batches on a hot barbecue
flatplate or grill.

Add the bok choy to the reserved marinade in
the pan, cover and cook until wilted.

INVOLTINI OF SWORDFISH

Preparation time: 30 minutes
Total cooking time: 10 minutes
Serves 4

1 kg (2 lb) swordfish, skin removed, cut into four 5 cm (2 inch) pieces
3 lemons
4 tablespoons olive oil
1 small onion, chopped
3 cloves garlic, chopped
2 tablespoons chopped capers
2 tablespoons chopped pitted Kalamata olives
1/3 cup (35 g/1 oz) finely grated Parmesan
1 1/2 cups (120 g/4 oz) fresh breadcrumbs
2 tablespoons chopped fresh parsley
1 egg, lightly beaten
24 fresh bay leaves
2 small white onions, quartered and separated into pieces
2 tablespoons lemon juice, extra

1 Cut each swordfish piece horizontally into four slices to give you 16 slices. Place each piece between two pieces of plastic wrap and roll gently with a rolling pin to flatten without tearing. Cut each piece in half to give 32 pieces.
2 Peel the lemons with a vegetable peeler. Cut the peel into 24 even pieces. Squeeze the lemons to give 3 tablespoons of juice.
3 Heat 2 tablespoons olive oil in a pan, add the onion and garlic, and cook over medium heat for 2 minutes. Place in a bowl with the capers, olives, Parmesan, breadcrumbs and parsley. Season, add the egg and mix to bind.
4 Divide the stuffing among the fish pieces and, with oiled hands, roll up to form parcels. Thread four rolls onto each of eight skewers alternating with the bay leaves, lemon peel and onion.
5 Mix the remaining oil with the lemon juice in a small bowl. Cook the skewers on a hot barbecue flatplate for 3–4 minutes each side, basting with the oil and lemon mixture. Serve with a little extra lemon juice drizzled over the top.

NUTRITION PER SERVE
Protein 34 g; Fat 38 g; Carbohydrate 5.5 g;
Dietary Fibre 5 g; Cholesterol 193 mg;
2065 kJ (493 cal)

Roll the swordfish out between two pieces of plastic wrap.

Roll up the fish pieces and filling with oiled hands to form neat parcels.

Thread the rolls, bay leaves, lemon peel and onion onto skewers.

VEGETARIAN BURGERS WITH CORIANDER GARLIC CREAM

Preparation time: 30 minutes
Total cooking time: 20 minutes
Makes 10 burgers

1 cup (250 g/8 oz) red lentils
1 tablespoon oil
2 onions, sliced
1 tablespoon tandoori mix powder
425 g (14 oz) can chickpeas, drained
1 tablespoon grated fresh ginger
1 egg
3 tablespoons chopped fresh parsley
2 tablespoons chopped fresh
    coriander
2¼ cups (180 g/6 oz) fresh
    breadcrumbs
plain flour, for dusting

CORIANDER GARLIC CREAM
½ cup (125 g/4 oz) sour cream
½ cup (125 ml/4 fl oz) cream
1 clove garlic, crushed
2 tablespoons chopped fresh
    coriander
2 tablespoons chopped fresh parsley

1 Simmer the lentils in a large pan of water for 8 minutes or until tender. Drain well. Heat the oil in a pan and cook the onion until tender. Add the tandoori mix and stir until fragrant.
2 Put the chickpeas, half the lentils, the ginger, egg and onion mixture in a food processor. Process for 20 seconds or until smooth. Transfer to a bowl. Stir in the remaining lentils, parsley, coriander and breadcrumbs.
3 Divide into 10 portions and shape into burgers. (If the mixture is too soft, refrigerate for 15 minutes to firm.) Toss the burgers in flour and place on a hot,

lightly oiled barbecue grill or flatplate. Cook for 3–4 minutes each side or until browned.
4 For the coriander garlic cream, mix together the sour cream, cream, garlic and herbs. Serve with the burgers.

NUTRITION PER BURGER
Protein 11 g; Fat 14 g; Carbohydrate 26 g;
Dietary Fibre 5 g; Cholesterol 50 mg;
1155 kJ (276 cal)

STORAGE: The burgers can be prepared up to 2 days in advance and stored, covered, in the fridge. The cream can be stored, covered, in the fridge for up to 3 days.

NOTE: The coriander garlic cream is also delicious with chicken or fish burgers.

Heat the oil in a pan and cook the onion until tender, then add the tandoori mix.

Process the chickpea mixture, then transfer to a bowl and mix with the other ingredients.

Shape the portions into burgers and then toss in flour, shaking off the excess, before cooking.

CHILLI BEEF BURGERS

Preparation time: 25 minutes +
    2 hours marinating
Total cooking time: 10 minutes
Makes 18 burgers

1 kg (2 lb) beef mince
3 onions, grated
3 tablespoons chopped fresh parsley
1¹/₂ cups (150 g/5 oz) dry
    breadcrumbs
1 egg, lightly beaten
1 tablespoon milk
1 tablespoon malt vinegar

1 tablespoon tomato paste
2 tablespoons soy sauce
1 tablespoon chilli sauce
3 tablespoons dried oregano

MUSTARD BUTTER
125 g (4 oz) butter, softened
2 tablespoons sour cream
2 tablespoons German mustard

1 Mix together the beef, onion, parsley, breacrumbs, egg, milk, vinegar, tomato paste, sauces and oregano. Refrigerate, covered with plastic wrap, for 2 hours.
2 To make the mustard butter, beat the butter, sour cream and mustard in a small bowl for 2 minutes or until well combined. Leave for 20 minutes to let the flavours develop.
3 Divide the burger mixture into 18 portions and shape each one into a burger. Cook on a hot, lightly oiled barbecue grill or flatplate for 4 minutes on each side. Serve immediately with the mustard butter.

NUTRITION PER BURGER
Protein 13 g; Fat 13 g; Carbohydrate 6 g;
Dietary Fibre 1 g; Cholesterol 66 mg;
811 kJ (200 cal)

Mix together all the burger ingredients and then refrigerate for 2 hours.

Divide the mixture into 18 portions and shape each into a round burger.

Cook the burgers over high heat on a lightly oiled grill or flatplate.

LAMB SOUVLAKI

Preparation time: 20 minutes +
  overnight marinating
Total cooking time: 10 minutes
Serves 4

1 kg (2 lb) boned leg lamb, trimmed
  and cut into small cubes
3 tablespoons olive oil
2 teaspoons finely grated lemon rind
4 tablespoons lemon juice
2 teaspoons dried oregano
1/2 cup (125 ml/4 fl oz) dry white wine

2 large cloves garlic, finely chopped
2 fresh bay leaves
1 cup (250 g/8 oz) Greek-style plain
  yoghurt
2 cloves garlic, crushed, extra

1 Place the lamb in a non-metallic
bowl with 2 tablespoons of the olive
oil, the lemon rind and juice, oregano,
wine, garlic and bay leaves. Season
with black pepper and toss to coat.
Cover and refrigerate overnight.
2 Place the yoghurt and extra garlic in
a bowl, mix together well and leave
for 30 minutes. If using wooden

skewers, soak for 30 minutes
beforehand to prevent scorching.
3 Drain the lamb and pat dry. Thread
onto 8 skewers and cook on a hot
barbecue flatplate, brushing with the
remaining oil, for 7–8 minutes, or until
brown on the outside and still a little
rare in the middle. Drizzle with the
garlic yoghurt and serve with warm
pitta bread.

NUTRITION PER SERVE
Protein 43 g; Fat 20 g; Carbohydrate 4 g;
Dietary Fibre 0 g; Cholesterol 126 mg;
1660 kJ (397 cal)

Toss the lamb and marinade together in a non-metallic bowl.

Pat the drained lamb dry and thread the pieces onto the skewers.

Brush the remaining oil over the lamb skewers during cooking.

TUNA SKEWERS WITH MOROCCAN SPICES AND CHERMOULA

Preparation time: 20 minutes +
  10 minutes marinating
Total cooking time: 5 minutes
Serves 4

800 g (1 lb 10 oz) tuna steaks, cut into
  cubes
2 tablespoons olive oil
$^1/_2$ teaspoon ground cumin
2 teaspoons grated lemon rind

CHERMOULA
3 teaspoons ground cumin
$^1/_2$ teaspoon ground coriander
2 teaspoons paprika
pinch of cayenne pepper
4 garlic cloves, crushed
$^1/_2$ cup (15 g/$^1/_2$ oz) chopped fresh
  flat-leaf parsley
$^1/_2$ cup (30 g/1 oz) chopped fresh
  coriander
4 tablespoons lemon juice
$^1/_2$ cup (125 ml/4 fl oz) olive oil

1 If using wooden skewers, soak for 30 minutes beforehand to prevent scorching. Place the tuna in a shallow non-metallic dish. Combine the olive oil, ground cumin and lemon rind and pour over the tuna. Toss to coat and leave to marinate for 10 minutes.

2 To make the chermoula, place the cumin, coriander, paprika and cayenne in a frying pan and cook over medium heat for 30 seconds, or until fragrant. Combine with the remaining ingredients and leave for the flavours to develop.

3 Thread the tuna onto the skewers. Cook on a hot, lightly oiled barbecue grill or flatplate until cooked to your

taste (about 1 minute on each side for rare and 2 minutes for medium). Serve on couscous with the chermoula drizzled over the skewers.

NUTRITION PER SERVE
Protein 50 g; Fat 40 g; Carbohydrate 0 g;
Dietary Fibre 0 g; Cholesterol 70 mg;
2186 kJ (520 cal)

Pour the combined olive oil, cumin and lemon rind over the tuna cubes.

Combine the chermoula ingredients in a small bowl and leave for the flavours to develop.

Thread the tuna onto the skewers and barbecue until cooked to your liking.

MUSTARD BURGERS WITH TOMATO AND ONION SALSA

Preparation time: 20 minutes
Total cooking time: 10 minutes
Makes 8 burgers

1 kg (2 lb) beef mince
3 tablespoons wholegrain mustard
2 teaspoons Dijon mustard
1 teaspoon beef stock powder
1 cup (90 g/3 oz) fresh breadcrumbs
   (see NOTE)
1 egg
1 teaspoon black pepper
1/4 red capsicum, chopped

TOMATO AND ONION SALSA
1 small red onion, diced
4 tomatoes, diced
2 tablespoons red wine vinegar
1 1/2 teaspoons caster sugar
2 teaspoons lemon juice

1 Mix together the beef mince, mustards, stock powder, breadcrumbs, egg, pepper and capsicum with your hands. Divide into eight portions and shape into burgers.
2 Cook the burgers on a hot, lightly oiled barbecue grill or flatplate for 2–3 minutes each side.
3 To make the tomato and onion salsa, put all the ingredients in a bowl and mix together well.

NUTRITION PER BURGER
Protein 27 g; Fat 14 g; Carbohydrate 13 g;
Dietary Fibre 1.5 g; Cholesterol 80 mg;
1210 kJ (290 cal)

NOTE: The breadcrumbs are best if made from slightly stale bread.

STORAGE: The burgers can be made a day in advance and kept, covered, in the fridge. The salsa will also keep, covered, in the fridge for a day.

VARIATION: Instead of Dijon, use German or American mustard for a mild-tasting burger. English mustard will make a strong-tasting, hot burger.

Put all the burger ingredients in a bowl and mix together thoroughly with your hands.

Divide the mixture into eight portions and shape each one into a burger.

To make the tomato and onion salsa, simply mix together all the ingredients.

HERB BURGERS

Preparation time: 20 minutes
Total cooking time: 20 minutes
Makes 8 burgers

750 g (1½ lb) beef or lamb mince
2 tablespoons chopped fresh basil
1 tablespoon chopped fresh chives
1 tablespoon chopped fresh rosemary
1 tablespoon chopped fresh thyme
2 tablespoons lemon juice
1 cup (90 g/3 oz) fresh breadcrumbs
1 egg
2 long crusty bread sticks
lettuce leaves
2 tomatoes, sliced
tomato sauce

1 Combine the mince with the herbs, juice, breadcrumbs, egg and season well with salt and pepper. Mix well with your hands. Divide the mixture into eight portions and shape into thick rectangular patties.
2 Place the burgers on a hot, lightly oiled barbecue grill or flatplate. Cook for 5–10 minutes each side until well browned and just cooked through.
3 Cut the bread sticks in half and sandwich with the burgers, lettuce, tomato and tomato sauce.

NUTRITION PER BURGER
Protein 26 g; Fat 12 g; Carbohydrate 32 g;
Dietary Fibre 2 g; Cholesterol 32 mg;
1455 kJ (350 cal)

STORAGE: The burger mixture can be kept refrigerated for a day.

Put the mince, herbs, juice, breadcrumbs, egg and seasoning in a bowl and mix well.

Shape the mixture into rectangular patties and cook on the barbecue for 10–20 minutes.

Make sandwiches from the bread sticks, burgers and salad ingredients.

TOFU KEBABS WITH MISO PESTO

Preparation time: 30 minutes +
  1 hour marinating
Total cooking time: 10 minutes
Serves 4

1 large red capsicum, cubed
12 button mushrooms, halved
6 pickling onions, quartered
3 zucchini, cut into chunks
450 g (14 oz) firm tofu, cubed
1/2 cup (125 ml/4 fl oz) light olive oil
3 tablespoons light soy sauce
2 cloves garlic, crushed
2 teaspoons grated fresh ginger

MISO PESTO
1/2 cup (90 g/3 oz) unsalted roasted
  peanuts
2 cups (60 g/2 oz) firmly packed fresh
  coriander leaves
2 tablespoons white miso paste
2 cloves garlic
100 ml (3 1/2 oz) olive oil

1 If using wooden skewers, soak them in water for 30 minutes to prevent scorching. Thread the vegetables and tofu alternately onto 12 skewers, then place in a large non-metallic dish.

2 Mix together the olive oil, soy sauce, garlic and ginger, then pour half over the kebabs. Cover and leave to marinate for 1 hour.

3 To make the miso pesto, finely chop the peanuts, coriander leaves, miso paste and garlic in a food processor. Slowly add the olive oil while the machine is still running and blend to a smooth paste.

4 Cook the kebabs on a hot, lightly oiled barbecue flatplate or grill, turning and brushing with the remaining marinade, for 4–6 minutes, or until the edges are slightly brown. Serve with the miso pesto.

NUTRITION PER SERVE
Protein 8 g; Fat 64 g; Carbohydrate 10 g;
Dietary Fibre 4 g; Cholesterol 0 mg;
2698 kJ (645 cal)

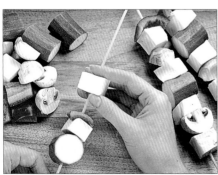

Thread the vegetable pieces and tofu cubes alternately onto the skewers.

Mix the nuts, coriander leaves, miso and garlic in a food processor until finely chopped.

Brush the kebabs with the remaining marinade during cooking.

YAKITORI CHICKEN

Preparation time: 30 minutes
Total cooking time: 20 minutes
Serves 4

3 tablespoons yellow or red miso
    paste
2 tablespoons sugar
3 tablespoons sake
2 tablespoons mirin
1 kg (2 lb) chicken thighs, boned
1 cucumber
2 spring onions, sliced

1 If using wooden skewers, soak them in water for 30 minutes to prevent scorching. Place the miso, sugar, sake and mirin in a small saucepan over medium heat and cook, stirring well, for 2 minutes, or until the sauce is smooth and the sugar has dissolved completely.

2 Cut the chicken into cubes. Seed the cucumber and cut into small batons. Thread the chicken, cucumber and spring onion alternately onto the skewers—you should have about three pieces of each per skewer.

3 Cook on a hot, lightly oiled barbecue flatplate, turning occasionally, for 10 minutes, or until the chicken is almost cooked. Brush with the miso sauce and continue cooking, then turn and brush the other side. Repeat once or twice until the chicken and vegetables are cooked.

NUTRITION PER SERVE
Protein 58 g; Fat 6.5 g; Carbohydrate 9 g;
Dietary Fibre 0.5 g; Cholesterol 126 mg;
1377 kJ (329 cal)

Buy ready-boned chicken thighs or remove the bones yourself with a sharp knife.

Remove the seeds from the centre of the cucumber, then cut into batons.

Brush the chicken and vegetables with the miso sauce during cooking.

LAMB PITTA

Preparation time: 20 minutes +
  15 minutes marinating
Total cooking time: 5 minutes
Serves 4

400 g (13 oz) lamb leg steaks
2 teaspoons finely grated lemon rind
3 teaspoons finely chopped fresh
  oregano
2 cloves garlic, finely chopped
2 tablespoons olive oil
1 red onion, thinly sliced
4 small pitta breads

1/2 cup (125 g/4 oz) hummus
1/2 cup (125 g /4 oz) plain yoghurt
1 small Lebanese cucumber, thinly
  sliced
1 small red chilli, seeds removed,
  finely chopped
snow pea sprouts

1 Trim the lamb of excess fat and cut into thin strips. Mix together the lemon rind, oregano, garlic, olive oil and some cracked black pepper in a non-metallic bowl. Add the lamb and refrigerate for 15 minutes.

2 Cook the lamb and onion on a very hot, lightly oiled barbecue flatplate for 2–3 minutes, turning to brown the meat quickly and soften the onion. Remove from the plate and keep warm. Place the pitta breads on the flatplate and warm both sides.

3 Spread each round of bread with a little of the hummus and yoghurt. Add the barbecued lamb and onion and scatter with the cucumber, chilli and a few snow pea sprouts.

NUTRITION PER SERVE
Protein 40 g; Fat 20 g; Carbohydrate 65 g;
Dietary Fibre 5 g; Cholesterol 70 mg;
2550 kJ (605 cal)

The seeds contain the heat of the chilli. Scrape them out with a knife.

Mix together the lemon rind, oregano, garlic, olive oil and some ground pepper.

Cook the lamb and onion for 2–3 minutes, turning to brown the meat quickly.

KIDNEY KEBABS

Preparation time: 15 minutes
  + 20 minutes marinating
Total cooking time: 5–10 minutes
Serves 4

200 g (61/2 oz) lamb kidneys
3 cloves garlic, finely chopped
2 bay leaves, torn into small pieces
3 tablespoons olive oil
300 g (10 oz) chicken breast fillets
150 g (5 oz) double-smoked ham
2 small onions
2 tablespoons dry sherry

1 Soak 8 bamboo skewers in water to prevent scorching. Trim the kidneys of any sinew or fat and cut into bite-sized pieces. Combine the garlic, bay leaves and olive oil. Add the kidneys, cover and marinate in the refrigerator for about 20 minutes.

2 Cut the chicken and ham into bite-sized pieces and cut the onions into small wedges.

3 Drain the kidneys, keeping the marinade. Thread the pieces of onion, kidney, chicken and ham alternately onto the skewers.

4 Cook the kebabs on a hot, lightly oiled barbecue grill or flatplate for about 5–10 minutes, brushing lightly with the marinade and sherry as they cook and turning them regularly. Cook until golden brown.

NUTRITION PER SERVE
Protein 35 g; Fat 20 g; Carbohydrate 2 g;
Dietary Fibre 1 g; Cholesterol 225 mg;
1335 kJ (315 cal)

VARIATION: Chicken livers can be used instead of the lamb kidneys.

Trim the kidneys of any sinew or fat and cut into bite-sized pieces.

Thread the pieces of onion, kidney, chicken and ham alternately onto the skewers.

While the skewers are cooking, brush them lightly with the marinade and sherry.

TERIYAKI FISH WITH MANGO SALSA

Preparation time: 30 minutes +
30 minutes marinating
Total cooking time: 10 minutes
Serves 4

750 g (1¹/₂ lb) swordfish fillets, cut into cubes

MARINADE
¹/₂ cup (125 ml/4 fl oz) teriyaki sauce
¹/₄ cup (60 ml/2 fl oz) pineapple juice
2 tablespoons honey
1 tablespoon grated fresh ginger
2 cloves garlic, crushed
1 teaspoon sesame oil

SALSA
1 red onion, chopped
2 teaspoons sugar
2 tablespoons lime juice
1 firm mango, diced
1 cup (150 g/5 oz) diced pineapple
1 kiwi fruit, diced
2 small red chillies, seeded and finely chopped
2 tablespoons finely chopped fresh coriander leaves

1 Soak 8 wooden skewers in water to prevent scorching. Place the cubes of fish in a non-metallic bowl. Combine the marinade ingredients, pour over the fish and stir to coat. Cover and refrigerate for 30 minutes.
2 Thread the fish onto the skewers, keeping the marinade.

3 To make the salsa, put the onion in a bowl and sprinkle with sugar. Add the other ingredients and mix together gently.
4 Cook the skewers on a hot, lightly oiled barbecue flatplate or grill for 6–8 minutes, turning often and basting with the reserved marinade. Serve with the salsa.

NUTRITION PER SERVE
Protein 50 g; Fat 18 g; Carbohydrate 40 g;
Dietary Fibre 3 g; Cholesterol 145 mg;
2153 kJ (515 cal)

NOTE: You should only marinate fish for 30 minutes; any longer and the fish flesh will begin to 'cook' in the marinade and break down.

Swordfish is a firm, meaty fish, perfect for barbecuing. Cut it into cubes.

Sprinkle the onion with sugar and then mix with all the other salsa ingredients.

Cook the swordfish for 6–8 minutes, turning often and basting with the marinade.

CHICKEN SATAY WITH PEANUT SAUCE

Preparation time: 40 minutes +
30 minutes marinating
Total cooking time: 15–20 minutes
Makes 20 skewers

500 g (1 lb) chicken thigh fillets,
trimmed
1 onion, roughly chopped
2 stems lemon grass (white part only),
thinly sliced
4 cloves garlic
2 red chillies, chopped
2 teaspoons ground coriander
1 teaspoon ground cumin
1/2 teaspoon salt
1 tablespoon soy sauce
1/4 cup (60 ml/2 fl oz) oil
1 tablespoon soft brown sugar

PEANUT SAUCE
1/2 cup (125 g/4 oz) crunchy peanut
butter
1 cup (250 ml/8 fl oz) coconut milk
1/2 cup (125 ml/4 fl oz) water
1–2 tablespoons sweet chilli sauce
1 tablespoon soy sauce
2 teaspoons lemon juice

1 Soak 20 wooden skewers in water
for 30 minutes to prevent scorching.
Cut the chicken into 20 strips and
thread one onto each skewer.
2 Process the onion, lemon grass,
garlic, chilli, coriander, cumin, salt and
soy sauce in a food processor in short
bursts until smooth, adding a little oil
to assist the processing. Spread over
the chicken, cover and refrigerate for
30 minutes.
3 Stir all the sauce ingredients in a
pan over low heat until the mixture
boils. Remove from the heat. The
sauce will thicken on standing.
4 Cook the chicken on a hot, lightly
oiled barbecue flatplate or grill for
2–3 minutes on each side, sprinkling
with a little oil and brown sugar. Serve
topped with peanut sauce.

NUTRITION PER SKEWER
Protein 30 g; Fat 35 g; Carbohydrate 9 g;
Dietary Fibre 6 g; Cholesterol 55 mg;
1945 kJ (465 cal)

Thread one chicken strip onto each skewer,
flattening it out on the skewer.

Add a little oil to the paste to give some moisture
to assist the processing.

The peanut sauce will thicken when it has been
left to stand.

During cooking, sprinkle the chicken with oil and
brown sugar.

SPICY BURGERS WITH AVOCADO SALSA

Preparation time: 25 minutes
Total cooking time: 10 minutes
Serves 6

1 kg (2 lb) beef mince
1 small onion, finely chopped
3 teaspoons chopped chilli
1 teaspoon ground cumin
2 tablespoons tomato paste
2 tablespoons chopped fresh
    coriander
6 bread rolls

AVOCADO SALSA
1 avocado
2 tablespoons lime juice
1 small tomato, chopped
125 g (4 oz) can corn kernels, drained

1 With your hands, mix together the mince, onion, chilli, cumin, tomato paste and coriander. Divide into six portions and shape into burgers.
2 Cook on a hot, lightly oiled grill or flatplate for 4–5 minutes each side.
3 To make the salsa, dice the avocado and toss with lime juice. Add the tomato and corn and toss lightly. Sandwich the burgers in the bread rolls and serve with the salsa.

NUTRITION PER SERVE
Protein 44 g; Fat 29 g; Carbohydrate 49 g;
Dietary Fibre 5 g; Cholesterol 105 mg;
2649 kJ (633 cal)

The most thorough way to mix the ingredients together is to use your hands.

Cook the burgers on a lightly oiled barbecue grill or flatplate, turning once.

Mix together the salsa ingredients: the lime juice will prevent the avocado browning.

PORK SAUSAGE BURGERS WITH MUSTARD CREAM

Preparation time: 20 minutes
Total cooking time: 10 minutes
Serves 6

1 kg (2 lb) pork mince
1 small onion, finely chopped
1 cup (90 g/3 oz) fresh breadcrumbs
2 cloves garlic, crushed
1 egg, lightly beaten
1 teaspoon dried sage
6 bread sticks

MUSTARD CREAM
1/2 cup (125 g/4 oz) sour cream
1 tablespoon wholegrain mustard
2 teaspoons lemon juice

1 Mix together the mince, onion, breadcrumbs, garlic, egg and sage with your hands. Divide into six portions and shape into sausages.
2 Cook the sausages on a hot, lightly oiled barbecue flatplate or grill for 5–10 minutes, turning occasionally.
3 To make the mustard cream, put the sour cream, mustard and juice in a small bowl and stir together. Sandwich the sausage burgers in the bread sticks and serve with the mustard cream.

NUTRITION PER SERVE
Protein 51 g; Fat 15 g; Carbohydrate 55 g;
Dietary Fibre 4 g; Cholesterol 140 mg;
2342 kJ (559 cal)

Divide the mixture into six portions and shape each one into a sausage.

Cook the burgers on a hot, lightly oiled barbecue flatplate or grill.

Stir together the sour cream, mustard and lemon juice and serve with the burgers.

BEEF SATAY STICKS WITH PEANUT SAUCE

Preparation time: 30 minutes +
    at least 3 hours marinating
Total cooking time: 15 minutes
Serves 4

800 g (1 lb 10 oz) rump steak
1/3 cup (80 ml/2³/₄ fl oz) soy sauce
2 tablespoons oil
2 cloves garlic, crushed
1 teaspoon grated fresh ginger

PEANUT SAUCE
1 cup (250 ml/8 fl oz) pineapple juice
1 cup (250 g/8 oz) peanut butter
1/2 teaspoon garlic powder

1/2 teaspoon onion powder
2 tablespoons sweet chilli sauce
3 tablespoons soy sauce

1 Trim the steak of excess fat and sinew. Slice across the grain evenly into long, thin strips. Thread onto skewers, bunching them thickly along three-quarters of the skewer. Place in a shallow non-metal dish.
2 Mix the soy sauce, oil, garlic and ginger together and pour over the satays. Cover with plastic wrap and refrigerate for several hours or overnight, turning occasionally.
3 Cook on a hot, lightly oiled barbecue grill or flatplate for 8–10 minutes or until tender, turning the skewers occasionally.

4 To make the peanut sauce, combine the juice, peanut butter, garlic and onion powders and sauces in a small pan and stir over medium heat for 5 minutes or until smooth. Serve warm with the satay sticks.

NUTRITION PER SERVE
Protein 70 g; Fat 55 g; Carbohydrate 17 g;
Dietary Fibre 9 g; Cholesterol 134 mg;
3500 kJ (838 cal)

STORAGE: The sauce can be made a day in advance and stored in the fridge. If it thickens too much on standing, add a little warm water when reheating.

Trim the meat and then slice across the grain into long, thin strips.

Thread the meat onto skewers and then leave to marinate in a non-metallic dish.

To make the peanut sauce, stir all the ingredients over medium heat until smooth.

LAMB SATAYS WITH CHILLI PEANUT SAUCE

Preparation time: 25 minutes +
  1 hour marinating
Total cooking time: 15 minutes
Serves 4

600 g (1 1/4 lb) lamb fillet
2 cloves garlic, crushed
1/2 teaspoon ground black pepper
6 teaspoons finely chopped lemon
    grass
2 tablespoons soy sauce
2 teaspoons sugar
1/4 teaspoon ground turmeric

CHILLI PEANUT SAUCE
1 1/2 cups (250 g/8 oz) unsalted
    roasted peanuts
2 tablespoons vegetable oil
1 onion, roughly chopped
1 clove garlic, roughly chopped
1 tablespoon sambal oelek
1 tablespoon soft brown sugar
1 tablespoon kecap manis
    or soy sauce
1 teaspoon grated fresh ginger
1 1/2 teaspoons ground coriander
1 cup (250 ml/8 fl oz) coconut cream
1/4 teaspoon ground turmeric

1 Trim the lamb, cut into thin strips and thread onto skewers, bunching along three-quarters of the length. Place in a shallow non-metallic dish. Mix together the garlic, pepper, lemon grass, soy sauce, sugar and turmeric and brush over the meat. Leave to marinate for 1 hour.
2 To make the chilli peanut sauce, roughly grind the peanuts in a food processor for 10 seconds. Heat the oil in a small pan. Add the onion and garlic and cook over medium heat for

3–4 minutes or until translucent. Add the sambal oelek, sugar, kecap manis, ginger and coriander. Cook, stirring, for 2 minutes. Add the coconut cream, turmeric and ground peanuts. Reduce the heat and cook for 3 minutes, or until thickened. Season well and then process for 20 seconds, or until the sauce is almost smooth.
3 Cook the skewers on a hot, lightly oiled barbecue grill or flatplate for 2–3 minutes on each side.

NUTRITION PER SERVE
Protein 51 g; Fat 57 g; Carbohydrate 16 g;
Dietary Fibre 7 g; Cholesterol 99 mg;
3241 kJ (774 cal)

STORAGE: Satays can be marinated for up to 2 days, covered in the fridge. The sauce will keep for 3–4 days in a screw-top jar in the fridge.

Thread the strips of lamb onto the skewers and then marinate for 1 hour.

Coarsely grind the peanuts in a processor and then heat with the other sauce ingredients.

Process the sauce until it is almost smooth and then serve with the skewers.

LAMB KOFTAS WITH TAHINI DRESSING

Preparation time: 25 minutes
Total cooking time: 10 minutes
Serves 4–6

600 g (1 1/4 lb) lean lamb
1 onion, roughly chopped
2 cloves garlic, roughly chopped
1 teaspoon cracked black pepper
1 1/2 teaspoons ground cumin
1/2 teaspoon ground cinnamon
1 teaspoon sweet paprika
1 teaspoon salt
2 slices bread, crusts removed
1 egg, lightly beaten
olive oil, for coating

TAHINI DRESSING
2 tablespoons tahini (sesame paste)
3 teaspoons lemon juice
1 small garlic clove, crushed
pinch of salt
2 tablespoons sour cream
1 tablespoon chopped fresh parsley

1 Soak 12 wooden skewers in water for 30 minutes to prevent scorching. Trim the meat of any excess fat and sinew. Cut into small pieces and put in a food processor with the onion, garlic, pepper, cumin, cinnamon, paprika, salt, bread and egg. Process for 20–30 seconds, or until the mixture becomes a smooth paste.
2 Divide the mixture into 12 portions. Using oil-coated hands, shape into sausages around the skewers.
3 To make the dressing, stir together the tahini, lemon juice, garlic, salt, sour cream, parsley and 2–3 table-spoons water until creamy.
4 Arrange the kebabs on a hot, lightly oiled barbecue grill or flatplate. Cook for 10 minutes, turning frequently, until browned and cooked through. Serve with the dressing.

NUTRITION PER SERVE (6)
Protein 23 g; Fat 10 g; Carbohydrate 6 g;
Dietary Fibre 1 g; Cholesterol 75 mg;
856 kJ (205 cal)

STORAGE: The dressing will keep for a day in the fridge.

Mix the kofta ingredients in a food processor until a smooth paste forms.

Shape the kofta mixture into sausages around the skewers.

To make the dressing, simply stir together the ingredients until creamy.

SWEET-AND-SOUR PORK KEBABS

Preparation time: 30 minutes +
  3 hours marinating
Total cooking time: 20 minutes
Serves 6

1 kg (2 lb) pork fillets, cubed
1 large red capsicum, cubed
1 large green capsicum, cubed
425 g (14 oz) can pineapple pieces,
  drained, juice reserved
1 cup (250 ml/8 fl oz) orange juice
3 tablespoons white vinegar
2 tablespoons soft brown sugar
2 teaspoons chilli garlic sauce
2 teaspoons cornflour

1 Soak wooden skewers in water for 30 minutes to prevent scorching. Thread pieces of meat alternately with pieces of capsicum and pineapple onto the skewers. Mix the pineapple juice with the orange juice, vinegar, sugar and sauce. Place the kebabs in a shallow non-metallic dish and pour half the marinade over them. Cover and refrigerate for at least 3 hours, turning occasionally.
2 Put the remaining marinade in a small pan. Mix the cornflour with a tablespoon of the marinade until smooth, then add to the pan. Stir over medium heat until the mixture boils and thickens. Transfer to a bowl, cover the surface with plastic wrap and leave to cool.
3 Cook the kebabs on a hot, lightly oiled barbecue flatplate or grill for 15 minutes, turning occasionally, until tender. Serve with the sauce.

NUTRITION PER SERVE
Protein 40 g; Fat 3 g; Carbohydrate 18 g;
Dietary Fibre 2 g; Cholesterol 82 mg;
1073 kJ (256 cal)

Thread pieces of pork onto the skewers, alternating with capsicum and pineapple.

Mix the cornflour with a little of the marinade and then add to the sauce to thicken.

Cook the kebabs on a hot flatplate or grill until the pork is tender.

CHICKEN BURGERS WITH TARRAGON MAYONNAISE

Preparation time: 25 minutes
Total cooking time: 15 minutes
Serves 6

1 kg (2 lb) chicken mince
1 small onion, finely chopped
2 teaspoons finely grated lemon rind
2 tablespoons sour cream
1 cup (90 g/3 oz) fresh breadcrumbs
6 onion bread rolls

TARRAGON MAYONNAISE
1 egg yolk
1 tablespoon tarragon vinegar
1/2 teaspoon French mustard
1 cup (250 ml/8 fl oz) olive oil

1 Mix together the mince, onion, rind, sour cream and breadcrumbs with your hands. Divide into six portions and shape into burgers.
2 To make the mayonnaise, put the yolk, half the vinegar and the mustard in a small bowl. Whisk for 1 minute until light and creamy. Add the oil about 1 teaspoon at a time, whisking constantly until the mixture thickens. Increase the flow of oil to a thin stream and continue whisking until it has all been incorporated. Stir in the remaining vinegar and season well with salt and white pepper.
3 Cook the burgers on a hot, lightly oiled barbecue flatplate or grill for 7 minutes each side, turning once. Serve on a roll with the mayonnaise.

NUTRITION PER SERVE
Protein 49 g; Fat 50 g; Carbohydrate 54 g; Dietary Fibre 4 g; Cholesterol 122 mg; 3600 kJ (860 cal)

The easiest way to mix all the burger ingredients thoroughly is to use your hands.

Add the oil a teaspoon at a time until the mayonnaise thickens, then pour a thin stream.

Cook the burgers on a hot, lightly oiled barbecue flatplate or grill.

SPICY SEAFOOD SKEWERS

Preparation time: 40 minutes
Total cooking time: 15 minutes
Serves 4

SPICE PASTE
2 large red chillies, seeded and
    chopped
1 clove garlic, chopped
2 spring onions, finely chopped
1 teaspoon grated fresh ginger
1 tablespoon grated fresh turmeric
1 small tomato, peeled and seeded
1/2 teaspoon coriander seeds
2 tablespoons chopped roasted
    peanuts
1/2 teaspoon dried shrimp paste
2 teaspoons vegetable oil
1 tablespoon tamarind concentrate
1 tablespoon finely chopped lemon
    grass

350 g (11 oz) skinned boneless
    snapper fillet
350 g (11 oz) raw prawns, peeled and
    deveined
1 egg, lightly beaten
2 cups (120 g/4 oz) flaked coconut
4 kaffir lime leaves, shredded
2 tablespoons brown sugar
3/4 cup (185 g/6 oz) whole egg
    mayonnaise
3 teaspoons grated lime rind
1 tablespoon chopped fresh coriander

1 Soak 6 thick wooden skewers in water for 30 minutes.
2 To make the paste, coarsely grind the chilli, garlic, spring onion, ginger, turmeric, tomato, coriander, peanuts and shrimp paste in a food processor. Heat the oil in a frying pan and cook the chilli mixture, tamarind and lemon grass for 5 minutes over medium heat, stirring frequently, until golden. Put aside to cool before using.
3 Finely mince the fish and prawns in a food processor. Add the egg, coconut, kaffir lime leaves, sugar and spice paste. Season well with salt and pepper. Process until well combined.
4 Using wet hands, shape 1/4 cup of mixture around each skewer, then cook on a hot, lightly oiled barbecue flatplate or grill for 8–10 minutes, turning often, until golden. Mix the mayonnaise, lime rind and coriander in a bowl and serve with the skewers.

NUTRITION PER SERVE
Protein 45 g; Fat 50 g; Carbohydrate 25 g;
Dietary Fibre 5 g; Cholesterol 245 mg;
2965 kJ (710 cal)

HINT: For extra flavour, try using trimmed stalks of lemon grass instead of wooden skewers.

Cook the spice paste in a frying pan until it becomes golden.

Add the egg, coconut, lime leaves, sugar and spice paste to the food processor.

Shape the skewers with wet hands so that the mixture doesn't stick.

VEGETABLE AND TOFU KEBABS

Preparation time: 40 minutes +
    30 minutes marinating
Total cooking time: 30 minutes
Serves 4

500 g (1 lb) firm tofu, cubed
1 red capsicum, cubed
3 zucchini, thickly sliced
4 small onions, cut into quarters
300 g (10 oz) button mushrooms, cut
    into quarters
1/2 cup (125 ml/4 fl oz) tamari
1/2 cup (125 ml/4 fl oz) sesame oil
2.5 cm (1 inch) piece fresh ginger,
    peeled and grated
1/2 cup (180 g/6 oz) honey
1 tablespoon sesame oil, extra
1 small onion, finely chopped
1 clove garlic, crushed
2 teaspoons chilli paste
1 cup (250 g/8 oz) smooth peanut
    butter
1 cup (250 ml/8 fl oz) coconut milk
1 tablespoon soft brown sugar
1 tablespoon tamari
1 tablespoon lemon juice
3 tablespoons peanuts, roasted and
    chopped
3 tablespoons sesame seeds, toasted

1 Preheat the oven to hot 220°C (425°F/Gas 7). Soak 12 bamboo skewers in water to prevent scorching. Thread the tofu, capsicum, zucchini, onions and mushrooms onto the skewers. Arrange in a shallow, non-metallic dish.
2 Combine the tamari, oil, ginger and honey and pour over the kebabs. Leave for 30 minutes.
3 To make the peanut sauce, heat the extra oil in a large frying pan over medium heat and cook the onion, garlic and chilli paste for 1–2 minutes, or until the onion is soft. Reduce the heat, add the peanut butter, coconut milk, sugar, tamari and lemon juice and stir. Bring to the boil, then reduce the heat and simmer for 10 minutes, or until just thick. Stir in the peanuts. If the sauce is too thick, add water.
4 Cook the kebabs on a hot, lightly oiled barbecue grill or flatplate, basting with the marinade and turning occasionally, for 10–15 minutes, or until tender. Drizzle peanut sauce over the kebabs and sprinkle with sesame seeds to serve.

NUTRITION PER SERVE
Protein 31.5 g; Fat 65 g; Carbohydrate 25.5 g;
Dietary Fibre 15 g; Cholesterol 0 mg;
3334 kJ (795 cal)

Thread alternating pieces of tofu and vegetables onto the skewers.

Simmer the peanut sauce for 10 minutes, or until just thickened.

Cook the skewers, occasionally turning and basting with the marinade.

MUSHROOM AND EGGPLANT SKEWERS WITH TOMATO SAUCE

Preparation time: 20 minutes +
   15 minutes marinating
Total cooking time: 30 minutes
Serves 4

12 long fresh rosemary sprigs
18 Swiss brown mushrooms,
   halved
1 small eggplant, cubed
3 tablespoons olive oil
2 tablespoons balsamic vinegar
2 cloves garlic, crushed
1 teaspoon sugar

TOMATO SAUCE
5 tomatoes
1 tablespoon olive oil
1 small onion, finely chopped
1 clove garlic, crushed
1 tablespoon tomato paste
2 teaspoons sugar
2 teaspoons balsamic vinegar
1 tablespoon chopped fresh
   flat-leaf parsley

1 Remove the leaves from the lower part of the rosemary sprigs. Reserve a tablespoon of the leaves. Put the mushrooms and eggplant in a large non-metallic bowl. Pour on the combined oil, vinegar, garlic and sugar and toss. Marinate for 15 minutes.
2 To make the tomato sauce, score a cross in the base of each tomato. Put in a bowl of boiling water for 30 seconds, then plunge into cold water. Peel the skin away from the cross. Cut in half and scoop out the seeds with a teaspoon. Dice the flesh.
3 Heat the oil in a saucepan. Cook the onion and garlic over medium heat for 2–3 minutes, or until soft. Reduce the heat, add the tomato, tomato paste, sugar, vinegar and parsley and simmer for 10 minutes, or until thick.
4 Thread alternating mushroom halves and eggplant cubes onto the rosemary sprigs. Cook on a hot, lightly oiled barbecue grill or flatplate for 7–8 minutes, or until the eggplant is tender, turning occasionally. Serve with the sauce.

NUTRITION PER SERVE
Protein 3 g; Fat 24 g; Carbohydrate 8.5 g;
Dietary Fibre 4 g; Cholesterol 0 mg;
1100 kJ (263 cal)

Simmer the tomato sauce until the liquid has evaporated and the sauce is thick.

Thread alternating mushrooms and eggplant cubes onto the skewers.

CHICKEN TIKKA KEBABS

Preparation time: 10 minutes +
   2 hours marinating
Total cooking time: 10 minutes
Serves 4

10 chicken thigh fillets, cubed
1 red onion, cut into wedges
3 tablespoons tikka paste
1/2 cup (125 ml/4 fl oz) coconut milk
2 tablespoons lemon juice

1 Soak 8 skewers in water to prevent scorching. Thread 2 pieces of chicken and a wedge of onion alternately along each skewer. Place the skewers in a shallow, non-metallic dish.
2 Combine the tikka paste, coconut milk and lemon juice in a jar with a lid. Season and shake well to combine. Pour the mixture over the skewers and marinate for at least 2 hours, or overnight if time permits.
3 Cook the skewers on a hot, lightly oiled barbecue grill or flatplate for 4 minutes on each side, or until the

chicken is cooked through. Put any leftover marinade in a small pan and bring to the boil. Serve as a sauce with the tikka kebabs.

NUTRITION PER SERVE
Protein 50 g; Fat 13 g; Carbohydrate 4 g;
Dietary Fibre 1.5 g; Cholesterol 114 mg;
1457 kJ (350 cal)

Thread a couple of pieces of chicken and then a wedge of onion and repeat until the skewer is full.

Mix the tikka marinade in a screw-top jar and then pour over the kebabs.

Cook the kebabs on a barbecue grill or flatplate until the chicken is cooked through.

SKEWERED LAMB WITH CHILLI AIOLI

Preparation time: 25 minutes + 3 hours marinating
Total cooking time: 15 minutes
Makes 12 skewers

1.5 kg (3 lb) leg of lamb, boned and cubed
1/2 cup (125 ml/4 fl oz) olive oil
1/2 cup (125 ml/4 fl oz) lemon juice
2 cloves garlic, crushed
1 teaspoon cracked black pepper
1 tablespoon Dijon mustard
1 tablespoon chopped fresh oregano

CHILLI AIOLI
2–3 small red chillies, seeds and stems removed
3 cloves garlic
1/2 teaspoon ground black pepper
3 egg yolks
2 tablespoons lemon juice
200 ml (6 1/2 fl oz) olive oil

1 Put the lamb in a large, non-metallic bowl. Add the combined olive oil, lemon juice, garlic, pepper, mustard and oregano. Toss well, cover and refrigerate for at least 3 hours.
2 Soak 12 wooden skewers in water to prevent scorching. Drain the lamb, reserving the marinade. Thread the lamb onto the skewers and cook on a hot, lightly oiled barbecue grill or flatplate until well browned, brushing with the marinade occasionally.
3 To make the chilli aioli, chop the chillies and garlic for 30 seconds in a food processor. Add the black pepper, egg yolks and 2 teaspoons of lemon juice. With the motor running, slowly pour in the oil in a fine stream. Increase the flow as the aioli thickens. Add the remaining lemon juice and season to taste. Serve with the skewered lamb.

NUTRITION PER SKEWER
Protein 20 g; Fat 15 g; Carbohydrate 0 g;
Dietary Fibre 0 g; Cholesterol 55 mg;
810 kJ (190 cal)

Mix the lamb pieces with the marinade to thoroughly coat the meat.

Thread four pieces of marinated lamb onto each soaked skewer.

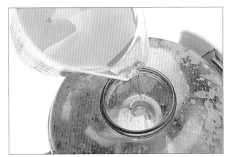
Pour the oil in a fine stream into the food processor with the motor running.

41

SESAME CHICKEN KEBABS

Preparation time: 10 minutes +
  2 hours marinating
Total cooking time: 10 minutes
Serves 4

3 tablespoons oil
2 tablespoons soy sauce
2 tablespoons honey
1 tablespoon grated fresh ginger
1 tablespoon sesame oil
4 large chicken breast fillets, cubed
8 spring onions, cut into short lengths
1 tablespoon toasted sesame seeds
  (see HINT)

1 Soak 12 wooden skewers in water to prevent scorching. To make the marinade, whisk together the oil, soy sauce, honey, ginger and sesame oil.

Thread the chicken and spring onion onto the skewers and put in a non-metallic dish. Add the marinade, cover and refrigerate for at least 2 hours.
2 Place the skewers on a hot, lightly oiled barbecue flatplate or grill and baste with the remaining marinade. Cook for 4 minutes on each side, or until the chicken is cooked through. Sprinkle with the sesame seeds.

NUTRITION PER SERVE
Protein 55 g; Fat 25 g; Carbohydrate 13 g; Dietary Fibre 1 g; Cholesterol 120 mg; 2180 kJ (520 cal)

HINT: To toast sesame seeds, place in a dry pan and shake over moderate heat until golden.

Spread the pieces of chicken and spring onion alternately onto the skewers.

Once the kebabs are cooked through, sprinkle with the sesame seeds to serve.

PERSIAN CHICKEN SKEWERS

Preparation time: 10 minutes +
  overnight marinating
Total cooking time: 10 minutes
Serves 4

2 teaspoons ground cardamom
1/2 teaspoon ground turmeric
1 teaspoon ground allspice
4 cloves garlic, crushed
3 tablespoons lemon juice
3 tablespoons olive oil
4 large chicken thigh fillets, excess fat
  removed
lemon wedges, to serve
plain yoghurt, to serve

1 Soak 8 wooden skewers in water to prevent scorching. To make the marinade, whisk together the cardamom, turmeric, allspice, garlic, lemon juice and oil. Season with salt and ground black pepper.
2 Cut each chicken thigh fillet into 3–4 cm cubes. Toss the cubes in the spice marinade. Thread the chicken onto skewers and place on a tray. Cover and refrigerate overnight.
3 Cook the skewers on a hot, lightly oiled barbecue grill or flatplate for 4 minutes on each side, or until the chicken is cooked through. Serve with lemon wedges and plain yoghurt.

NUTRITION PER SERVE
Protein 35 g; Fat 18 g; Carbohydrate 0.5 g;
Dietary Fibre 0.5 g; Cholesterol 75 mg;
1259 kJ (300 cal)

Whisk together the spices, garlic, lemon juice and oil to make a marinade.

Cut the chicken into bite-sized cubes and then toss in the marinade.

Cook the skewers for 4 minutes on each side, or until the chicken is cooked through.

MEDITERRANEAN CHICKEN SKEWERS

Preparation time: 20 minutes +
  2 hours marinating
Total cooking time: 10 minutes
Makes 8 skewers

32 chicken tenderloins
24 cherry tomatoes
6 cap mushrooms, cut into quarters
2 cloves garlic, crushed
rind of 1 lemon, grated

2 tablespoons lemon juice
2 tablespoons olive oil
1 tablespoon fresh oregano leaves,
  chopped

1 Soak 8 wooden skewers in water to prevent scorching. Thread a piece of chicken onto each skewer, followed by a tomato, then a piece of mushroom. Repeat three times for each skewer. Put the skewers in a shallow, non-metallic dish.
2 Combine the garlic, lemon rind, lemon juice, olive oil and chopped

oregano, pour over the skewers and toss well. Marinate for at least 2 hours, or overnight if time permits.
3 Cook the skewers on a hot, lightly oiled barbecue grill or flatplate for 4 minutes on each side, basting occasionally, until the chicken is cooked and the tomatoes have shrivelled slightly.

NUTRITION PER SKEWER
Protein 34 g; Fat 8 g; Carbohydrate 1 g;
Dietary Fibre 1 g; Cholesterol 75 mg;
909 kJ (217 cal)

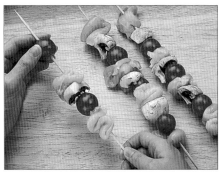

Thread the chicken tenderloins, cherry tomatoes and pieces of mushroom on the skewers.

Put the skewers in a shallow, non-metallic dish and marinate for at least 2 hours.

Cook the skewers for 4 minutes on each side, basting occasionally.

THAI MEATBALL SKEWERS

Preparation time: 25 minutes
Total cooking time: 10 minutes
Serves 4

350 g (11 oz) beef mince
3 French shallots, finely chopped
3 cloves garlic, chopped
2.5 cm (1 inch) piece fresh ginger,
    grated
1 tablespoon green or pink
    peppercorns, crushed

2 teaspoons Golden Mountain sauce
2 teaspoons fish sauce
2 teaspoons soft brown sugar
lime wedges, to serve

1 Soak wooden skewers in water to prevent scorching. Chop the mince with a cleaver or large knife until the mince is very fine. Mix together the mince, French shallots, garlic, ginger, peppercorns, Golden Mountain sauce, fish sauce and brown sugar with your hands until well combined.
2 Using 2 teaspoons of mixture at a time, form into balls. Thread three of the balls onto each of the skewers.
3 Cook the skewers on a hot, lightly oiled barbecue grill or flatplate, turning frequently, for 7–8 minutes or until the meat is cooked. Serve with the lime wedges.

NUTRITION PER SERVE
Protein 78 g; Fat 10 g; Carbohydrate 4 g;
Dietary Fibre 1 g; Cholesterol 55 mg;
728 kJ (174 cal)

Use a large, sharp knife or a cleaver to chop the mince until very fine.

Form 2 teaspoonsful of mixture at a time into small, compact balls.

Cook the skewered meatballs, turning frequently, for 7–8 minutes.

INDIAN SEEKH KEBABS

Preparation time: 40 minutes
Total cooking time: 12 minutes
Serves 4

pinch of ground cloves
pinch of ground nutmeg
1/2 teaspoon chilli powder
1 teaspoon ground cumin
2 teaspoons ground coriander
3 cloves garlic, finely chopped
5 cm (2 inch) piece fresh ginger,
    grated
500 g (1 lb) lean beef mince
1 tablespoon oil
2 tablespoons lemon juice

ONION AND MINT RELISH
1 red onion, finely chopped
1 tablespoon white vinegar
1 tablespoon lemon juice
1 tablespoon chopped fresh mint

1 Soak 12 thick wooden skewers in cold water to prevent scorching. Dry-fry the cloves, nutmeg, chilli, cumin and coriander in a heavy-based frying pan, over low heat, for 2 minutes, shaking the pan constantly. Transfer to a bowl with the garlic and ginger and set aside.
2 Knead the mince firmly with your fingertips and the base of your hand for 3 minutes, or until very soft and a little sticky (this gives the kebabs the correct soft texture when cooked). Add the mince to the spice and garlic mixture and mix well, seasoning with plenty of salt and pepper.
3 Form tablespoons of the meat into small, round patties. Wet your hands and press two portions of the meat around a skewer, leaving a small gap at the top. Smooth the outside gently,

place on baking paper and refrigerate while making the remaining kebabs.
4 To make the relish, mix the onion, vinegar and lemon juice and refrigerate for 10 minutes. Stir in the mint and season with pepper.
5 Cook the skewers on a hot, lightly oiled barbecue grill or flatplate for about 8 minutes, turning regularly and sprinkling with a little lemon juice. Serve with the relish.

NUTRITION PER SERVE
Protein 16 g; Fat 13 g; Carbohydrate 2 g;
Dietary Fibre 1 g; Cholesterol 47 mg;
798 kJ (190 cal)

NOTE: These kebabs freeze very well —simply defrost before barbecuing.

Peel and chop the garlic and peel and grate the piece of fresh ginger.

Dry-fry the cloves, nutmeg, chilli, cumin and coriander in a heavy-based pan.

Form the meat mixture into small patties and then press two around each skewer.

TANDOORI PRAWN STICKS

Preparation time: 20 minutes + 1 hour
 refrigeration
Total cooking time: 15 minutes
Serves 6

1 tablespoon oil
1 clove garlic, crushed
1 tablespoon grated fresh ginger
1 tablespoon finely chopped lemon
 grass
1 onion, finely chopped
1 tablespoon tandoori paste
4 kaffir lime leaves, finely shredded

1 tablespoon coconut cream
2 teaspoons grated lime rind
600 g (1¼ lb) raw prawns, peeled and
 deveined
3 stems lemon grass, cut into
 15 cm (6 inch) lengths

1 Heat the oil in a frying pan, add the garlic, ginger, lemon grass and onion and cook over medium heat for 3 minutes, or until golden.
2 Add the tandoori paste and kaffir lime leaves and cook for 5 minutes, or until the tandoori paste is fragrant. Cool slightly. Transfer to a food processor, add the coconut cream, lime rind and prawns and process until

finely minced. Divide the mixture into six portions and shape around the middle of the lemon grass stems with wet hands. The mixture is quite soft, so take care when handling it (using wet hands will prevent it sticking). Refrigerate for 1 hour.
3 Cook the satays on a moderately hot, lightly oiled barbecue grill or flatplate for 5 minutes, or until they are cooked through.

NUTRITION PER SERVE
Protein 21 g; Fat 5 g; Carbohydrate 1 g;
Dietary Fibre 0.5 g; Cholesterol 1 mg;
560 kJ (134 cal)

Add the tandoori paste and kaffir lime leaves to the pan and cook until fragrant.

Transfer the mixture to a food processor and add the coconut cream, lime rind and prawns.

Wet your hands to prevent sticking, and shape the mixture around the stems.

Sausage Marinades

The following recipes make enough marinade for about 12 sausages. Leave to marinate for at least a few hours, and overnight if time permits. Some of the marinades are also suitable to use as bastes—simply brush over the sausages during cooking to add extra flavour.

There are many flavoured sausages available today that need no enhancement, just barbecue and serve with a salad, bread or vegetables. But for creative cooks, who want their traditional beef or pork sausages to take pride of place on the barbecue menu, a simple marinade or baste can change an ordinary sausage into something extra special.

Marinades add flavour to meat or vegetables and, when they have an acid ingredient such as lemon juice, wine or vinegar, they also work to tenderise the meat. Leave the sausages in the marinade for several hours (or preferably overnight) to give them time to absorb the flavours of the marinade. The longer you leave them, the more intense the flavours will be when the sausages are cooked.

A baste is similar to a marinade, but is brushed over the food while it cooks. The result is a lovely, subtle flavour. Basting will also keep sausages moist while they cook.

To use the following marinades as bastes, brush the mixture over the sausages while they are cooking, rather than marinating the sausages first.

FRESH HERB MARINADE

Mix the following ingredients thoroughly in a bowl: 1/4 cup (60 ml/2 fl oz) olive oil, 2–3 tablespoons lemon juice or balsamic vinegar, 1–2 crushed cloves garlic, 3 teaspoons soft brown sugar, some salt and freshly ground black pepper and 4 tablespoons of chopped fresh mixed herbs (use any combination you have handy—chives, lemon thyme, rosemary, parsley, basil, coriander, mint, oregano or marjoram). Prick the sausages all over and marinate, covered in a non-metallic dish, for at least 3 hours or overnight in the refrigerator. Turn the sausages occasionally. Use with any type of sausage. This mixture is also suitable for use as a baste.

HONEY AND CHILLI MARINADE

Mix the following ingredients thoroughly in a bowl:
1/4 cup (60 ml/2 fl oz) soy sauce, 1 tablespoon grated fresh ginger, 2 teaspoons grated lemon rind, 1/4 cup (90 g/3 oz) honey, 1–2 crushed cloves garlic, 1 tablespoon sherry or rice wine and 3 tablespoons sweet chilli sauce. Prick the sausages all over and marinate, covered in a non-metallic dish, for at least 3 hours or overnight in the refrigerator. Turn the sausages occasionally. This marinade goes well with any kind of sausage. It is also suitable for basting.

APRICOT AND ONION MARINADE

Mix the following ingredients thoroughly in a bowl: 1/3 cup (80 ml/2 3/4 fl oz) apricot nectar, 3 tablespoons lime marmalade, 2 crushed cloves garlic, 2 tablespoons olive oil, 1–2 tablespoons French onion soup mix, 1 tablespoon chopped fresh chives, a dash of Worcestershire sauce. Prick the sausages all over and marinate, covered, for at least 3 hours or overnight in the refrigerator. Turn the sausages occasionally. This mixture is also suitable for use as a baste.

SPICY TANDOORI MARINADE

Mix the following ingredients thoroughly in a bowl: 1 tablespoon oil, 2 teaspoons each of ground cumin, coriander and paprika, 3 teaspoons turmeric, 2 teaspoons each of fresh grated ginger and tamarind sauce, 2 crushed cloves garlic, 1/2–1 teaspoon chilli powder, 1/2 teaspoon salt, 3 tablespoons tomato sauce and 200 g (6 1/2 oz) plain yoghurt. Prick the sausages all over and marinate, covered, for at least 3 hours or overnight in the refrigerator. Turn the sausages occasionally. Use for lamb or chicken sausages. This mixture is also suitable for basting.

PLUM AND CORIANDER MARINADE

Mix the following ingredients thoroughly in a bowl: 1/4 cup (60 ml/2 fl oz) plum sauce, 1–2 crushed cloves garlic, 1 tablespoon each of Worcestershire and soy sauce, 2 tablespoons each of lime juice and chopped fresh coriander and 1/4 cup (60 ml/2 fl oz) tomato sauce. Prick the sausages all over and marinate, covered, for at least 3 hours or overnight in the refrigerator. Turn the sausages occasionally. This mixture is also suitable for basting.

Clockwise, from top left: Fresh Herb Marinade; Honey and Chilli Marinade; Spicy Tandoori Marinade; Plum and Coriander Marinade; Apricot and Onion Marinade

Meatballs with Sauces & Dips

Meatballs on skewers or spiked on toothpicks are great fun at barbecues, especially if you serve them up with an array of sauces for dipping. The following recipe makes about 45 meatballs, and two or three choices of sauce would be about right to accompany them.

MEATBALLS

Combine 750 g (1¹/₂ lb) lean beef mince, 1 very finely chopped onion, 1 lightly beaten egg, 2 crushed garlic cloves, 2–3 tablespoons fresh breadcrumbs and lots of salt and freshly ground black pepper in a large bowl. Use your hands to mix well. Then wet your hands and roll tablespoons of the mince mixture into balls. You can thread the meatballs onto wooden skewers that have been soaked in water to prevent scorching. Cook on a hot, lightly oiled barbecue grill or flatplate for about 10 minutes, or until the meat is cooked through. Serve the meatballs with the sauces.

BARBECUE SAUCE

Finely chop 1 small onion. Put a little oil in a frying pan and add the onion. Cook over low heat for 3 minutes, or until the onion is soft but not browned. Add 1 tablespoon each of malt vinegar, Worcestershire sauce and soft brown sugar, plus ¹/₃ cup (80 ml/2³/₄ fl oz) tomato sauce. Bring the mixture to the boil and then reduce the heat and simmer for about 3 minutes, or until the sauce has slightly thickened. Serve the barbecue sauce warm or at room temperature with the meatballs.

DILL SAUCE

Combine $^1/_2$ cup (125 g/4 oz) each of plain yoghurt and sour cream, 1 tablespoon horseradish cream, $^1/_4$ cup (15 g/$^1/_2$ oz) chopped fresh dill, 2 finely chopped spring onions and salt and pepper. Mix well and serve chilled.

CAPSICUM MAYONNAISE

Cut a large red capsicum in half, remove the seeds and membrane and brush the skin lightly with oil. Grill, skin-side-up, until the skin blisters and blackens. Cover the capsicum with a tea towel or put in a paper or plastic bag to cool. When cool enough to handle, peel away the skin and place the flesh in a food processor. Add $^3/_4$ cup (185 g/6 oz) whole egg mayonnaise, 1–2 cloves garlic, salt, pepper and a squeeze of lemon juice. Process until smooth. You could also add some chopped fresh basil.

HERB SAUCE

Mix together 200 g (6$^1/_2$ oz) plain yoghurt, 1 tablespoon each of chopped fresh mint, coriander and lemon thyme, 2 tablespoons cream and 1 teaspoon freshly grated ginger. You could also add 1 small peeled, seeded and finely chopped Lebanese cucumber.

CHILLI AND LIME SAUCE

Combine $^1/_4$ cup (60 ml/2 fl oz) sweet chilli sauce, 2 teaspoons soft brown sugar, 1 teaspoon finely grated lime rind, 3–4 teaspoons lime juice and 1 tablespoon freshly chopped basil.

PEANUT SAUCE

Heat 3 teaspoons peanut oil in a pan. Add 1 small, finely chopped onion and cook for 3 minutes, or until soft. Stir in 2 crushed cloves garlic, 2 teaspoons each of grated fresh ginger and ground cumin and 1 teaspoon red curry paste. Cook, stirring, for 1 minute. Stir in 1$^1/_2$ cups (375 ml/ 12 fl oz) coconut milk, $^1/_2$ cup (80 g/2$^3/_4$ oz) very finely chopped peanuts and 2 tablespoons soft brown sugar. Simmer over low heat for 5 minutes, or until slightly thickened. Add a little lemon juice. Serve the sauce warm.

CORIANDER SAUCE

In a bowl, combine $^1/_4$ cup (60 ml/2 fl oz) fish sauce, 1 tablespoon white vinegar, 2–3 teaspoons finely chopped fresh red chillies, 1 teaspoon sugar and 3 teaspoons chopped fresh coriander. Add a good squeeze of lime juice, mix well and serve.

Left to right: Meatballs; Barbecue Sauce; Dill Sauce; Capsicum Mayonnaise; Herb Sauce; Chilli and Lime Sauce; Peanut Sauce; Coriander Sauce

Meat

TANGY BEEF RIBS

Preparation time: 20 minutes +
  3 hours marinating
Total cooking time: 15–20 minutes
Serves 4

1 kg (2 lb) beef ribs
1/2 cup (125 ml/4 fl oz) tomato sauce
2 tablespoons Worcestershire sauce
2 tablespoons soft brown sugar
1 teaspoon paprika
1/4 teaspoon chilli powder
1 clove garlic, crushed

1 Chop the ribs into individual serving pieces, if necessary (see NOTES). Bring a large pan of water to the boil. Cook the ribs in boiling water for 5 minutes and then drain.
2 Combine the tomato sauce, Worcestershire sauce, sugar, paprika, chilli powder and garlic in large non-metallic bowl and mix together well. Add the ribs, cover and marinate in the fridge for at least several hours or overnight if time permits.
3 Cook the ribs on a hot, lightly oiled barbecue grill or flatplate, brushing frequently with the marinade, for 10–15 minutes, or until the ribs are well browned and cooked through. Serve with slices of grilled fresh pineapple.

NUTRITION PER SERVE
Protein 28 g; Fat 10 g; Carbohydrate 21 g; Dietary Fibre 1 g; Cholesterol 84 mg; 982 kJ (235 cal)

HINT: If time is short, toss the ribs in the marinade and leave at room temperature, covered, for up to 2 hours. The meat will absorb the flavours of the marinade more quickly at room temperature. (This principle applies to all marinades.)

NOTES: Ribs can be bought as a long piece or cut into individual pieces. If chopping ribs yourself, you will need a sharp cleaver. Alternatively, ribs can be cooked in one piece and chopped into pieces after cooking, when the bone is softer. A longer cooking time will be required if the ribs are to be cooked as a single piece.

Pork ribs can also be used in this recipe. Use either the thick, meaty ribs, which are like beef ribs, or the long thin spare ribs, also known as American-style ribs. Pork spare ribs have less meat so a shorter cooking time is required.

Cook the ribs in a large pan of boiling water for 5 minutes before marinating.

Cook the ribs until they are well browned and cooked through, basting frequently.

CHILLI PORK RIBS

Preparation time: 15 minutes +
  overnight marinating
Total cooking time: 20 minutes
Serves 4–6

1 kg (2 lb) pork spareribs
125 g (4 oz) can puréed tomatoes
2 tablespoons honey
2 tablespoons chilli sauce
2 tablespoons hoisin sauce
2 tablespoons lime juice
2 cloves garlic, crushed
1 tablespoon oil

1 Cut each rib into thirds, then lay them in a single layer in a shallow non-metallic dish.
2 Mix together all the other ingredients except the oil and pour over the meat, turning to coat well. Cover with plastic wrap and refrigerate overnight, turning occasionally.
3 Drain the ribs, reserving the marinade, and cook them over medium heat on a lightly oiled barbecue grill or flatplate. Baste often with the marinade and cook for 15–20 minutes, or until the ribs are tender and well browned, turning occasionally. Season to taste before serving immediately.

NUTRITION PER SERVE (6)
Protein 15 g; Fat 26 g; Carbohydrate 9 g;
Dietary Fibre 0 g; Cholesterol 90 mg;
1399 kJ (333 cal)

Use a sharp knife to cut each of the pork ribs into thirds, then place in a shallow dish.

Mix together all the ingredients for the marinade and then pour over the ribs.

Turn the ribs and baste often with the marinade while they are cooking.

LAMB SOUVLAKI ROLL

Preparation time: 20 minutes +
  4 hours marinating
Total cooking time: 10 minutes
Serves 4

500 g (1 lb) lamb backstrap or loin fillet
100 ml (3$^{1}/_{2}$ fl oz) olive oil
3 tablespoons dry white wine
1 tablespoon fresh oregano
3 tablespoons roughly chopped fresh
  basil
3 cloves garlic, crushed
2 bay leaves, crushed
2$^{1}/_{2}$ tablespoons lemon juice
1 large loaf Turkish bread

1 cup (250 g/8 oz) baba ganouj
1 tablespoon roughly chopped fresh
  parsley

1 Place the lamb in a shallow non-metallic dish. Mix together the oil, wine, oregano, basil, garlic, bay leaves and 2 tablespoons of the lemon juice and pour over the lamb, turning to coat well. Cover with plastic wrap and marinate for 4 hours.
2 Cook the lamb on a hot, lightly oiled barbecue grill or flatplate for 6–8 minutes, or until seared but still pink in the centre. Remove from the heat and rest for 10 minutes, then cut into slices.
3 Split the Turkish bread lengthways and spread the bottom thickly with the baba ganouj. Top with the lamb, sprinkle with the parsley and remaining lemon juice, then season with salt and pepper. Replace the top of the loaf, then cut into quarters to serve.

NUTRITION PER SERVE
Protein 40 g; Fat 43 g; Carbohydrate 33 g;
Dietary Fibre 8.5 g; Cholesterol 82 mg;
2870 kJ (686 cal)

Chop the fresh basil with a sharp knife and then measure out 3 tablespoons.

Turn the lamb in the marinade so that it is well coated, then cover and leave.

After cooking, let the meat settle for 10 minutes before slicing.

FILLET STEAK WITH ONION MARMALADE

Preparation time: 20 minutes
Total cooking time: 1 hour
Serves 4

4 thick rib-eye steaks
30 g (1 oz) butter
2 red onions, thinly sliced
2 tablespoons soft brown sugar
1 tablespoon balsamic vinegar

1 Trim any fat from the steaks, then sprinkle liberally with freshly ground black pepper. Cover and refrigerate until ready to cook.
2 To make the onion marmalade, heat the butter in a heavy-based pan. Add the onion and cook, stirring often, for 10 minutes over low heat, or until the onion is soft but not brown. Stir in the brown sugar and balsamic vinegar and continue to cook for about 30 minutes, stirring frequently. The mixture will become thick and glossy.

3 Place the steaks on a hot, lightly oiled barbecue grill or flatplate and cook for 3 minutes each side to seal, turning once only. For rare steaks, cook a further minute. For medium, cook for another few minutes and for well done, about 5 minutes. Serve at once with the onion marmalade.

NUTRITION PER SERVE
Protein 30 g; Fat 10 g; Carbohydrate 25 g;
Dietary Fibre 4 g; Cholesterol 100 mg;
1355 kJ (320 cal)

Trim any fat from the steaks and then sprinkle liberally with black pepper.

Cook the onion marmalade for about 30 minutes, or until it is thick and glossy.

Cook the steaks for 3 minutes on each side to seal them, then cook to your taste.

SESAME AND GINGER BEEF

Preparation time: 15 minutes +
  2 hours marinating
Total cooking time: 25 minutes
Serves 4–6

1/4 cup (60 ml/2 fl oz) sesame oil
1/4 cup (60 ml/2 fl oz) soy sauce
2 cloves garlic, crushed
2 tablespoons grated fresh ginger
1 tablespoon lemon juice
2 tablespoons chopped spring onions

1/4 cup (60 g/2 oz) firmly packed soft
  brown sugar
500 g (1 lb) beef fillet (see NOTE)

1 Combine the sesame oil, soy sauce, garlic, ginger, lemon juice, spring onion and brown sugar in a non-metallic dish. Add the beef and coat well with the marinade. Cover and refrigerate for at least 2 hours, or overnight if possible.
2 Brown the beef on all sides on a very hot, lightly oiled barbecue grill or flatplate. When the beef is sealed, remove, wrap in foil and return to the

barbecue, turning occasionally, for a further 15–20 minutes, depending on how well done you like your meat. Leave for 10 minutes before slicing.
3 Put the leftover marinade in a pan and boil for 5 minutes. Serve as a sauce with the beef.

NUTRITION PER SERVE (6)
Protein 20 g; Fat 15 g; Carbohydrate 10 g;
Dietary Fibre 0 g; Cholesterol 55 mg;
975 kJ (230 cal)

NOTE: Steaks can be used instead—there is no need to wrap them in foil.

Combine the marinade ingredients in a non-metallic dish.

Brown the beef on all sides until the meat is sealed, then remove from the barbecue.

Wrap the beef in foil and then cook on the barbecue, turning occasionally.

VEAL STEAKS WITH CAPER BUTTER

Preparation time: 10 minutes
Total cooking time: 6 minutes
Serves 4

50 g (1¾ oz) butter, softened
2 tablespoons dry white wine
2 tablespoons capers, finely chopped
2 teaspoons finely grated lemon rind
8 small veal steaks, about 500 g (1 lb)

1 Mix together the butter, white wine, capers, lemon rind and some salt and black pepper with a wooden spoon. Cover and refrigerate until required.
2 Cook the veal steaks on a hot, lightly oiled barbecue flatplate or grill for 2–3 minutes on each side. Remove, place on warm plates and top with the caper butter. Serve immediately.

NUTRITION PER SERVE
Protein 30 g; Fat 15 g; Carbohydrate 0 g; Dietary Fibre 0 g; Cholesterol 135 mg; 990 kJ (235 cal)

Use a sharp knife to finely chop the capers so that they mix smoothly with the butter.

Mix the butter, white wine, capers, lemon rind and salt and pepper.

Cook the veal for 2–3 minutes on each side on a hot barbecue flatplate.

MOROCCAN LAMB WITH PISTACHIO COUSCOUS

Preparation time: 40 minutes +
 2 hours marinating
Total cooking time: 20 minutes
Serves 4

MOROCCAN MARINADE
3 tablespoons olive oil
1 tablespoon lemon juice
2 teaspoons honey
1–2 cloves garlic, crushed
1 teaspoon ground cumin
1/2 teaspoon ground turmeric
1/2 teaspoon ground
 cinnamon
1/4 teaspoon cayenne pepper

8–10 small lamb fillets
pinch of saffron
1 1/2 cups (375 ml/12 fl oz) hot chicken
 stock
250 g (8 oz) couscous
1 tablespoon olive oil
1 red onion, chopped
1 red chilli, seeded and chopped
2 cloves garlic, crushed
1/2 cup (75 g/2 1/2 oz) currants
100 g (3 1/2 oz) shelled pistachio nuts
grated rind of 1 lemon
grated rind of 1 orange
3 tablespoons chopped fresh mint

1 Mix together all the marinade ingredients. Put the lamb in a shallow, non-metallic dish, add the marinade, cover and refrigerate for 2 hours.

2 Add the saffron to the hot stock and pour over the couscous. Set aside for 10 minutes, then stir to remove lumps.
3 Heat the oil in a frying pan, add the onion, chilli and garlic and cook for 3 minutes. Add the currants and nuts and cook for 5 minutes. Stir in the lemon and orange rind and the mint. Stir through the couscous.
4 Cook the lamb on a hot, lightly oiled barbecue grill or flatplate, turning once, until browned all over. Cook for 2–3 minutes more, turning frequently. Serve with the couscous.

NUTRITION PER SERVE
Protein 45 g; Fat 40 g; Carbohydrate 50 g;
Dietary Fibre 5 g; Cholesterol 110 mg;
3030 kJ (720 cal)

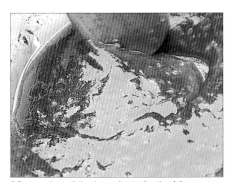

Mix together all the ingredients for the Moroccan marinade and pour over the lamb.

Stir the onion, chilli, garlic, currants, nuts, rind and mint through the couscous.

Cook the lamb on a hot barbecue until browned all over and then cook for a little longer.

LAMB WITH EGGPLANT, TOMATO AND PESTO

Preparation time: 30 minutes
Total cooking time: 25 minutes
Serves 4

PESTO
2 cups (100 g/3¹/₂ oz) fresh basil
    leaves
2 cloves garlic, crushed
¹/₃ cup (50 g/1³/₄ oz) pine nuts
³/₄ cup (185 ml/6 fl oz) olive oil
³/₄ cup (75 g/2¹/₂ oz) grated
    Parmesan

1 eggplant
4 Roma tomatoes, halved
6 lamb fillets
60 g (2 oz) goats cheese

1 To make the pesto, finely chop the basil, garlic and pine nuts in a food processor. With the motor running slowly, gradually pour in the olive oil. Add the Parmesan and process briefly.
2 Cut the eggplant into thick slices and brush with some olive oil. Cook the eggplant on a hot barbecue grill or flatplate, brushing with a little more oil, for 3–4 minutes each side, or until golden brown and softened. Remove

and keep warm. Add the tomatoes and cook, brushing with olive oil, until soft. Remove and keep warm.
3 Sprinkle each lamb fillet liberally with black pepper. Wipe the barbecue clean and lightly oil. Cook the lamb for 3–4 minutes, until cooked through but still pink inside. Slice diagonally and serve with the eggplant, tomato and a little pesto. Crumble the goats cheese over the top.

NUTRITION PER SERVE
Protein 35 g; Fat 75 g; Carbohydrate 5 g;
Dietary Fibre 5 g; Cholesterol 95 mg;
3490 kJ (830 cal)

Make the pesto in a food processor, finely chopping the basil, garlic and pine nuts first.

Brush the slices of eggplant with olive oil and then grill until golden brown and softened.

The lamb should be cooked through but still pink inside. Slice diagonally to serve.

LAMB CHOPS WITH CITRUS POCKETS

Preparation time: 25 minutes
Total cooking time: 15 minutes
Serves 4

4 lamb chump chops, about 250 g
   (8 oz) each
2 tablespoons lemon juice

CITRUS FILLING
3 spring onions, finely chopped
1 celery stick, finely chopped
2 teaspoons grated fresh ginger
3/4 cup (60 g/2 oz) fresh breadcrumbs
2 tablespoons orange juice
2 teaspoons finely grated orange rind
1 teaspoon chopped fresh rosemary

1 Cut a deep, long pocket in the side of each lamb chop.
2 Mix together all the filling ingredients and spoon into the pockets in the lamb.
3 Cook on a hot, lightly oiled barbecue flatplate or grill, turning once, for 15 minutes, or until the lamb is cooked through but still pink in the centre. Drizzle with the lemon juice.

NUTRITION PER SERVE
Protein 35 g; Fat 5 g; Carbohydrate 15 g;
Dietary Fibre 1 g; Cholesterol 105 mg;
1080 kJ (335 cal)

Cut a deep, long pocket in the side of each lamb chop, right through the skin and fat.

Mix together all the filling ingredients and then spoon into the lamb pockets.

Cook the lamb chops on a hot barbecue flatplate, turning once.

PORK WITH APPLE AND ONION WEDGES

Preparation time: 25 minutes
Total cooking time: 15 minutes
Serves 4

2 pork fillets, about 400 g (13 oz) each
12 pitted prunes
2 green apples, cored, unpeeled, cut
    into wedges
2 red onions, cut into wedges
50 g (1³/₄ oz) butter, melted
2 teaspoons caster sugar
¹/₂ cup (125 ml/4 fl oz) cream
2 tablespoons brandy
1 tablespoon chopped chives

1 Trim the pork of any excess fat and sinew and cut each fillet in half. Make a slit with a knife through the centre of each fillet and push 3 prunes into each one. Brush the pork, the apple and onion wedges with the melted butter and sprinkle the apple and onion with the caster sugar.
2 Brown the pork on a hot, lightly oiled barbecue flatplate. Add the apple and onion wedges (you may need to cook in batches if your flatplate isn't large enough). Cook, turning frequently, for 5–7 minutes, or until the pork is cooked through and the apple and onion pieces are softened. Remove the pork, apple and onion from the barbecue and keep warm.

3 Mix together the cream, brandy and chives in a pan. Transfer to the stove top and simmer for 3 minutes, or until slightly thickened. Season with salt and black pepper.
4 Slice the meat, apple and onion wedges and serve with the brandy cream sauce.

NUTRITION PER SERVE
Protein 25 g; Fat 25 g; Carbohydrate 25 g;
Dietary Fibre 4 g; Cholesterol 130 mg;
1920 kJ (455 cal)

Make a slit through the centre of the pork and fill with three prunes.

Brush the apple and onion with melted butter and then sprinkle with caster sugar.

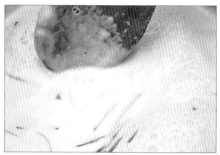
Simmer the brandy cream sauce until is has slightly thickened.

T-BONE STEAK WITH SWEET ONIONS

Preparation time: 10 minutes
Total cooking time: 20 minutes
Serves 4

4 tablespoons oil
6 onions, sliced into rings (see
    NOTE)
3 tablespoons barbecue sauce
4 T-bone steaks

1 Heat 2 tablespoons of the oil on a hot barbecue flatplate or grill. Add the onions and barbecue sauce and cook, stirring regularly, for 10 minutes, or until the onions are very soft and brown. Push to one side of the hot plate to keep warm.
2 Brush the T-bone steaks with the remaining oil and add to the hot plate. Cook over high heat, turning once or twice, until tender and cooked to your liking. Arrange the steaks on warm plates, spoon over some of the sweet caramelised onions, and serve.

NUTRITION PER SERVE
Protein 40 g; Fat 30 g; Carbohydrate 15 g;
Dietary Fibre 2 g; Cholesterol 85 mg;
1995 kJ (475 cal)

NOTE: The onions in this dish are caramelised, which means they are cooked very slowly over low heat until they are soft and sweet. Use common brown onions for caramelising, not the red variety.

You will need six onions for this recipe—they shrink down once they're carmelised

Cook the onions with the barbecue sauce until they are fully caramelised.

Brush the T-bone steaks with the remaining oil and then cook over high heat.

STEAK IN RED WINE

Preparation time: 10 minutes + 3 hours
  marinating
Total cooking time: 10 minutes
Serves 4

750 g (1¹/₂ lb) rump steak
1 cup (250 ml/8 fl oz) good red wine

2 teaspoons garlic salt
1 tablespoon dried oregano leaves
cracked black pepper

1 Trim the steak of any fat. Mix
together the wine, salt, oregano and
pepper. Put the steak in a shallow,
non-metallic dish and add the
marinade. Toss well, cover and
refrigerate for at least 3 hours.

2 Cook the steak on a hot, lightly
oiled barbecue flatplate or grill for
3–4 minutes on each side, brushing
frequently with the marinade.

NUTRITION PER SERVE
Protein 44 g; Fat 5 g; Carbohydrate 0 g;
Dietary Fibre 0 g; Cholesterol 126 mg;
1100 kJ (264 cal)

Trim the steak of any excess fat and sinew
before marinating.

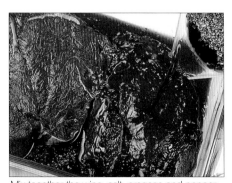

Mix together the wine, salt, oregano and pepper
and pour over the steak.

Cook the steak on a hot barbecue, brushing
frequently with the wine marinade.

PEPPER STEAKS WITH HORSERADISH SAUCE

Preparation time: 15 minutes
Total cooking time: 15 minutes
Serves 4

4 sirloin steaks
3 tablespoons seasoned cracked
   pepper

HORSERADISH SAUCE
2 tablespoons brandy
3 tablespoons beef stock
4 tablespoons cream
1 tablespoon horseradish cream
1/2 teaspoon sugar

1 Coat the steaks on both sides with pepper, pressing it into the meat. Cook on a hot, lightly oiled barbecue grill or flatplate for 5–10 minutes, until cooked to your taste.

2 To make the sauce, put the brandy and stock in a pan. Bring to the boil, then reduce the heat. Stir in the cream, horseradish and sugar and heat through. Serve with the steaks.

NUTRITION PER SERVE
Protein 43 g; Fat 21 g; Carbohydrate 2 g;
Dietary Fibre 0 g; Cholesterol 130 mg;
1615 kJ (386 cal)

Press the cracked pepper firmly into both sides of the steaks.

Cook the steaks on a hot, lightly oiled barbecue grill until they are cooked to your taste.

Add the cream, horseradish and sugar to the brandy and stock in the pan.

FILLET STEAK WITH FLAVOURED BUTTERS

Preparation time: 30 minutes
Total cooking time: 15 minutes
Serves 4

4 fillet steaks

CAPSICUM BUTTER
1 small red capsicum
125 g (4 oz) butter
2 teaspoons chopped fresh oregano
2 teaspoons chopped chives

GARLIC BUTTER
125 g (4 oz) butter
3 cloves garlic, crushed
2 spring onions, finely chopped

1 Cut a pocket in each steak.
2 For the capsicum butter, cut the capsicum into large pieces and place, skin-side-up, under a hot grill until the skin blisters and blackens. Put in a plastic bag until cool. Peel away the skin and dice the flesh. Beat the butter until creamy. Add the capsicum and herbs, season and beat until smooth.
3 For the garlic butter, beat the butter until creamy, add the garlic and spring onions and beat until smooth.
4 Push capsicum butter into the pockets in two of the steaks and garlic butter into the other two.
5 Cook on a hot, lightly oiled barbecue grill or flatplate for 4–5 minutes each side, turning once. Brush frequently with any remaining flavoured butter while cooking.

NUTRITION PER SERVE
Protein 28 g; Fat 57 g; Carbohydrate 2 g; Dietary Fibre 1 g; Cholesterol 244 mg; 2595 kJ (620 cal)

To make the garlic butter, beat the butter, garlic and spring onions until smooth.

Spoon the flavoured butter into the pocket cut in the side of the steak.

Brush the steaks with any remaining flavoured butter while barbecuing.

VEAL WITH SKORDALIA AND TOMATO BEANS

Preparation time: 45 minutes
Total cooking time: 40 minutes
Serves 4

SKORDALIA
350 g (11 oz) potatoes
3 tablespoons toasted blanched
    almonds
2 cloves garlic
1 tablespoon white wine vinegar
1/3 cup (80 ml/2¾ fl oz) olive oil

TOMATO BEANS
6 tomatoes, peeled, seeded and
    chopped
3 cloves garlic, chopped
1 teaspoon caster sugar
300 g (10 oz) can cannellini beans
1/3 cup (20 g/¾ oz) chopped fresh
    parsley

8 veal cutlets
lemon pepper seasoning
Parmesan shavings, to garnish

1 To make the skordalia, cut the potatoes into large pieces and boil for 15–20 minutes, or until tender. Drain and cool. Finely chop the toasted almonds in a food processor. Mash the potato and stir in the almonds, garlic and vinegar. Gradually pour in the olive oil, stirring constantly, until all the oil is incorporated. Season well.
2 To make the beans, heat a little olive oil in a heavy-based pan and add the tomato, garlic and sugar. Bring to the boil, reduce the heat and simmer, stirring frequently, for 15 minutes, or until thickened. Stir in the rinsed and drained beans and parsley. Season.
3 Trim the veal of fat and sinew and coat liberally with the lemon pepper. Cook on a hot, lightly oiled barbecue grill or flatplate for 3 minutes each side, depending on the thickness of the cutlets. Serve with the beans and skordalia, topped with Parmesan.

NUTRITION PER SERVE
Protein 35 g; Fat 25 g; Carbohydrate 35 g;
Dietary Fibre 5 g; Cholesterol 85 mg;
2200 kJ (525 cal)

Peel the cooked potatoes, then mash with a potato masher.

Mix the beans, parsley and salt and pepper into the tomatoes.

Trim the veal cutlets of any excess fat and sinew before they are barbecued.

KOREAN BEEF

Preparation time: 20 minutes
  + 30 minutes freezing
  + 2 hours marinating
Total cooking time: 15 minutes
Serves 4–6

500 g (1 lb) scotch fillet or sirloin steak
1/4 cup (40 g/1 1/4 oz) sesame seeds
1/2 cup (125 ml/4 fl oz) shoyu
   (Japanese soy sauce)
2 cloves garlic, finely chopped
3 spring onions, finely chopped
1 tablespoon sesame oil
1 tablespoon oil

1 Freeze the steak for 30 minutes for ease of slicing. Dry-fry the sesame seeds over low heat for 3–4 minutes, shaking the pan until golden. Cool and then grind in a food processor or with a mortar and pestle.

2 Slice the steak into thin strips, cutting across the grain. Combine the meat, shoyu, garlic, spring onion and half the crushed seeds in a non-metallic bowl and toss until the meat is well coated. Cover and marinate in the fridge for 2 hours.

3 Combine the oils and use to brush a very hot barbecue flatplate. Cook the meat in batches, searing each side for about 1 minute (don't overcook or the steak will be chewy). Oil and reheat the grill between batches. Sprinkle the steak with the remaining crushed seeds to serve.

NUTRITION PER SERVE (6)
Protein 19 g; Fat 15 g; Carbohydrate 0.5 g;
Dietary Fibre 1 g; Cholesterol 42 mg;
893 kJ (213 cal)

Freeze the meat for 30 minutes and then thinly slice across the grain.

Combine the meat with shoyu, garlic, spring onion and half the sesame seeds.

Take care not to overcook the meat when searing it on both sides.

PEPPERED STEAKS WITH MANGO SALSA

Preparation time: 10 minutes
  + 30 minutes chilling
Total cooking time: 15 minutes
Serves 6

6 fillet steaks
2 tablespoons black peppercorns
1 tablespoon white mustard seeds
2 tablespoons oil

MANGO AND AVOCADO SALSA
1 large ripe mango
1 large ripe avocado
1 spring onion, finely sliced
1 tablespoon lime juice
dash of Tabasco sauce

1 Trim the meat of excess fat and flatten with a meat mallet to even thickness. Nick the edges to prevent curling. Crush the peppercorns and mustard seeds briefly in a blender until coarsely cracked.

2 Rub oil over the steaks, then press on the peppercorn mixture to coat both sides. Store in the fridge, covered in plastic, for 30 minutes.

3 To make the salsa, peel the mango and dice the flesh. Peel the avocado and dice the flesh. Mix together the mango, avocado and remaining ingredients and toss well. Refrigerate, covered, until needed.

4 Cook the steaks on a hot, lightly oiled barbecue flatplate or grill for 2 minutes on each side to sear, turning only once. For rare steaks, cook for a further minute each side. For medium and well done, move the steaks to a cooler part of the barbecue and cook for a further 3–6 minutes each side. Serve with the salsa.

NUTRITION PER SERVE
Protein 28 g; Fat 20 g; Carbohydrate 3.5 g;
Dietary Fibre 1 g; Cholesterol 84 mg;
1302 kJ (311 cal)

Place the steaks between two sheets of plastic and flatten with a meat mallet.

Mix together the black pepper and white mustard seeds and press onto the steaks.

Cook the steaks on a hot barbecue flatplate for 3–6 minutes each side, depending on taste.

FILLET STEAK WITH LEMON BUTTER

Preparation time: 5 minutes
Total cooking time: 15 minutes
Serves 6

6 fillet steaks
1 tablespoon olive oil
2 cloves garlic, crushed
1 teaspoon dried rosemary

LEMON BUTTER
125 g (4 oz) butter
1 tablespoon French mustard
1 tablespoon lemon juice
2 teaspoons finely grated lemon rind
1 tablespoon chopped chives

1 Trim the meat of excess fat and flatten with a meat mallet to even thickness. Nick the edges to prevent curling. Combine the oil, garlic and rosemary and rub over the meat.
2 To make the lemon butter, cream the butter with the mustard, lemon juice and rind. Stir in the chives. Shape into a log, wrap in plastic and keep in the fridge.
3 Cook the steaks on a hot, lightly oiled barbecue flatplate or grill for 2 minutes on each side to sear, turning only once. For rare steaks, cook for a further minute each side. For medium and well done, move the steaks to a cooler part of the barbecue and cook for a further 3–6 minutes each side. Serve topped with a slice of the lemon butter.

NUTRITION PER SERVE
Protein 22 g; Fat 25 g; Carbohydrate 1 g; Dietary Fibre 0 g; Cholesterol 120 mg; 1293 kJ (309 cal)

Place the steaks between two sheets of plastic and flatten with a meat mallet.

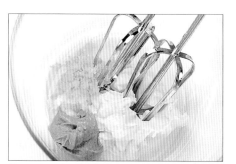
Cream together the butter, mustard, lemon juice and lemon rind to make the flavoured butter.

Cook the meat over high heat for 2 minutes on each side to seal.

LAMB CHOPS WITH PINEAPPLE SALSA

Preparation time: 20 minutes
Total cooking time: 10 minutes
Serves 6

12 lamb loin chops
2 tablespoons oil
1 teaspoon cracked black pepper

PINEAPPLE SALSA
1/2 ripe pineapple (or 400 g/13 oz
   drained canned pineapple)
1 large red onion, finely chopped

1 fresh red chilli, seeded and diced
1 tablespoon cider or rice vinegar
1 teaspoon sugar
2 tablespoons chopped fresh mint

1 Trim the meat of excess fat and sinew. Brush the chops with oil and season with pepper.
2 To make the salsa, peel the pineapple, remove the core and eyes and dice the flesh. Toss with the onion, chilli, vinegar, sugar, salt, pepper and mint and mix well.
3 Cook the lamb chops on a hot, lightly greased barbecue flatplate or grill for 2–3 minutes each side, turning

once, until just tender. Serve with the pineapple salsa.

NUTRITION PER SERVE
Protein 33 g; Fat 9 g; Carbohydrate 7 g;
Dietary Fibre 2 g; Cholesterol 116 mg;
994 kJ (237 cal)

STORAGE: The salsa can be made and stored for up to a day in the fridge. Add the mint just before serving and be aware that the red onion may affect the colour of the pineapple.

Trim the lamb chops of excess fat and season, brush with oil and season with pepper.

It is a good idea to wear gloves when seeding chillies to avoid the hot juice on your fingers.

Cook the lamb chops for just 2–3 minutes on each side, turning once.

PORK LOIN CHOPS WITH APPLE CHUTNEY

Preparation time: 20 minutes
    + 3 hours marinating
Total cooking time: 25 minutes
Serves 6

6 pork loin chops
2/3 cup (80 ml/2³/4 fl oz) white wine
2 tablespoons oil
2 tablespoons honey
1¹/2 teaspoons ground cumin
2 cloves garlic, crushed

APPLE CHUTNEY
3 green apples
¹/2 cup (125 ml/4 fl oz) apple juice
¹/2 cup (125 g/4 oz) fruit chutney
15 g (¹/2 oz) butter

1 Trim the chops of excess fat and sinew. Combine the wine, oil, honey, cumin and garlic. Put the chops in a shallow non-metallic dish and then pour in the marinade and toss well to cover. Store, covered with plastic wrap, in the fridge for at least 3 hours, turning occasionally.
2 To make the chutney, peel and dice the apples. Place in a small pan with the apple juice. Bring to the boil, reduce the heat and simmer, covered, for 7 minutes or until completely soft. Stir in the chutney and butter and serve warm.
3 Cook the chops on a hot, lightly oiled barbecue grill or flatplate for 8 minutes on each side or until tender, turning once. Serve immediately with the chutney.

NUTRITION PER SERVE
Protein 25 g; Fat 10 g; Carbohydrate 29 g;
Dietary Fibre 2 g; Cholesterol 55 mg;
1304 kJ (311 cal)

STORAGE: The chutney can be kept in the fridge for 1 day before use. It is also delicious with roast pork, lamb chops, chicken cutlets or as a relish with a cheese plate. It can be served warm or cold.

Mix together the white wine, oil, honey, cumin and garlic to make a marinade.

Simmer until the apple is soft and then stir in the chutney and butter.

Cook the chops on a hot barbecue for 8 minutes on each side.

GINGER-ORANGE PORK

Preparation time: 15 minutes + 3 hours
    marinating
Total cooking time: 20 minutes
Serves 6

6 pork butterfly steaks
1 cup (250 ml/8 fl oz) ginger wine
¹/2 cup (150 g/5 oz) orange
    marmalade
2 tablespoons oil
1 tablespoon grated fresh ginger

1 Trim the pork steak of excess fat and sinew. Mix together the wine, marmalade, oil and ginger. Place the steaks in a shallow non-metallic dish and add the marinade. Store, covered with plastic wrap, in the fridge for at least 3 hours, turning occasionally. Drain, reserving the marinade.
2 Cook the pork on a hot, lightly oiled barbecue flatplate or grill for 5 minutes each side or until tender, turning once.
3 While the meat is cooking, place the reserved marinade in a small pan. Bring to the boil, reduce the heat and simmer for 5 minutes, or until the marinade has reduced and thickened slightly. Pour over the pork.

NUTRITION PER SERVE
Protein 45 g; Fat 10 g; Carbohydrate 14 g;
Dietary Fibre 0 g; Cholesterol 98 mg;
1461 kJ (349 cal)

HINT: Steaks of uneven thickness may curl when cooked. Prevent this by leaving a layer of fat on the outside and making a few deep cuts in it prior to cooking. Remove before serving.

Put the pork in a shallow non-metallic dish so that the marinade doesn't react.

Cook the pork on a hot barbecue for 5 minutes on each side, or until tender.

Place the leftover marinade in a small pan and boil until reduced and thickened to a sauce.

LAMB CUTLETS WITH ROSEMARY MARINADE

Preparation time: 15 minutes +
  20 minutes marinating
Total cooking time: 10 minutes
Serves 4

12 lamb cutlets
3 tablespoons olive oil
2 tablespoons chopped fresh
  rosemary
1½ teaspoons cracked black pepper
1 bunch fresh rosemary, extra

1 Trim the cutlets of excess fat and sinew. Place in a shallow, non-metallic dish and brush with oil.
2 Scatter half the chopped rosemary and pepper on the meat and set aside for 20 minutes. Turn the meat over and brush with the remaining oil. Scatter with the remaining rosemary and pepper. Tie the extra bunch of rosemary to the handle of a wooden spoon.
3 Cook the cutlets on a hot, lightly oiled barbecue grill or flatplate for 2–3 minutes on each side. As the cutlets cook, bat frequently with the rosemary spoon. This will release flavoursome oils into the cutlets. When the cutlets are almost done, remove the rosemary from the spoon and drop it on the fire, where it will flare up briefly and infuse rosemary smoke into the cutlets. Serve with barbecued lemon slices.

NUTRITION PER SERVE
Protein 23 g; Fat 22 g; Carbohydrate 0 g; Dietary Fibre 0 g; Cholesterol 71 mg; 1195 kJ (285 cal)

Trim the lamb cutlets of excess fat and sinew and then place in a shallow dish.

Scatter half the chopped rosemary and pepper over the meat.

As the lamb is cooking, bat it frequently with the rosemary spoon to add flavour.

LAMB WITH SALSA VERDE AND POLENTA WEDGES

Preparation time: 40 minutes +
  20 minutes
Total cooking time: 35 minutes
Serves 4

SALSA VERDE
1 cup (20 g/³/₄ oz) fresh parsley leaves
1 cup (50 g/1³/₄ oz) fresh basil leaves
1 cup (20 g/³/₄ oz) fresh mint leaves
¹/₂ cup (30 g/1 oz) fresh dill
2 tablespoons capers
1–2 cloves garlic
1 tablespoon caster sugar
1 teaspoon grated lemon rind
1 tablespoon lemon juice
1 slice white bread
2–3 anchovy fillets
¹/₃ cup (80 ml/2³/₄ fl oz) olive oil

POLENTA WEDGES
2 cups (500 ml/16 fl oz) chicken stock
1 cup (150 g/5 oz) polenta (cornmeal)
50 g (1³/₄ oz) butter
¹/₂ cup (125 ml/4 fl oz) cream

12 lamb cutlets, trimmed

1 To make the salsa verde, chop the herbs, capers, garlic, sugar, lemon rind, juice, bread and anchovies in a food processor. With the motor running, add the oil in a thin stream and blend until smooth.
2 To make the polenta, heat the stock until boiling. Add the polenta, stirring over low heat for 20 minutes until it leaves the side of the pan. Stir in the butter and cream and season. Grease a deep 23 cm (9 inch) round cake tin, spoon in the polenta and smooth the top. Set in the fridge for 20 minutes.
3 Turn out the polenta, cut into wedges and brush with melted butter. Cook on a hot, lightly oiled barbecue grill or flatplate for 2–3 minutes each side, or until brown.
4 Cook the lamb for 2 minutes on each side, or until cooked through but still just pink inside.

NUTRITION PER SERVE
Protein 30 g; Fat 50 g; Carbohydrate 35 g;
Dietary Fibre 3 g; Cholesterol 150 mg;
2985 kJ (710 cal)

Trimming the lamb bones of any excess fat or sinew makes them easier to hold.

Finely chop the ingredients for the salsa verde in a food processor.

When the polenta leaves the side of the pan, stir in the butter and cream.

Cut the polenta into wedges and brush with melted butter.

Marinades & Butters
for Meat

Soak beef, lamb or pork in the following tangy marinades for a few hours, or overnight, to tenderise and flavour, or brush with the bastes while the meat is cooking. The butters need to be prepared a few hours in advance to give them time to firm up again in the fridge before slicing.

ASIAN MARINADE

Mix together 2 crushed cloves garlic, 3 tablespoons each of soy sauce, sweet chilli sauce and teriyaki marinade, 1 tablespoon lemon juice and 1 teaspoon each of sesame oil and peanut oil. Place in a shallow, non-metallic dish, add the meat and toss well to coat. Marinate in the fridge overnight before cooking on the barbecue.
Makes 1 cup (250 ml/8 fl oz)

TANDOORI MARINADE

Combine 1 cup (250 g/8 oz) yoghurt, 1 tablespoon each of grated onion and ginger, 2 crushed cloves garlic and 1 teaspoon each of brown sugar, ground turmeric, cumin, chilli and coriander. Place in a shallow, non-metallic dish, add the meat and toss well to coat. Marinate in the fridge overnight before cooking on the barbecue.
Makes 1 cup (250 ml/8 fl oz)

ROSEMARY MUSTARD BUTTER

Beat 125 g (4 oz) butter until light and creamy, add
3 tablespoons wholegrain mustard,1 tablespoon chopped
fresh rosemary and 1 teaspoon each of lemon juice, lemon
rind and honey. Mix together until well combined. Spoon
the butter down the middle of a piece of plastic wrap, fold
up the edges over the butter and roll the mixture into a log
shape. Refrigerate until firm. Slice the butter into rounds and
serve on top of barbecued lamb or beef. Serves 6

ORANGE BUTTER

Beat 125 g (4 oz) butter until light and creamy, add
1 tablespoon chopped fresh mint and 1 teaspoon each of
orange marmalade and Dijon mustard and mix until smooth.
Roll the butter out between 2 pieces of baking paper and
refrigerate until firm. Using small cookie cutters, cut out
shapes from the butter and chill until ready to use. Delicious
with barbecued lamb or beef. Serves 6

CAJUN SPICE MIX

Place 2 tablespoons each of freshly ground black pepper,
sweet paprika and white pepper into a bowl, add
1 tablespoon each of onion powder and garlic powder,
2 teaspoons dried oregano leaves and 1 teaspoon each of
dried thyme leaves and cayenne pepper. Place in a shallow
dish, add the meat and toss well to coat. Marinate in the
fridge for at least 3 hours before cooking on the barbecue.
Makes $1/3$ cup (80 g/$2^3/4$ oz)

SUN-DRIED TOMATO
AND BASIL BUTTER

Beat 125 g (4 oz) butter until light and creamy, then add 30 g
(1 oz) finely chopped sun-dried tomatoes, 1 tablespoon
finely shredded fresh basil and 20 g ($3/4$ oz) finely grated
Parmesan and mix together well. Spoon the butter into small
pots and swirl the surface with a flat-bladed knife. Serve in
small slices on top of barbecued meats. Serves 6

From left: Asian Marinade; Tandoori Marinade; Cajun Spice Mix; Rosemary Mustard Butter; Orange Butter; Sun-dried Tomato and Basil Butter

Chicken

HONEY-GLAZED CHICKEN BREASTS

Preparation time: 6 minutes +
  20 minutes marinating
Total cooking time: 10 minutes
Serves 6

6 chicken breast fillets
50 g (1³/₄ oz) butter, softened
3 tablespoons honey
3 tablespoons barbecue sauce
2 teaspoons wholegrain mustard

1 Trim the chicken of excess fat and sinew and remove the skin. Use a sharp knife to make three or four diagonal slashes across one side of each chicken breast.
2 Mix together the butter, honey, barbecue sauce and mustard. Spread half of the marinade thickly over the slashed side of the chicken and cover. Set the remaining marinade aside.

Leave the chicken at room temperature for 20 minutes.
3 Place the chicken breasts, slashed-side-up, on a hot, lightly oiled barbecue flatplate or grill. Cook for 2–3 minutes each side or until tender. Brush with the reserved marinade several times during cooking.

NUTRITION PER SERVE
Protein 50 g; Fat 18 g; Carbohydrate 0 g;
Dietary Fibre 0.5 g; Cholesterol 110 mg;
1510 kJ (360 cal)

STORAGE: The chicken can be marinated overnight, covered, in the fridge. The longer the chicken is marinated, the more it will take on the marinade flavour, which is quite sweet. If the sweetness is not to your taste, marinate for a shorter time.

Cut three or four slashes in the chicken breasts so that they cook evenly.

Cook the chicken for 2–3 minutes on each side, brushing with marinade occasionally.

CHICKEN WITH SALSA VERDE

Preparation time: 10 minutes
Total cooking time: 10 minutes
Serves 6

SALSA VERDE
1 clove garlic
2 cups (60 g/2 oz) firmly packed fresh
flat-leaf parsley
1/3 cup (80 ml/2 3/4 fl oz) extra virgin
olive oil

3 tablespoons chopped fresh dill
1 1/2 tablespoons Dijon mustard
1 tablespoon sherry vinegar
1 tablespoon baby capers, drained

6 large chicken breast fillets

1 Place all the ingredients for the salsa verde in a food processor or blender and process until almost smooth.
2 Cook the chicken fillets on a very hot, lightly oiled barbecue grill or flatplate for 4–5 minutes each side, or until cooked through.

3 Cut each chicken fillet into three on the diagonal and arrange on serving plates. Top with a spoonful of salsa verde and season to taste.

NUTRITION PER SERVE
Protein 50 g; Fat 18 g; Carbohydrate 0 g;
Dietary Fibre 0.5 g; Cholesterol 110 mg;
1510 kJ (360 cal)

STORAGE: The salsa verde can be kept for a day in the fridge.

Put all the salsa verde ingredients in the food processor and process until almost smooth.

Cook the chicken on a very hot barbecue until it is cooked through.

To serve, slice each fillet into three on the diagonal and top with salsa verde.

THAI SPICED CHICKEN WITH POTATO ROSTI

Preparation time: 30 minutes +
  2 hours marinating
Total cooking time: 20 minutes
Serves 6

600 g (1¼ lb) chicken tenderloin
  pieces
1 tablespoon chopped fresh lemon
  grass
2 tablespoons lime juice
1½ tablespoons oil
2 cloves garlic, crushed
1 tablespoon grated fresh ginger
2 teaspoons sweet chilli sauce
2 spring onions, chopped

POTATO ROSTI
600 g (1¼ lb) potatoes
3 tablespoons plain flour
1 egg, lightly beaten

1 Remove any excess fat or sinew from the chicken and put the chicken in a shallow, non-metallic dish. Mix together the lemon grass, lime juice, oil, garlic, ginger, sweet chilli sauce and spring onion. Pour over the chicken pieces, cover and refrigerate for at least 2 hours.

2 To make the potato rosti, peel and grate the potatoes. Squeeze the excess moisture from the potato with your hands until it feels quite dry. Mix the potato with the flour and egg and season well. Divide into six equal portions. Cook on a hot, lightly oiled barbecue flatplate for 10 minutes, or until golden brown on both sides, flattening them down with the back of a spatula during cooking.

3 Drain the chicken and reserve the marinade. Cook on a barbecue grill or

flatplate for 3 minutes each side, or until tender and golden brown. Brush with the reserved marinade while cooking. Serve with the rosti.

NUTRITION PER SERVE
Protein 25 g; Fat 10 g; Carbohydrate 20 g;
Dietary Fibre 2 g; Cholesterol 100 mg;
1125 kJ (265 cal)

Peel the potatoes and then grate them for making the rosti.

As you cook the rosti, flatten them down with the back of a spatula.

Cook the chicken until it is golden brown, brushing with the marinade.

MIRIN AND SAKE CHICKEN

Preparation time: 10 minutes +
    15 minutes marinating
Total cooking time: 10 minutes
Serves 4

4 large chicken breast fillets
2 tablespoons mirin
2 tablespoons sake
1 tablespoon oil
5 cm (2 inch) piece of fresh ginger,
    very finely sliced
3 teaspoons soy sauce

1 Put the chicken in a non-metallic dish. Combine the mirin, sake and oil and pour over the chicken. Marinate for 15 minutes, then drain the chicken, reserving the marinade.
2 Cook the chicken on a hot, lightly oiled barbecue grill or flatplate for 4 minutes on each side, or until tender.
3 Put the ginger in a pan and add the reserved marinade. Boil for about 7 minutes, or until thickened.
4 Drizzle the soy sauce over the chicken and top with the ginger. Serve immediately.

NUTRITION PER SERVE
Protein 35 g; Fat 10 g; Carbohydrate 1 g;
Dietary Fibre 0 g; Cholesterol 80 mg;
995 kJ (235 cal)

Put the chicken in a shallow, non-metallic dish and leave to marinate.

Cook the chicken for 4 minutes on each side, or until tender.

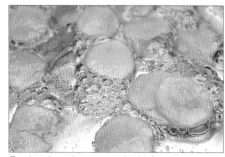

Put the ginger in a pan and add the reserved marinade. Boil until thickened.

HONEY CHICKEN WINGS

Preparation time: 10 minutes +
  2 hours marinating
Total cooking time: 15 minutes
Serves 4

12 chicken wings
4 tablespoons soy sauce
1 clove garlic, crushed
3 tablespoons sherry
3 tablespoons vegetable oil
3 tablespoons honey

1 Rinse the chicken wings and pat dry with paper towels. Tuck the wing tips to the underside and put in a shallow, non-metallic dish. Combine the soy sauce, garlic, sherry and oil and pour over the chicken. Cover with plastic wrap and refrigerate for 2 hours, turning occasionally.

2 Cook the chicken on a hot, lightly oiled barbecue grill or flatplate for 5 minutes on each side or until cooked through, turning occasionally. Place the honey in a small heatproof bowl on the edge of the barbecue to warm and thin down a little.

3 Brush the wings with honey and grill for 2 minutes more.

NUTRITION PER SERVE
Protein 46 g; Fat 8 g; Carbohydrate 21 g;
Dietary Fibre 2 g; Cholesterol 100 mg;
1411 kJ (337 cal)

VARIATION: Try apricot jam instead of the honey for basting. If you prefer a slightly hotter flavour, add some bottled crushed chilli pepper.

Put the chicken wings in a shallow, non-metallic dish and leave to marinate.

During the 2 hours of marinating, turn the chicken wings occasionally.

Once the wings are cooked through, brush with the honey and cook for a little longer.

THAI CHILLI GARLIC QUAIL

Preparation time: 15 minutes + 2 hours
  marinating
Total cooking time: 20 minutes
Serves 6

6 quails
1 small red chilli, finely chopped
2 tablespoons chopped fresh
  coriander leaves and stems
4 cloves garlic, crushed
2 teaspoons soft brown sugar
2 teaspoons Thai red curry paste

1 tablespoon grated fresh ginger
2 teaspoons light soy sauce
2 teaspoons chilli sauce
2 teaspoons oil
lime wedges, to serve

1 Using poultry shears or kitchen
scissors, cut each quail down either
side of the backbone and then open
out flat. Cut each one in half through
the breastbone.
2 Using a mortar and pestle or
blender, blend the chilli, coriander
leaves and stems, garlic, brown sugar,
paste, ginger, soy sauce, chilli sauce
and oil, until smooth.

3 Brush the mixture all over the
quails. Place them in a shallow, non-
metallic dish, cover and refrigerate for
at least 2 hours.
4 Cook the quails on a hot, lightly
oiled barbecue grill or flatplate for
15–20 minutes, turning once, until
browned and cooked through. Serve
with lime wedges.

NUTRITION PER SERVE
Protein 30 g; Fat 5 g; Carbohydrate 5.5 g;
Dietary Fibre 0 g; Cholesterol 55 mg;
820 kJ (198 cal)

Cut the quails down either side of the backbone
and then open out flat.

Blend the ingredients until smooth, using a mortar
and pestle or blender.

Use a pastry brush to spread the mixture all over
the quails.

THAI GARLIC CHICKEN

Preparation time: 20 minutes +
 2 hours marinating
Total cooking time: 10 minutes
Serves 4

6 cloves garlic, crushed
1^1/$_2$ tablespoons cracked black
 peppercorns
^{1}/$_2$ cup (30 g/1 oz) chopped fresh
 coriander leaves and stems
4 coriander roots, chopped
^{1}/$_3$ cup (80 ml/2^3/$_4$ fl oz) lime juice
1 teaspoon soft brown sugar
1 teaspoon ground turmeric
2 teaspoons light soy sauce
4 chicken breast fillets

CUCUMBER AND TOMATO SALAD
1 small green cucumber
1 large Roma tomato
^{1}/$_4$ small red onion, thinly sliced
1 small red or green chilli, diced
2 tablespoons fresh coriander leaves
2 tablespoons lime juice
1 teaspoon soft brown sugar
1 tablespoon fish sauce

1 Blend the garlic, peppercorns,
coriander, lime juice, sugar, turmeric
and soy sauce until smooth in a food
processor or mortar and pestle.
2 Separate the tenderloins from the
fillets. Put the chicken in a shallow,
non-metallic dish, add the marinade;
cover and refrigerate for 2 hours or
overnight, turning occasionally.
3 To make the salad, halve the
cucumber and scoop out the seeds
with a teaspoon. Cut into slices. Halve
the tomato lengthways and slice.
Combine the cucumber, tomato,
onion, chilli and coriander. Drizzle
with the combined lime juice, sugar
and fish sauce.
4 Cook the chicken on a hot, lightly
oiled barbecue grill or flatplate for
4 minutes on each side or until tender.
The tenderloins will take less time to
cook. Serve with the salad.

NUTRITION PER SERVE
Protein 26 g; Fat 3 g; Carbohydrate 6 g;
Dietary Fibre 2 g; Cholesterol 55 mg;
664 kJ (159 cal)

Add the chopped coriander roots to the other
ingredients and blend until smooth.

Separate the tenderloins from the chicken fillets by
pulling them away.

Use a teaspoon to scoop the seeds out of the
halved cucumber.

Drizzle the combined lime juice, sugar and fish
sauce over the salad ingredients.

DRUMSTICKS IN TOMATO AND MANGO CHUTNEY

Preparation time: 10 minutes + 2 hours
  marinating
Total cooking time: 20 minutes
Serves 4

8 chicken drumsticks, scored
1 tablespoon mustard powder
2 tablespoons tomato sauce
1 tablespoon sweet mango chutney
1 teaspoon Worcestershire sauce
1 tablespoon Dijon mustard
1/4 cup (30 g/1 oz) raisins
1 tablespoon oil

1 Toss the chicken in the mustard powder and season.
2 Combine the tomato sauce, chutney, Worcestershire sauce, mustard, raisins and oil. Spoon over the chicken and toss well. Marinate for at least 2 hours, turning once.
3 Cook the chicken on a hot, lightly oiled barbecue flatplate for about 20 minutes, or until cooked through.

NUTRITION PER SERVE
Protein 25 g; Fat 15 g; Carbohydrate 3.5 g;
Dietary Fibre 0.5 g; Cholesterol 103 mg;
1005 kJ (240 cal)

HINT: Serve with toasted Turkish bread and a cool raita.

The cleanest way to toss the chicken with mustard powder is to put them in a bag.

Marinate the chicken in a shallow, non-metallic dish, turning once.

Cook the chicken on a hot flatplate until it is cooked through.

CHICKEN SALAD WITH ROCKET AND CANNELLINI BEANS

Preparation time: 10 minutes
Total cooking time: 10 minutes
Serves 4

^{1}/3 cup (80 ml/2^3/4 fl oz) lemon juice
3 cloves garlic, crushed
1 teaspoon soft brown sugar
^{1}/4 cup (15 g/^{1}/2 oz) fresh basil, finely
  chopped
^{1}/2 cup (125 ml/4 fl oz) olive oil
4 chicken breast fillets
400 g (13 oz) can cannellini beans,
  rinsed and drained
100 g (3^1/2 oz) small rocket leaves

1 Whisk together the lemon juice, garlic, sugar, basil and olive oil.
2 Pour a third of the dressing over the chicken to coat. Cook the chicken on a hot, lightly oiled barbecue grill or flatplate for 4 minutes on each side, or until cooked through.
3 Meanwhile, combine the beans and rocket with the remaining dressing, toss well and season. Slice the chicken and serve over the rocket and beans.

NUTRITION PER SERVE
Protein 35 g; Fat 35 g; Carbohydrate 13 g;
Dietary Fibre 7.5 g; Cholesterol 60 mg;
2045 kJ (490 cal)

Whisk together the lemon juice, garlic, sugar, basil and olive oil.

Cook the chicken on a hot grill or flatplate until cooked through.

Slice the chicken and serve on top of the rocket and cannellini beans.

TANDOORI CHICKEN

Preparation time: 10 minutes + 1 hour
  marinating
Total cooking time: 10 minutes
Serves 4

¹/₂ cup (125 g/4 oz) Greek-style
  plain yoghurt
2 tablespoons tandoori paste
2 cloves garlic, crushed

2 tablespoons lime juice
1¹/₂ teaspoons garam masala
2 tablespoons finely chopped fresh
  coriander leaves
6 chicken thigh fillets

1 Combine the yoghurt, tandoori
paste, garlic, lime juice, garam masala
and coriander in a bowl and mix well.
2 Add the chicken, coat well, cover
and refrigerate for at least 1 hour.
3 Cook the chicken on a hot, lightly

oiled barbecue grill or flatplate for
5 minutes on each side, basting with
the remaining marinade, until golden
and cooked through. Serve with
cucumber raita and naan bread.

NUTRITION PER SERVE
Protein 27 g; Fat 3.5 g; Carbohydrate 2 g;
Dietary Fibre 0 g; Cholesterol 60 mg;
635 kJ (150 cal)

Mix together the yoghurt, tandoori paste, garlic,
lime juice, garam masala and coriander.

Add the chicken to the marinade and leave for at
least an hour.

Cook the chicken on a barbecue grill or flatplate
for 5 minutes on each side.

CHERMOULA CHICKEN

Preparation time: 10 minutes +
  2 hours marinating
Total cooking time: 15 minutes
Serves 4

¹/₂ cup (15 g/¹/₂ oz) firmly packed
  fresh flat-leaf parsley
¹/₄ cup (7 g/¹/₄ oz) firmly packed
  fresh coriander leaves
2 cloves garlic, roughly chopped
3 tablespoons lemon juice
1 tablespoon chopped preserved
  lemon

3 teaspoons ground cumin
¹/₂ cup (125 ml/4 fl oz) olive oil
4 chicken breast fillets, flattened (see
  NOTE)

1 Mix the parsley, coriander, garlic, lemon juice, preserved lemon and cumin in a food processor until well combined. With the motor running, gradually add the oil in a thin stream until smooth. Season well.
2 Place the chicken in a shallow, non-metallic dish and pour over the marinade. Marinate for at least 2 hours.
3 Grease four sheets of foil and place a chicken breast in the centre of each.

Spoon any extra marinade over the chicken. Fold the foil over to seal. Cook the parcels on a hot, lightly oiled barbecue flatplate for 10–12 minutes without turning, until cooked through. Remove from the foil and slice.

NUTRITION PER SERVE
Protein 25 g; Fat 33 g; Carbohydrate 0.5 g;
Dietary Fibre 0.5 g; Cholesterol 60 mg;
1690 kJ (405 cal)

NOTE: To flatten chicken fillets, place between two pieces of plastic wrap and hit with a meat mallet or the palm of your hand.

Put all the ingredients except the chicken in a food processor and mix until smooth.

Put the chicken in a shallow, non-metallic dish and add the marinade.

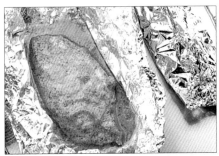

Once the chicken is cooked, remove from the barbecue onto a tray and open the parcels.

BLACKENED CAJUN SPICED CHICKEN

Preparation time: 15 minutes +
  30 minutes standing
Total cooking time: 1 hour
Serves 4

1¹/2 tablespoons onion powder
1¹/2 tablespoons garlic powder
2 teaspoons paprika
1 teaspoon white pepper
2 teaspoons dried thyme
¹/2–1 teaspoon chilli powder (see
  NOTE)
8 chicken drumsticks, scored

1 Combine the herbs, spices and
1 teaspoon salt in a plastic bag. Place
the drumsticks in the bag and shake
until all the pieces are coated. Leave

the chicken in the fridge for at least
30 minutes to allow the flavours to
develop, or overnight if time permits.
2 Cook the chicken on a lightly oiled
barbecue grill for 55–60 minutes, or
until slightly blackened and cooked
through. Brush lightly with some oil to
prevent drying out during cooking.

Put the herbs, spices and salt in a freezer bag,
add the chicken and shake to coat.

NUTRITION PER SERVE
Protein 25 g; Fat 7 g; Carbohydrate 0 g;
Dietary Fibre 0 g; Cholesterol 103 mg;
660 kJ (160 cal)

NOTE: Chilli powder is very hot, so
only use ¹/2 teaspoon if you prefer a
milder flavour.

Cook the chicken for 55–60 minutes, or until
slightly blackened.

ASIAN BARBECUED CHICKEN

Preparation time: 10 minutes +
  2 hours marinating
Total cooking time: 25 minutes
Serves 6

2 cloves garlic, finely chopped
1/4 cup (60 ml/2 fl oz) hoisin sauce
3 teaspoons light soy sauce
3 teaspoons honey
2 tablespoons tomato sauce
  or sweet chilli sauce
1 teaspoon sesame oil
2 spring onions, finely sliced
1.5 kg (3 lb) chicken wings

1 To make the marinade, mix together the garlic, hoisin sauce, soy, honey, tomato sauce, sesame oil and spring onion.
2 Put the chicken wings in a shallow, non-metallic dish, add the marinade, cover and leave in the fridge for at least 2 hours.
3 Cook the chicken on a hot, lightly oiled barbecue grill, turning once, for 20–25 minutes, or until cooked and golden brown. Baste with the marinade during cooking. Heat any remaining marinade in a pan until boiling and serve as a sauce.

NUTRITION PER SERVE
Protein 26 g; Fat 8.5 g; Carbohydrate 9 g; Dietary Fibre 1.5 g; Cholesterol 111 mg; 916 kJ (219 cal)

Mix together the garlic, hoisin sauce, soy, honey, tomato sauce, sesame oil and spring onions.

Pour the marinade over the chicken, cover the dish and leave in the fridge.

Cook the chicken for 20–25 minutes, or until cooked and golden brown.

THAI DRUMSTICKS

Preparation time: 10 minutes +
  2 hours marinating
Total cooking time: 1 hour
Serves 6

3 tablespoons Thai red curry paste
1 cup (250 ml/8 fl oz) coconut milk
2 tablespoons lime juice
4 tablespoons finely chopped fresh
    coriander leaves
12 chicken drumsticks, scored
2 bunches (1 kg/2 lb) baby bok choy
2 tablespoons soy sauce
1 tablespoon oil

1 Combine the curry paste, coconut milk, lime juice and coriander. Place the chicken in a shallow, non-metallic dish and pour on the marinade. Cover and marinate in the fridge for at least 2 hours.
2 Cook the chicken on a lightly oiled barbecue grill for 50–60 minutes, or until cooked through.
3 Trim the bok choy and combine with the soy sauce and oil, then cook on the barbecue or in a wok for 3–4 minutes, or until just wilted. Serve the chicken on a bed of bok choy.

NUTRITION PER SERVE
Protein 30 g; Fat 20 g; Carbohydrate 3 g;
Dietary Fibre 5 g; Cholesterol 105 mg;
1250 kJ (300 cal)

Pour the marinade over the chicken, make sure it is well coated then leave in the fridge.

Cook the chicken on a lightly oiled barbecue grill until cooked through.

Cook the bok choy on the barbecue or in a wok until it is just wilted.

PIRI-PIRI CHICKEN

Preparation time: 5 minutes +
   1 hour marinating
Total cooking time: 1 hour
Serves 4

6 bird's eye chillies, with seeds left in,
   finely chopped
1 teaspoon coarse salt
1/2 cup (125 ml/4 fl oz) olive oil
3/4 cup (185 ml/6 fl oz) cider vinegar
1 clove garlic, crushed
4 chicken Maryland pieces (see NOTE)
lemon wedges, to serve

1 Combine the chilli, salt, olive oil,
vinegar and garlic in a screw-top jar.
Seal and shake well to combine.
2 Place the chicken pieces in a
shallow, non-metallic dish and pour
on the marinade. Cover and marinate
for at least 1 hour.
3 Cook the chicken on a hot, lightly
oiled barbecue grill or flatplate,
basting regularly with the marinade,
for 50–60 minutes, or until the chicken
is cooked through and the skin begins
to crisp. Serve with lemon wedges.

NUTRITION PER SERVE
Protein 27 g; Fat 30 g; Carbohydrate 0.5 g;
Dietary Fibre 0.5 g; Cholesterol 60 mg;
1705 kJ (405 cal)

NOTE: Marylands are the drumstick
and thigh pieces of the chicken. Any
chicken cut that is still on the bone can
be used in this recipe. Piri-piri is also
excellent for barbecuing prawns. Seed
the chillies for a milder tasting dish.

Put the marinade ingredients in a screw-top jar
and shake well to combine.

Pour the marinade over the chicken pieces in the
shallow dish.

Cook the chicken on a hot barbecue grill until the
skin begins to crisp.

CHICKEN CUTLETS WITH CORN RELISH

Preparation time: 20 minutes
Total cooking time: 30 minutes
Serves 4

8 chicken thigh cutlets with skin
1 tablespoon olive oil
1 small clove garlic, crushed
1/4 teaspoon ground turmeric
1/2 teaspoon salt

CORN RELISH
1 cup (200 g/6 1/2 oz) corn kernels,
   fresh or canned
1 tablespoon olive oil
1 red chilli, seeded and chopped
1 small green capsicum, finely
   chopped
1 onion, finely chopped
4 tablespoons white vinegar
3 tablespoons sugar
1 teaspoon wholegrain mustard
3 teaspoons cornflour
1 teaspoon paprika
1 teaspoon finely chopped fresh
   coriander leaves
1 tablespoon olive oil, extra

1 Prick the chicken skin and put in a large pan of boiling water. Simmer for 5 minutes. Drain and cool. Mix the olive oil, garlic, turmeric and salt and rub over the skin of the chicken.
2 To make the relish, cook the fresh corn in boiling water for 2–3 minutes or until tender, then drain. (If using canned corn, drain, but do not cook.) Heat the oil in a pan. Add the chilli, capsicum and onion and cook until tender. Add the corn, vinegar, sugar and mustard and cook, stirring, for a further 5 minutes. Blend the cornflour with 125 ml (4 fl oz) water until

smooth and add to the relish. Bring to the boil, reduce the heat and stir until thickened. Stir in the paprika, coriander and extra oil. Leave to cool.
3 Cook the chicken, skin-side-up, on a hot, lightly oiled barbecue grill or flatplate for 2 minutes, then turn and cook for 4 minutes. Continue cooking for another 5–10 minutes, turning frequently, until the chicken is well

browned and cooked through. Serve with the corn relish.

NUTRITION PER SERVE
Protein 36 g; Fat 39 g; Carbohydrate 14 g; Dietary Fibre 1 g; Cholesterol 110 mg; 2280 kJ (545 cal)

STORAGE: The corn relish will keep for up to 4 days in a jar in the fridge.

Prick the chicken skin and simmer in water for 5 minutes to remove the fat.

Mix the cornflour with water until smooth and then add to the relish.

Cook the cutlets skin-side-up, then turn frequently during the cooking time.

CITRUS CHICKEN DRUMSTICKS

Preparation time: 20 minutes +
  3 hours marinating
Total cooking time: 20 minutes
Serves 4

8 chicken drumsticks
4 tablespoons orange juice
4 tablespoons lemon juice
1 teaspoon grated orange rind
1 teaspoon grated lemon rind
1 teaspoon sesame oil
1 tablespoon olive oil
1 spring onion, finely chopped

1 Score the thickest part of the chicken so that it cooks evenly. Place in a shallow non-metallic dish.
2 Combine the juices, rinds, oils and spring onion and pour over the chicken. Cover and leave in the fridge for at least 3 hours, turning occasionally. Drain the chicken, reserving the marinade.
3 Cook the drumsticks on a hot, lightly oiled barbecue grill or flatplate for 15–20 minutes, or until tender. Brush occasionally with the reserved marinade. Serve immediately.

NUTRITION PER SERVE
Protein 24 g; Fat 13 g; Carbohydrate 3 g; Dietary Fibre 0 g; Cholesterol 103 mg; 949 kJ (227 cal)

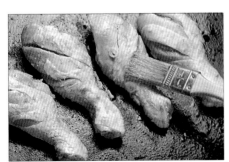

Score the thickest part of the chicken with a knife so that it cooks evenly.

Put the chicken in a non-metallic dish so that the citrus in the marinade doesn't react.

While the chicken is cooking, brush it occasionally with the marinade.

SPICY CHICKEN WITH CHILLI GARLIC DIP

Preparation time: 20 minutes + 1 hour
    marinating
Total cooking time: 25 minutes
Serves 4–6

6 cloves garlic
1 teaspoon black peppercorns
3 coriander roots and stems, roughly
    chopped
1/4 teaspoon salt
12 chicken thigh fillets

CHILLI GARLIC DIP
4–5 dried red chillies
2 large cloves garlic, chopped
3 tablespoons sugar
4 tablespoons cider or rice vinegar
pinch of salt
3 tablespoons boiling water

1 Put the garlic, peppercorns, coriander and salt in a food processor and process for 20–30 seconds or until a smooth paste forms, or grind in a mortar and pestle. Put the chicken in a shallow, non-metallic dish and spread the paste over the chicken. Cover and leave in the fridge for 1 hour.
2 To make the dip, soak the chillies in hot water for 20 minutes. Drain the chillies and chop finely. Place in a mortar with the garlic and sugar and grind to a smooth paste. Place in a small pan, add the vinegar, salt and water and bring to the boil. Reduce the heat, simmer for 2–3 minutes and cool.
3 Cook the chicken on a hot, lightly oiled barbecue grill or flatplate for 5–10 minutes each side, turning once. Serve with the dip.

NUTRITION PER SERVE (6)
Protein 47 g; Fat 5 g; Carbohydrate 0.5 g;
Dietary Fibre 1 g; Cholesterol 105 mg;
1005 kJ (240 cal)

STORAGE: The chicken can be kept in the marinade in the fridge for up to a day. The dip can be made 3 days in advance.

Trim the chicken of excess fat and sinew before you put it in the marinade.

Mix together the garlic, peppercorns, coriander and salt in a food processor.

Grind the chillies, garlic and sugar to a smooth paste with a mortar and pestle.

Barbecue the chicken on a hot, lightly oiled grill for 5–10 minutes on each side, turning once.

MIDDLE-EASTERN BAKED CHICKEN

Preparation time: 30 minutes
Total cooking time: 1 hour 15 minutes
Serves 6

1.6 kg (3¹/₄ lb) chicken
¹/₂ cup (90 g/3 oz) instant couscous
4 pitted dates, chopped
4 dried apricots, chopped
1 tablespoon lime juice
1 tablespoon olive oil
1 tablespoon butter
1 onion, chopped
1–2 cloves garlic, chopped
1 teaspoon ground coriander
2 tablespoons chopped fresh parsley
1 teaspoon salt
¹/₄ teaspoon cracked black pepper
1 teaspoon ground cumin
1 tablespoon olive oil, extra

1 Wipe and pat dry the chicken with paper towel. Pour 125 ml (4 fl oz) boiling water over the couscous and set aside for 15 minutes for it to swell and soften. Soak the dates and apricots in the lime juice.
2 Heat the oil and butter in a pan, add the onion and garlic and cook for 3–4 minutes, or until translucent. Remove from the heat, add the couscous, soaked dried fruit, coriander and parsley. Mix well and season. Spoon into the chicken cavity and close with a skewer. Tie the legs together with string.
3 Rub the chicken skin all over with a mixture of salt, pepper, cumin and the extra oil. Place in the centre of a large piece of greased foil. Gather the edges together and wrap securely.
4 Place on a barbecue grill over a drip tray. Cover the barbecue and cook for 50 minutes. Open the foil, crimping the edges to form a tray to retain most of the cooking liquid. Cook for a further 20 minutes or until the chicken is tender and golden. Remove from the heat and leave for 5–6 minutes before carving.

NUTRITION PER SERVE
Protein 46 g; Fat 14 g; Carbohydrate 5.5 g; Dietary Fibre 1 g; Cholesterol 110 mg; 1378 kJ (329 cal)

Mix the couscous with the other flavourings to make a stuffing.

Remove the giblets from the chicken and cut away any large pieces of fat.

Rub the chicken skin all over with a mixture of cumin, oil, salt and pepper.

Open the parcel, crimping the edges to make a baking tray for the juices.

BUFFALO CHICKEN WINGS WITH RANCH DRESSING

Preparation time: 25 minutes + 3 hours
    marinating
Total cooking time: 10 minutes
Serves 4

8 large chicken wings
2 teaspoons black pepper
2 teaspoons garlic salt
2 teaspoons onion powder
olive oil, for deep-frying
1/2 cup (125 g/4 oz) tomato sauce
2 tablespoons Worcestershire sauce
1 tablespoon melted butter
2 teaspoons sugar
Tabasco sauce, to taste

RANCH DRESSING
1/2 cup (125 g/4 oz) mayonnaise
1/2 cup (125 g/4 oz) sour cream
2 tablespoons lemon juice
2 tablespoons chopped chives

1 Wash the wings thoroughly and pat dry with paper towels. Cut the tip off each wing and discard. Bend each wing back to snap the joint and cut through to create two pieces. Combine the pepper, garlic salt and onion powder and rub into the wings.
2 Heat the oil to moderately hot in a deep heavy-based pan. Deep-fry the chicken in batches for 2 minutes. Drain on paper towels.
3 Transfer the chicken to a shallow, non-metallic dish. Combine the sauces, butter, sugar and Tabasco and pour over the chicken, stirring to coat. Cover and refrigerate for at least 3 hours.
4 Cook the chicken on a hot, lightly oiled barbecue grill or flatplate for 5 minutes, turning and brushing with the marinade.
5 To make the ranch dressing, combine the mayonnaise, cream, juice, chives, salt and pepper and serve with the chicken wings.

NUTRITION PER SERVE
Protein 24 g; Fat 47 g; Carbohydrate 19 g;
Dietary Fibre 1 g; Cholesterol 132 mg;
2478 kJ (592 cal)

Cut the tips off the wings, then snap them in the middle and cut into two pieces.

Deep-fry the wings for 2 minutes and then drain on paper towels.

Marinate the chicken in a mixture of butter, sugar, tomato and Worcestershire sauces and Tabasco.

While the chicken is cooking, turn it often and baste with the marinade.

CHICKEN WITH FRUIT SALSA

Preparation time: 25 minutes + 3 hours
  marinating
Total cooking time: 20 minutes
Serves 4

4 chicken breast fillets
3/4 cup (185 ml/6 fl oz) white wine
3 tablespoons olive oil
2 teaspoons grated fresh ginger
1 clove garlic, crushed

FRUIT SALSA
220 g (7 oz) can pineapple slices,
  drained
1 small mango, peeled
2 small kiwi fruit, peeled
150 g (5 oz) watermelon, peeled,
  seeds removed
1 tablespoon finely chopped fresh
  mint

1 Put the chicken in a shallow non-metallic dish. Combine the wine, oil, ginger and garlic and pour over the chicken. Refrigerate, covered with plastic wrap, for at least 3 hours, turning occasionally.
2 To make the fruit salsa, chop the fruit finely and combine with the mint in a small serving bowl.
3 Cook the chicken fillets on a hot, lightly oiled barbecue grill or flatplate for 5–10 minutes each side, or until well browned.

NUTRITION PER SERVE
Protein 51 g; Fat 20 g; Carbohydrate 14 g;
Dietary Fibre 3 g; Cholesterol 110 mg;
1993 kJ (476 cal)

STORAGE: The chicken can be left in the marinade in the fridge for up to 2 days. The fruit salsa needs to be served within 2 hours of making.

VARIATION: You can use any seasonal fruits for the salsa, but you do need to use at least one ingredient with a firm flesh, for example, apple or pear.

Mix together the wine, oil, ginger and garlic and use to marinate the chicken.

To make the salsa, simply dice all the fresh fruit and mix with the mint.

Cook the chicken on a hot barbecue grill until well browned on both sides.

TERIYAKI CHICKEN WINGS

Preparation time: 15 minutes + 3 hours
   marinating
Total cooking time: 15 minutes
Serves 4

8 chicken wings
3 tablespoons soy sauce
2 tablespoons sherry
2 teaspoons grated fresh ginger
1 clove garlic, crushed
1 tablespoon honey

1 Wash the chicken wings and pat dry with paper towels. Trim any excess fat from the wings and tuck the tips under to form a triangle. Place in a shallow non-metallic dish.

2 Mix together the soy sauce, sherry, ginger, garlic and honey in a jug. Pour over the chicken and store, covered with plastic wrap, in the fridge for at least 3 hours. Lightly brush two sheets of foil with oil. Place 4 wings in a single layer on each piece of foil and wrap completely in a parcel.

3 Cook the parcels on a hot barbecue grill or flatplate for 10 minutes. Unwrap, then place the wings directly on a lightly greased grill and cook for 3 minutes or until brown. Turn them frequently and brush with any remaining marinade.

NUTRITION PER SERVE
Protein 16 g; Fat 7 g; Carbohydrate 6 g;
Dietary Fibre 0 g; Cholesterol 46 mg;
700 kJ (167 cal)

STORAGE: The chicken can be left in the marinade in the fridge for up to 2 days.

Trim the excess fat from the wings and tuck the tips under to make triangles.

Place four wings in a single layer on each sheet of foil and make a parcel.

Unwrap the wings from the parcels and place directly on the barbecue grill.

CHICKEN FAJITAS

Preparation time: 35 minutes + 3 hours
    marinating
Total cooking time: 10 minutes
Serves 4

4 chicken breast fillets
2 tablespoons olive oil
3 tablespoons lime juice
2 cloves garlic, crushed
1 teaspoon ground cumin
$1/4$ cup (15 g/$1/4$ oz) chopped fresh
    coriander leaves
8 flour tortillas
1 tablespoon olive oil, extra
2 onions, sliced

2 green capsicums, cut into thin strips
1 cup (125 g/4 oz) grated Cheddar
    cheese
1 large avocado, sliced
1 cup (250 g/8 oz) bottled tomato
    salsa

1 Cut the chicken into thin strips and place in a shallow, non-metallic dish. Combine the oil, lime juice, garlic, cumin and coriander and pour over the chicken. Store, covered, in the fridge for at least 3 hours.
2 Wrap the tortillas in foil and place on a cooler part of the barbecue for 10 minutes to warm through. Heat the oil on a flatplate. Cook the onion and capsicum for 5 minutes or until soft.

Push over to a cooler part of the plate to keep warm.
3 Place the chicken and marinade on the flatplate and cook for 5 minutes, or until just tender. Transfer the chicken, vegetables and wrapped tortillas to a serving platter. Make up individual fajitas by placing the chicken, cooked onion and capsicum, grated cheese and avocado over the flat tortillas. Top with the salsa and roll up.

NUTRITION PER SERVE
Protein 65 g; Fat 52 g; Carbohydrate 126 g;
Dietary Fibre 9 g; Cholesterol 118 mg;
5170 kJ (1236 cal)

Put the chicken in a shallow, non-metallic bowl and marinate for at least 3 hours.

Cook the onion and capsicum on the flatplate for 5 minutes, or until soft.

Cook the chicken on the flatplate for 5 minutes, or until it is tender.

CRISPY CHICKEN WINGS

Preparation time: 10 minutes + 2 hours
  marinating
Total cooking time: 15 minutes
Serves 6

12 chicken wings
3 tablespoons soy sauce
3 tablespoons hoisin sauce
1/2 cup (125 g/4 oz) tomato sauce
2 tablespoons honey
1 tablespoon brown sugar
1 tablespoon cider vinegar
2 cloves garlic, crushed
1/4 teaspoon Chinese five-spice
  powder
2 teaspoons sesame oil

1 Tuck the chicken wing tips to
the underside and place in a non-
metallic bowl.
2 Mix together all the remaining
ingredients and pour over the wings,
tossing to coat. Cover and leave
in the fridge for at least 2 hours,
turning occasionally. Drain, reserving
the marinade.
3 Cook the wings on a hot, lightly
oiled barbecue grill or flatplate for
5 minutes, or until cooked through,
brushing with the reserved marinade
several times.

NUTRITION PER SERVE
Protein 46 g; Fat 8 g; Carbohydrate 21 g;
Dietary Fibre 2 g; Cholesterol 100 mg;
1411 kJ (337 cal)

Tuck the chicken wing tips to the underside so
the wings form triangle shapes.

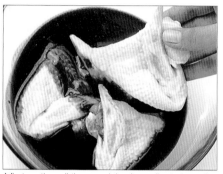

Mix together all the remaining ingredients to make
a marinade for the chicken.

Place the chicken on a hot, lightly oiled barbecue
grill and cook for 5 minutes.

GINGER-CHILLI DRUMSTICKS WITH CUCUMBER YOGHURT

Preparation time: 10 minutes + 3 hours
  marinating
Total cooking time: 20 minutes
Serves 6

1 tablespoon grated fresh ginger
1 tablespoon brown sugar
1 teaspoon bottled crushed red
  chilli peppers
1/4 teaspoon ground turmeric
1 teaspoon lemon juice
1 teaspoon finely grated lemon rind
1 cup (250 g/8 oz) plain yoghurt
12 chicken drumsticks

CUCUMBER YOGHURT
1 cup (250 g/8 oz) plain yoghurt
1/2 teaspoon bottled crushed red chlili
  peppers
1 cucumber, finely chopped
1/2 teaspoon sugar

1 Mix together the ginger, brown
sugar, crushed chilli pepper, turmeric,
lemon juice and lemon rind. Stir in the
yoghurt. Add the chicken, stirring well
to coat. Cover and refrigerate for at
least 3 hours, stirring occasionally.
Drain, reserving the marinade.
2 Cook the drumsticks on a hot,
lightly oiled barbecue grill or flatplate
for 15–20 minutes, or until tender.
Brush occasionally with the
reserved marinade.
3 To make the cucumber yoghurt,
mix together the yoghurt, crushed
chilli pepper, cucumber, sugar and salt
and serve with the drumsticks.

NUTRITION PER SERVE
Protein 45 g; Fat 14 g; Carbohydrate 6 g;
Dietary Fibre 0 g; Cholesterol 190 mg;
1403 kJ (333 cal)

Mix together the ginger, sugar, chilli, turmeric,
lemon juice and rind and yoghurt.

Cook the drumsticks for 15–20 minutes,
brushing occasionally with marinade.

To make the cucumber yoghurt, mix together all
the ingredients.

BACON-WRAPPED CHICKEN

Preparation time: 15 minutes
Total cooking time: 10 minutes
Serves 6

2 tablespoons olive oil
2 tablespoons lime juice
1/4 teaspoon ground coriander
6 chicken breast fillets
4 tablespoons fruit chutney
3 tablespoons chopped pecan nuts
6 slices bacon

1 Mix together the oil, lime juice, coriander and salt and pepper. Using a sharp knife, cut a pocket in the thickest section of each fillet. Mix together the chutney and nuts. Spoon 1 tablespoon of the chutney mixture into each chicken breast pocket.
2 Turn the tapered ends of the fillets to the underside. Wrap a bacon slice around each fillet to enclose the filling and secure with a toothpick.
3 Put the chicken parcels on a hot, lightly oiled barbecue grill or flatplate and cook for 5 minutes on each side, or until cooked through, turning once. Brush with the lime juice mixture several times during cooking and drizzle with any leftover lime juice mixture to serve.

NUTRITION PER SERVE
Protein 72 g; Fat 28 g; Carbohydrate 19 g;
Dietary Fibre 1 g; Cholesterol 164 mg;
2589 kJ (618 cal)

VARIATION: This recipe also works well with prosciutto, which is an Italian equivalent of bacon.

Mix together the fruit chutney and pecans to make a filling for the chicken.

Wrap a piece of bacon around each breast and secure with a toothpick or skewer.

Cook the chicken on a hot barbecue grill for 5 minutes on each side.

Brush the chicken with the lime juice mixture during cooking.

CHILLI CHICKEN WITH TOMATO SALSA

Preparation time: 10 minutes +
  3 hours marinating
Total cooking time: 20 minutes
Serves 4

8 chicken thighs
1/2 cup (125 ml/4 fl oz) lemon juice
1/4 teaspoon bottled crushed chilli
2 tablespoons oil
2 teaspoons sesame oil
3 tablespoons soy sauce
3 tablespoons honey
1 clove garlic, crushed
2 spring onions, chopped
3 tablespoons finely chopped
  fresh coriander

TOMATO SALSA
1 small cucumber, chopped
1 small red onion, finely chopped
1 tomato, chopped
2 tablespoons olive oil
1 tablespoon white wine vinegar
1/4 teaspoon sugar
1/4 cup (7 g/1/4 oz) chopped fresh
  coriander

1 Trim the chicken of excess fat and sinew and place in a shallow, non-metallic dish. Mix together the lemon juice, chilli, oils, soy sauce, honey, garlic, spring onion, coriander and salt. Pour over the chicken and toss to coat. Cover and refrigerate for at least 3 hours, stirring occasionally.
2 Drain the chicken, reserving the marinade. Cook on a hot, lightly oiled barbecue grill or flatplate for 5–10 minutes on each side or until tender and cooked through. Brush with reserved marinade occasionally.
3 To make the tomato salsa, mix together the cucumber, onion, tomato, olive oil, vinegar, sugar and fresh coriander in a serving bowl. Serve with the chicken.

NUTRITION PER SERVE
Protein 26 g; Fat 22 g; Carbohydrate 15 g;
Dietary Fibre 1 g; Cholesterol 55 mg;
1522 kJ (364 cal)

STORAGE: The salsa can be kept, covered, at room temperature for up to a day.

Mix together the marinade ingredients and soak the chicken for at least 3 hours.

While the chicken is cooking, baste it occasionally with the marinade.

To make the tomato salsa, simply mix together all the ingredients.

Marinades & Glazes for Chicken

Chicken should be left to marinate for at least 2 hours and overnight if you have the time. A good tip is to put chicken pieces in a plastic bag with the marinade and then freeze for future use. When you bring the chicken out to defrost, it can be marinating at the same time.

LIME AND GINGER GLAZE

Put $1/2$ cup (160 g/$5^1/2$ oz) lime marmalade, $1/4$ cup (60 ml/2 fl oz) lime juice, 2 tablespoons sherry, 2 tablespoons soft brown sugar and 2 teaspoons finely grated fresh ginger in a pan. Stir over low heat until liquid. Pour over 1 kg (2 lb) chicken wings and toss well to combine. Cover and refrigerate for 2 hours or overnight. Cook on a hot barbecue for 10 minutes, or until cooked through.

HONEY SOY MARINADE

Put $1/4$ cup (90 g/3 oz) honey, $1/4$ cup (60 ml/2 fl oz) soy sauce, 1 crushed garlic clove, 2 tablespoons sake and $1/2$ teaspoon Chinese five-spice powder in a pan. Pour over 500 g (1 lb) chicken thigh fillets and toss well. Cover and refrigerate for 2 hours or overnight. Cook on a hot barbecue for 10 minutes, or until cooked through.

REDCURRANT GLAZE

Put 340 g (11 oz) redcurrant jelly, 2 tablespoons lemon juice, 2 tablespoons brandy and 1 teaspoon chopped fresh thyme in a pan and stir over low heat until it becomes liquid. Pour over 500 g (1 lb) chicken breast fillets and toss well to combine. Cover and refrigerate for 2 hours or overnight. Cook on a hot barbecue for 8 minutes, turning once, or until cooked through.

TANDOORI MARINADE

Soak 8 bamboo skewers in water for 30 minutes to prevent scorching. Combine 2 tablespoons tandoori paste, 1 cup (250 g/8 oz) plain yoghurt and 1 tablespoon lime juice. Cut 500 g (1 lb) tenderloins in half lengthways and thread onto skewers. Pour over the marinade and toss well to combine. Cover and refrigerate for 1–2 hours. Cook on a hot barbecue, basting with the marinade, for 5–10 minutes, or until cooked through.

MEXICAN MARINADE

Combine 440 g (14 oz) bottled taco sauce, 2 tablespoons lime juice and 2 tablespoons chopped fresh coriander leaves. Pour the marinade over 1 kg (2 lb) scored chicken drumsticks and toss well to combine. Cover and refrigerate for 2 hours or overnight. Cook on a hot barbecue for 30 minutes, or until cooked through.

THAI MARINADE

Combine 2 tablespoons fish sauce, 2 tablespoons lime juice, 1 crushed garlic clove, 1 finely chopped lemon grass stem, 2 teaspoons soft brown sugar, $1/2$ cup (125 ml/4 fl oz) coconut cream and 2 tablespoons chopped fresh coriander leaves. Pour the marinade over 1 kg (2 lb) chicken drumettes and toss well to combine. Cover and refrigerate for 2 hours or overnight. Cook on a hot barbecue for 30 minutes, or until cooked through.

This page, from top: Tandoori Marinade; Mexican Marinade; Thai Marinade
Opposite, from top: Lime and Ginger Glaze; Honey Soy Marinade; Redcurrant Glaze

Seafood

MALAYSIAN BARBECUED SEAFOOD

Preparation time: 30 minutes +
  15 minutes marinating
Total cooking time: 10 minutes
Serves 6

1 onion, grated
4 cloves garlic, chopped
5 cm (2 inch) piece of fresh ginger,
  grated
3 stems lemon grass (white
  part only), chopped
2 teaspoons ground or grated fresh
  turmeric
1 teaspoon shrimp paste
1/3 cup (80 ml/2^{3}/4 fl oz) vegetable oil
1/4 teaspoon salt
4 medium calamari tubes
2 thick white boneless fish fillets
8 raw king prawns
banana leaves, for serving
2 limes, cut into wedges

1 Combine the onion, garlic, ginger, lemon grass, turmeric, shrimp paste, oil and salt in a small food processor. Process in short bursts until the mixture forms a paste.
2 Cut the calamari in half lengthways and lay it on the bench with the soft inside facing up. Score a very fine honeycomb pattern into the soft side,

taking care not to cut all the way through, and then cut into large pieces. Wash all the seafood under cold running water and pat dry with paper towels. Brush the seafood lightly with the spice paste. Place the seafood on a tray, cover and refrigerate for 15 minutes.
3 Lightly oil a barbecue hotplate and heat. When the plate is hot, arrange the fish fillets and prawns side by side on the plate. Cook for about 3 minutes on each side, turning them once only, or until the fish flesh is just firm and the prawns turn bright pink to orange. Add the calamari pieces and cook for about 2 minutes or until the flesh turns white and rolls up—take care not to overcook the seafood.
4 Arrange the seafood on a platter lined with the banana leaves, add the lime wedges and serve immediately, garnished with strips of lime rind and some fresh mint, if you like.

NUTRITION PER SERVE
Protein 33 g; Fat 3 g; Carbohydrate 1 g;
Dietary Fibre 1 g; Cholesterol 300 mg;
681 kJ (163 cal)

NOTE: Banana leaves are available from speciality fruit and vegetable shops. Alternatively, make friends with someone who has a banana tree.

Process in short bursts until the mixture forms a paste for coating the seafood.

Score a fine honeycomb pattern into the soft side of the calamari.

VIETNAMESE FISH

Preparation time: 25 minutes +
  20 minutes marinating
Total cooking time: 15 minutes
Serves 6

750 g (1¹/₂ lb) small, firm, white fish
2 teaspoons green peppercorns,
   finely crushed
2 teaspoons chopped red chilli
3 teaspoons fish sauce
2 teaspoons oil
1 tablespoon oil, extra
2 onions, finely sliced
4 cm (1¹/₂ inch) piece of fresh ginger,
   peeled and thinly sliced
3 cloves garlic, finely sliced

2 teaspoons sugar
4 spring onions, cut into short lengths,
   then finely shredded

LEMON AND GARLIC DIPPING
   SAUCE
3 tablespoons lemon juice
2 tablespoons fish sauce
1 tablespoon sugar
2 small red chillies, chopped
3 cloves garlic, crushed

1 Cut 2 diagonal slashes in the
thickest part of the fish on both sides.
In a food processor or mortar and
pestle, grind the peppercorns, chilli
and fish sauce to a paste and brush
over the fish. Leave for 20 minutes.
2 Cook on a hot, lightly oiled

barbecue grill or flatplate for 8 minutes
on each side, or until the flesh flakes
easily when tested.
3 While the fish is cooking, heat the
extra oil in a pan and stir the onion
over medium heat, until golden.
Add the ginger, garlic and sugar and
cook for 3 minutes. Place the fish
on a serving plate, top with the
onion mixture and sprinkle with
spring onion.
4 To make the dipping sauce, mix
together all the ingredients. Serve with
the barbecued fish.

NUTRITION PER SERVE
Protein 27 g; Fat 5 g; Carbohydrate 3 g;
Dietary Fibre 1 g; Cholesterol 88 mg;
705 kJ (168 cal)

Cut diagonal slashes into the thickest part of the
fish so that it cooks through evenly.

Lightly brush the chilli mixture over the surface of
the fish.

Cook the finely sliced onion over medium heat,
stirring until golden.

BALSAMIC BABY OCTOPUS

Preparation time: 15 minutes + 3 hours marinating
Total cooking time: 10 minutes
Serves 4

1 kg (2 lb) baby octopus
3/4 cup (185 ml/6 fl oz) red wine
2 tablespoons balsamic vinegar
2 tablespoons soy sauce
2 tablespoons hoisin sauce
1 clove garlic, crushed

1 Cut off the octopus heads, below the eyes, with a sharp knife. Discard the heads and guts. Push the beaks out with your index finger, remove and discard. Wash the octopus thoroughly under running water and drain on crumpled paper towels. If the octopus tentacles are large, cut into quarters.
2 Put the octopus in a large bowl. Stir together the wine, vinegar, soy sauce, hoisin sauce and garlic and pour over the octopus. Toss to coat, then cover and refrigerate for at least 3 hours. Drain the octopus, reserving the leftover marinade.

3 Cook on a very hot, lightly oiled barbecue grill or flatplate, in batches, for 3–5 minutes, or until the octopus flesh turns white. Brush the marinade over the octopus during cooking. Be careful not to overcook or the octopus will be tough. Serve warm or cold.

NUTRITION PER SERVE
Protein 42.5 g; Fat 3.5 g; Carbohydrate 4 g; Dietary Fibre 1 g; Cholesterol 497.5 mg; 1060 kJ (255 cal)

Remove and discard the head from each octopus using a sharp knife.

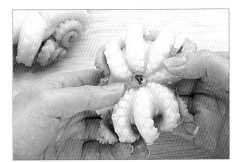

Push the beaks through the centre with your index finger.

Brush the octopus all over with the reserved marinade while cooking.

CORIANDER PRAWNS

Preparation time: 15 minutes +
    30 minutes marinating
Total cooking time: 5 minutes
Serves 4

8 very large raw prawns
1 tablespoon sweet chilli sauce
1 teaspoon ground coriander
1/2 cup (125 ml/4 fl oz) olive oil
1/3 cup (80 ml/2³/4 fl oz) lime juice
3 cloves garlic, crushed
1 tomato, peeled, seeded and
    chopped
2 tablespoons roughly chopped
    fresh coriander

1 Remove the heads from the prawns and, with a sharp knife, cut the prawns in half lengthways, leaving the tails attached. Pull out each dark vein.
2 Mix together the sweet chilli sauce and ground coriander with half the olive oil, half the lime juice and half the garlic. Add the prawns, toss to coat, then cover and marinate in the fridge for 30 minutes.
3 Meanwhile, to make the dressing, mix the remaining olive oil, lime juice and garlic in a bowl with the chopped tomato and fresh coriander.
4 Drain the prawns, reserving the marinade and cook, cut-side-down, on a hot, lightly oiled barbecue grill or flatplate for 1–2 minutes each side, or until cooked through, brushing occasionally with the marinade.
5 Spoon a little of the dressing over the prawns and season well before serving.

NUTRITION PER SERVE
Protein 42 g; Fat 31 g; Carbohydrate 2.5 g;
Dietary Fibre 2 g; Cholesterol 298 mg;
1930 kJ (460 cal)

Cut each prawn through the centre lengthways, leaving the tail attached.

Stir the dressing ingredients together in a bowl until well combined.

Cook both sides of the drained prawns on a hot barbecue grill.

TUNA WITH MEDITERRANEAN VEGETABLES

Preparation time: 15 minutes +
  30 minutes marinating
Total cooking time: 20 minutes
Serves 4

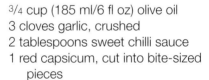

3/4 cup (185 ml/6 fl oz) olive oil
3 cloves garlic, crushed
2 tablespoons sweet chilli sauce
1 red capsicum, cut into bite-sized
    pieces
1 yellow capsicum, cut into bite-sized
    pieces
2 large zucchini, thickly sliced
2 slender eggplant, thickly sliced
olive oil, extra, for brushing
4 tuna steaks

LEMON AND CAPER MAYONNAISE
1 egg yolk
1 teaspoon grated lemon rind
2 tablespoons lemon juice
1 small clove garlic, chopped
3/4 cup (185 ml/6 fl oz) olive oil
1 tablespoon baby capers

1 Combine the olive oil, garlic and sweet chilli sauce in a large bowl. Add the capsicum, zucchini and eggplant, toss well, then marinate for 30 minutes.
2 For the mayonnaise, process the egg yolk, rind, lemon juice and garlic together in a food processor until smooth. With the motor running, gradually add the oil in a thin steady stream until the mixture thickens and is a creamy consistency. Stir in the capers and 1/2 teaspoon salt. Set aside.
3 Cook the drained vegetables on a hot, lightly oiled barbecue grill or flatplate for 4–5 minutes each side, or until cooked through. Keep warm.

4 Brush the tuna steaks with the extra oil and barbecue for 2–3 minutes each side, or until just cooked (tuna should be rare in the centre). Serve the vegetables and tuna steaks with the lemon and caper mayonnaise.

NUTRITION PER SERVE
Protein 68 g; Fat 69 g; Carbohydrate 6 g; Dietary Fibre 3 g; Cholesterol 151 mg; 3885 kJ (925 cal)

VARIATION: This recipe is also suitable for use with Atlantic salmon or swordfish.

Process the mayonnaise ingredients until smooth and creamy.

Turn the vegetables over when browned on one side, then cook through.

LEMON AND HERB TROUT

Preparation time: 20 minutes
Total cooking time: 15 minutes
Serves 4

3 tablespoons chopped fresh dill
2 tablespoons chopped fresh
   rosemary
3 tablespoons coarsely chopped fresh
   flat-leaf parsley
2 teaspoons thyme leaves
6 teaspoons crushed green
   peppercorns
$1/3$ cup (80 ml/$2^3/_4$ fl oz) lemon juice
1 lemon
4 whole fresh trout
$1/3$ cup (80 ml/$2^3/_4$ fl oz) dry white
   wine

HORSERADISH CREAM
1 tablespoon horseradish cream
$1/2$ cup (125 g/4 oz) sour cream
2 tablespoons cream

LEMON SAUCE
2 egg yolks
150 g (5 oz) butter, melted
3–4 tablespoons lemon juice

1 Lightly grease 4 large sheets of foil, each double-thickness. Mix together the herbs, peppercorns, juice and salt and pepper in a bowl. Cut the lemon into 8 slices, cut each slice in half. Place 2 lemon pieces in each fish cavity. Spoon the herb mixture into the fish cavities.
2 Place each fish on a piece of foil and sprinkle each with 1 tablespoon of wine. Seal the fish in foil to form neat parcels. Cook on a hot barbecue flatplate or grill for 10–15 minutes or until the fish is just cooked through and can be gently flaked with a fork. Leave the fish to stand, still wrapped in foil, for 5 minutes, before serving.
3 To make the horseradish cream, mix together all the ingredients and then season well.
4 To make the lemon sauce, process the yolks in a food processor for 20 seconds or until blended. With the motor running, add the butter slowly in a thin, steady stream. Continue processing until all butter has been added and the sauce is thick and creamy. Add the juice and season with salt and pepper.

NUTRITION PER SERVE
Protein 33 g; Fat 58 g; Carbohydrate 4 g;
Dietary Fibre 1 g; Cholesterol 334 mg;
2869 kJ (685 cal)

Mix together the herbs, peppercorns, juice and salt and pepper and use to stuff the fish.

Sprinkle each fish with a tablespoon of wine and then wrap up in foil.

Make the lemon sauce in a food processor, adding the butter in a slow stream.

LOBSTER TAILS WITH AVOCADO SAUCE

Preparation time: 15 minutes + 3 hours
 marinating
Total cooking time: 10 minutes
Serves 4

3 tablespoons dry white wine
1 tablespoon honey
1 teaspoon sambal oelek
1 clove garlic, crushed
1 tablespoon olive oil
4 raw lobster tails

AVOCADO SAUCE
1 ripe avocado, mashed
3 teaspoons lemon juice
2 tablespoons sour cream
1 small tomato, chopped finely

1 Mix together the wine, honey, sambal oelek, garlic and oil. Cut along the soft shell on the underside of the lobster. Gently pull the shell apart and ease out the flesh.
2 Put the lobster in a shallow, non-metallic dish. Add the marinade and toss to coat. Cover and refrigerate for at least 3 hours.
3 Cook the lobster on a hot, lightly oiled barbecue grill or flatplate for 5–10 minutes, turning frequently. Brush with the marinade until cooked through. Slice into medallions.
4 To make the sauce, mix together the avocado, juice and sour cream. Add the tomato and season well.

NUTRITION PER SERVE
Protein 24 g; Fat 23 g; Carbohydrate 7 g;
Dietary Fibre 1 g; Cholesterol 1 mg;
1421 kJ (339 cal)

STORAGE: The sauce will keep for 2–3 hours in the fridge with plastic wrap pressed over its surface.

Use a sharp knife or kitchen scissors to cut the soft shell on the underside of the lobster.

Put the lobster in a shallow, non-metallic dish and leave to marinate.

Mix together the avocado, juice and sour cream before combining with the tomato.

115

SQUID WITH PICADA DRESSING

Preparation time: 40 minutes +
    30 minutes chilling
Total cooking time: 10 minutes
Serves 6

500 g (1 lb) small squid (see NOTE)
1/4 teaspoon salt

PICADA DRESSING
2 tablespoons extra virgin olive oil
2 tablespoons finely chopped fresh
    flat-leaf parsley
1 clove garlic, crushed
1/4 teaspoon cracked black pepper

1 To clean the squid, gently pull the tentacles away from the hood (the intestines should come away at the same time). Remove the intestines from the tentacles by cutting under the eyes, then remove the beak, if it remains in the centre of the tentacles, by pushing up with your index finger. Pull away the soft bone.
2 Rub the hoods under cold running water and the skin should come away easily. Wash the hoods and tentacles and drain well. Place in a bowl, add the salt and mix well. Cover and refrigerate for about 30 minutes.
3 For the picada dressing, whisk together the olive oil, parsley, garlic, pepper and some salt.
4 Cook the squid hoods in small

batches on a very hot, lightly oiled barbecue flatplate for 2–3 minutes, or until white and tender. Barbecue or grill the squid tentacles, turning to brown them all over, for 1 minute, or until they curl up. Serve hot, drizzled with the picada dressing.

NUTRITION PER SERVE
Protein 20 g; Fat 10 g; Carbohydrate 1 g;
Dietary Fibre 1 g; Cholesterol 180 mg;
800 kJ (190 cal)

NOTE: A suitably small variety of squid is the bottleneck squid.

STORAGE: Make the picada dressing as close to serving time as possible so the parsley doesn't discolour.

Gently pull the tentacles away from the squid hoods and the intestines should follow.

Cut under the eyes to remove the intestines and then remove the beak.

Rub the hoods under cold running water and remove the skin.

SALMON WITH CHILLI-CORN SALSA

Preparation time: 25 minutes
Total cooking time: 5 minutes
Serves 4

1 tablespoon olive oil
1/2 teaspoon ground cumin
1/2 teaspoon paprika
4 salmon cutlets
4 limes, cut into quarters, to serve

CHILLI-CORN SALSA
2 corn cobs
4 spring onions, finely sliced
1 small clove garlic, crushed
1/2 red capsicum, finely diced
1 teaspoon diced red jalapeno chilli
1 teaspoon diced green jalapeno chilli
1 teaspoon ground cumin
2 tablespoons extra virgin olive oil
2 tablespoons lime juice
1 tablespoon finely chopped fresh
  parsley

1 Mix the oil, cumin and paprika.
2 To make the salsa, cook the corn cobs until tender in boiling water. Transfer to iced water to cool. Cut off the kernels and mix with the spring onion, garlic, capsicum, chilli, cumin, extra virgin olive oil, lime juice and parsley. Season to taste.
3 Brush the salmon with the spicy oil and cook on a hot, lightly oiled barbecue grill for 2 minutes on each side for rare, or a few extra minutes for well done. Take care not to overcook. Serve with the salsa and lime quarters.

NUTRITION PER SERVE
Protein 20 g; Fat 25 g; Carbohydrate 20 g;
Dietary Fibre 3 g; Cholesterol 70 mg;
1695 kJ (405 cal)

Combine the olive oil with the ground cumin and the paprika.

Slice the kernels from the cooled corn cobs with a sharp knife.

Cook the salmon cutlets for about 2 minutes on each side.

FISH WRAPPED IN BANANA LEAVES

Preparation time: 20 minutes
Total cooking time: 35 minutes
Serves 4–6

SPICE PASTE
1 red onion, finely chopped
3 small red chillies, seeded and
    chopped
1 teaspoon dried shrimp paste
1 cm (1/2 inch) piece fresh galangal,
    finely chopped
1 stem lemon grass, white part only,
    finely sliced
5 blanched almonds, chopped
4 kaffir lime leaves, finely shredded

2 teaspoons sesame oil
1 tablespoon vegetable oil
1 teaspoon soy sauce
1 banana leaf (about 50 x 30 cm/
    20 x 12 inches)
1 whole trout or silver bream
    (about 750 g/11/2 lb),
    cleaned and scaled

1 To make the spice paste, grind all
the ingredients except the kaffir lime
leaves in a food processor with
2 tablespoons water until smooth.
Transfer to a bowl and mix in the kaffir
lime leaves. Set aside.
2 Heat the sesame oil and vegetable
oil in a small frying pan and gently fry
the paste for 5 minutes. Mix in the soy
sauce. Remove from the heat and cool.
3 Cut a large rectangle from the
banana leaf and brush with oil. Score
the fish several times on both sides
and rub in the paste, pushing it well
into the cuts.
4 Place the fish on the banana leaf
and fold over to make a parcel. Wrap
again in foil to secure and protect.
Cook over medium heat on a hot,
lightly oiled barbecue grill or flatplate
for 20–30 minutes, or until the flesh
flakes easily when tested with a fork.

NUTRITION PER SERVE (6)
Protein 30 g; Fat 15 g; Carbohydrate 3 g;
Dietary Fibre 1 g; Cholesterol 75 mg;
1050 kJ (250 cal)

Add the shredded kaffir lime leaves to the smooth
spice paste.

Stir the soy sauce into the fried spice paste and
mix well.

Score the fish several times on both sides with a
sharp knife.

Wrap the fish in the banana leaf, folding the ends
securely to make a parcel.

THAI-STYLE WHOLE SNAPPER

Preparation time: 10 minutes
Total cooking time: 30 minutes
Serves 4–6

2 garlic cloves, crushed
1 tablespoon fish sauce
2 tablespoons lemon juice
1 tablespoon grated fresh ginger
2 tablespoons sweet chilli sauce

2 tablespoons chopped fresh
    coriander
1 tablespoon rice wine vinegar
2 tablespoons white wine
600 g (1¼ lb) whole snapper, cleaned
    and scaled
2 spring onions, cut into julienne strips

1 Mix together the garlic, fish sauce, lemon juice, ginger, chilli sauce, coriander, rice wine vinegar and wine.
2 Place the snapper on a large piece of double-thickness foil. Pour the

marinade over the fish and sprinkle with the spring onion.
3 Wrap the fish in the foil to make a parcel. Cook over medium heat on a barbecue grill or flatplate for 20–30 minutes, or until the flesh flakes easily when tested with a fork.

NUTRITION PER SERVE (6)
Protein 20 g; Fat 2 g; Carbohydrate 5 g;
Dietary Fibre 0 g; Cholesterol 60 mg;
495 kJ (120 cal)

Mix together the garlic, fish sauce, lemon juice, ginger, chilli sauce, coriander, vinegar and wine.

Pour the marinade over the snapper after you have placed it on the foil.

Cook the fish until the flesh flakes easily when tested with a fork.

THAI BABY OCTOPUS

Preparation time: 1 hour
Total cooking time: 15–25 minutes
Serves 6

500 g (1 lb) baby octopus
2 tablespoons oil
3 cloves garlic, chopped
1 tablespoon green or pink
    peppercorns
2–4 small red chillies, finely chopped
1 tablespoon fish sauce

1 Cut off the octopus heads, below the eyes, with a sharp knife. Discard the heads and guts. Push the beaks out with your index finger, remove and discard. Wash the octopus thoroughly under running water and drain on crumpled paper towels. If the octopus tentacles are large, cut into quarters. Put in a shallow dish.
2 Mix together the oil, garlic, peppercorns and chilli, add to the octopus and marinate for 30 minutes. Cook 3 octopus at a time, turning frequently, on a very hot, lightly oiled barbecue flatplate for 3 minutes or until they turn white. Do not overcook. Sprinkle the fish sauce over the top and serve immediately.

NUTRITION PER SERVE
Protein 14 g; Fat 7 g; Carbohydrate 0 g;
Dietary Fibre 0 g; Cholesterol 166 mg;
522 kJ (125 cal)

HINT: This recipe is also suitable for calamari. Wash the tubes, pat dry and cut into strips before marinating and cooking in the same way.

Use a sharp knife to slice off the head of the octopus so you can remove the gut.

Use your index finger to push the beak up so you can remove and discard it.

Cook the octopus, turning frequently, until they turn white.

THAI-STYLE STUFFED CALAMARI TUBES

Preparation time: 30 minutes
Total cooking time: 10 minutes
Serves 4

8 very small calamari tubes (see NOTE)
2 tablespoons oil
4 cloves garlic, chopped
2 stems lemon grass, finely chopped
4 coriander roots, chopped
1–2 teaspoons Thai green curry paste
125 g (4 oz) pork mince
100 g (3¹/₂ oz) chicken mince
2 tablespoons fish sauce
2 tablespoons rice flour
1 tablespoon Golden Mountain sauce
2 teaspoons soft brown sugar
chilli sauce, to serve

1 Pull the tentacles from the body of the calamari. Pull the quill from the pouch of the calamari. Pull the skin away from the flesh and discard it. Wash the tubes thoroughly.
2 Heat half the oil in a frying pan over medium heat. Add the garlic, lemon grass, coriander root and curry paste and stir-fry for 2 minutes. Remove from the heat; add both the minces, the fish sauce and rice flour and mix well.
3 Fill each tube with the mixture and secure the end with a toothpick. Mix together the Golden Mountain sauce, sugar and 1 tablespoon water and brush over the tubes.
4 Brush a barbecue flatplate with the remaining oil and then heat to very hot. Add the tubes and cook, turning frequently, for 4–6 minutes or until just firm to the touch. Leave for 2 minutes before slicing, or serve whole. Serve with chilli sauce.

NUTRITION PER SERVE
Protein 74 g; Fat 15 g; Carbohydrate 9 g; Dietary Fibre 1 g; Cholesterol 744 mg; 1974 kJ (472 cal)

NOTE: Don't use pre-cleaned calamari as the tip will have been removed and the stuffing will come out. Baby calamari is very tender and only about 8 cm (3 inches) long.

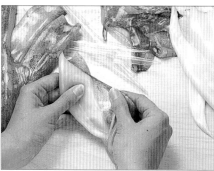

Hold one end of the calamari, pull the skin away from the flesh and discard it.

Remove the frying pan from the heat and stir in the minces, fish sauce and rice flour.

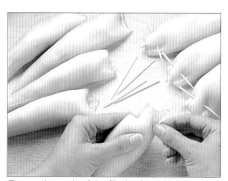

Secure the ends of the filled calamari tubes with toothpicks so the filling won't come out.

Leave the cooked tubes for 2 minutes before slicing, or serve them whole.

GARLIC CALAMARI WITH PARMESAN

Preparation time: 30 minutes +
    10 minutes marinating
Total cooking time: 5 minutes
Serves 2–4 (see NOTE)

350 g (11 oz) calamari tubes, cleaned
4 cloves garlic, chopped
2 tablespoons olive oil
2 tablespoons finely chopped fresh
    parsley
1 large tomato, peeled, seeded and
    finely chopped
1/4 cup (25 g/3/4 oz) grated Parmesan

1 Cut the calamari tubes in half lengthways, wash and pat dry. Lay them flat, with the soft, fleshy side facing upwards, and cut into rectangular pieces, about 6 x 2.5 cm (2¹/2 x 1 inch). Finely honeycomb by scoring the fleshy side with diagonal strips, one way and then the other, to create a diamond pattern.
2 Mix the garlic, oil, half the parsley, salt and pepper in a bowl. Add the calamari and refrigerate for at least 10 minutes.
3 Cook on a very hot, lightly oiled barbecue flatplate in 2 batches, tossing regularly, until they just turn white (take care never to overcook calamari or it can become tough). Add the chopped tomato and toss through to just heat.
4 Arrange the calamari on a plate and scatter with the Parmesan and remaining parsley.

NUTRITION PER SERVE (4)
Protein 20 g; Fat 15 g; Carbohydrate 2 g;
Dietary Fibre 1 g; Cholesterol 180 mg;
800 kJ (190 cal)

NOTE: This dish will serve four as a starter and two as a main course.

Honeycomb the soft fleshy side of the calamari with a sharp knife.

Combine the garlic, oil, parsley and some salt and pepper in a bowl.

Cook the calamari in batches, tossing regularly, until they turn white.

Serve the calamari topped with a little grated Parmesan and the remaining parsley.

SALMON CUTLETS WITH TROPICAL FRUIT SALSA

Preparation time: 20 minutes + 3 hours
  marinating
Total cooking time: 20 minutes
Serves 4

4 salmon cutlets
1¹⁄₂ tablespoons seasoned pepper
2 tablespoons lemon juice
¹⁄₂ cup (125 ml/4 fl oz) lime juice
1 tablespoon chopped fresh thyme

FRUIT SALSA
¹⁄₂ small pawpaw, peeled
¹⁄₄ small pineapple, peeled
3 spring onions, chopped
1 tablespoon chopped fresh coriander
2 tablespoons lime juice
3 teaspoons caster sugar
salt, to taste

1 Sprinkle the salmon all over with seasoned pepper. Place in a shallow non-metallic dish. Mix together the lemon juice, lime juice and thyme and pour over the salmon. Cover and refrigerate for at least 3 hours.
2 Cook the salmon on a hot, lightly oiled barbecue grill or flatplate, brushing with any remaining marinade. Cook for 5–10 minutes each side, turning once, until lightly browned and the flesh is just cooked.
3 To make the salsa, chop the pawpaw and pineapple into small dice. Mix with the spring onion, coriander, lime juice, caster sugar and salt and serve with the salmon.

NUTRITION PER SERVE
Protein 20 g; Fat 12 g; Carbohydrate 13 g;
Dietary Fibre 3 g; Cholesterol 70 mg;
980 kJ (235 cal)

STORAGE: Do not marinate fish for more than 3 hours as the citrus juices will begin to 'cook' the fish and turn the flesh opaque. If this should occur, reduce the cooking time by half. Salsa should be made just before serving.

NOTE: When buying pawpaw, look for a deep yellow skin colour and a firm flesh. (If pawpaw yields easily to gentle pressure in the thickest area, it is over-ripe and should not be used.) Smaller pawpaws with orange-red flesh are sometimes available—their flesh is more delicate than the large variety. Store uncut, ripe pawpaws in the fridge for up to a week. Serve as soon as possible after cutting as the flesh discolours unless tossed in lemon juice.

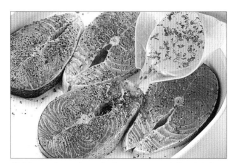

Put the salmon in a shallow, non-metallic dish for marinating with the citrus mixture.

Cook the salmon until it is lightly browned on the outside and the flesh is just cooked.

To make the salsa, simply dice the tropical fruit and mix with the other ingredients.

INTERNATIONAL BARBECUED SHELLFISH PLATTER

Preparation time: 40 minutes +
1 hour freezing
Total cooking time: 30 minutes
Serves 6

6 raw Balmain bugs (see NOTES)
30 g (1 oz) butter, melted
1 tablespoon oil
12 black mussels
12 scallops on their shells
12 oysters on their shells
18 raw large prawns, unpeeled

SALSA VERDE, FOR SCALLOPS
1 tablespoon finely chopped
preserved lemon (see NOTES)
1 cup (20 g/³/₄ oz) fresh
parsley leaves
1 tablespoon drained bottled capers
1 tablespoon lemon juice
3 tablespoons oil, approximately

VINEGAR AND SHALLOT DRESSING,
FOR MUSSELS
¹/₄ cup (60 ml/2 fl oz) white wine
vinegar
4 French shallots, finely chopped
1 tablespoon chopped fresh chervil

PICKLED GINGER AND WASABI
SAUCE, FOR OYSTERS
1 teaspoon soy sauce
¹/₄ cup (60 ml/2 fl oz) mirin
2 tablespoons rice wine vinegar
¹/₄ teaspoon wasabi paste
2 tablespoons finely sliced pickled
ginger

SWEET BALSAMIC DRESSING,
FOR BALMAIN BUGS
1 tablespoon olive oil
1 tablespoon honey
¹/₂ cup (125 ml/4 fl oz) balsamic
vinegar

THAI CORIANDER SAUCE,
FOR PRAWNS
¹/₂ cup (125 ml/4 fl oz) sweet chilli
sauce
1 tablespoon lime juice
2 tablespoons chopped fresh
coriander

1 Freeze the bugs for 1 hour to immobilise. Cut each bug in half with a sharp knife, then brush the flesh with the combined butter and oil. Set aside while you prepare the rest of the seafood.
2 Scrub the mussels with a stiff brush and pull out the hairy beards. Discard any broken mussels, or open ones that don't close when tapped on the bench. Rinse well.
3 Slice or pull off any vein, membrane or hard white muscle from the scallops, leaving any roe attached. Brush the scallops with the combined butter and oil.
4 Remove the oysters from the shells, then rinse the shells under cold water. Pat the shells dry and return the oysters to their shells. Cover and refrigerate all the seafood while you make the dressings.
5 For the salsa verde, combine all the ingredients except the oil in a food processor and process in short bursts until roughly chopped. Transfer to a bowl and add enough oil to moisten the mixture. Season with salt and pepper. Serve a small dollop on each cooked scallop.
6 For the vinegar and shallot dressing, whisk the vinegar, shallots and chervil in a bowl until combined. Pour over the cooked mussels.
7 For the pickled ginger and wasabi sauce, whisk all the ingredients in a bowl until combined. Spoon over the cooked oysters.
8 For the sweet balsamic dressing, heat the oil in a pan, add the honey and vinegar and bring to the boil, then boil until reduced by half. Drizzle over the cooked bugs.
9 For the Thai coriander sauce, combine all the ingredients in a jug or bowl and drizzle over the cooked prawns.
10 Cook the seafood on a hot, lightly oiled barbecue grill or flatplate. If necessary, do this in batches, depending on the size of your barbecue. The Balmain bugs will take the longest time to cook, about 5 minutes—they are cooked when the flesh turns white and starts to come away from the shells. The mussels, scallops, oysters and prawns all take about 2–5 minutes to cook.

NOTES: Balmain bugs, or Moreton Bay bugs, are also known as shovel-nosed or slipper lobsters. Recipes for Balmain bugs are usually suitable for large prawns or lobster.

Oysters are sold by fishmongers either freshly shucked on the half shell or alive and unshucked. (Shucked oysters are also sold in bottles of brine, canned, dried and frozen.) When buying fresh shucked oysters, look for a plump moist oyster. The flesh should be creamy with a clear liquid (oyster liquor) surrounding it. Oysters should smell fresh like the sea and have no traces of shell particles. If you prefer to shuck them yourself, look for tightly closed, unbroken shells.

To prepare the preserved lemon, remove the flesh and discard. Wash the skin to remove excess salt and then chop finely.

Mirin, rice wine vinegar and pickled ginger are all available from Asian food speciality stores.

KING PRAWNS WITH DILL MAYONNAISE

Preparation time: 40 minutes + 2 hours
   marinating
Total cooking time: 10–15 minutes
Serves 4

MARINADE
1/2 cup (125 ml/4 fl oz) olive oil
1/3 cup (80 ml/2 3/4 fl oz) lemon juice
2 tablespoons wholegrain mustard
2 tablespoons honey
2 tablespoons chopped fresh dill

16–20 raw king prawns

DILL MAYONNAISE
3/4 cup (185 g/6 oz) mayonnaise
2 tablespoons chopped fresh dill
1 1/2 tablespoons lemon juice
1 gherkin, finely chopped
1 teaspoon chopped capers
1 clove garlic, crushed

1 To make the marinade, combine the olive oil, lemon juice, mustard, honey and dill, pour over the unpeeled prawns and coat well. Cover and refrigerate for at least 2 hours, turning occasionally.
2 To make the dill mayonnaise, whisk together the mayonnaise, dill, lemon juice, gherkin, capers and garlic. Cover and refrigerate.
3 Cook the drained prawns on a hot, lightly oiled barbecue grill or flatplate in batches for 4 minutes, turning frequently until pink and cooked through. Serve with the mayonnaise.

NUTRITION PER SERVE
Protein 20 g; Fat 45 g; Carbohydrate 25 g;
Dietary Fibre 1 g; Cholesterol 155 mg;
405 kJ (570 cal)

Mix together the marinade ingredients and pour over the unpeeled prawns.

Whisk together the mayonnaise, dill, lemon juice, gherkin, capers and garlic.

Cook the prawns in batches so that they don't overcrowd the barbecue.

HERB-STUFFED TROUT

Preparation time: 15 minutes
Total cooking time: 10 minutes
Serves 4

4 rainbow trout, about 200 g
    (6¹/₂ oz) each
4 sprigs fresh dill
4 sprigs fresh lemon thyme
2 limes, thinly sliced
2 cloves garlic, thinly sliced

2 tablespoons olive oil
100 g (3¹/₂ oz) butter, softened
1 teaspoon grated lime rind
1 tablespoon lime juice
1 tablespoon chopped fresh dill

1 Wash the trout under cold water and pat dry with paper towels.
2 Place a sprig of each herb into the cavity of each fish along with the lime slices and garlic.
3 Lightly brush the outside of each fish with the olive oil. Cook on a hot, lightly oiled barbecue grill or flatplate for 5 minutes each side, or until the fish flakes when tested.
4 Place the butter, lime rind and juice and chopped dill into a bowl and mix together. Top each fish with a spoonful of the butter before serving.

NUTRITION PER SERVE
Protein 50 g; Fat 40 g; Carbohydrate 1 g;
Dietary Fibre 1 g; Cholesterol 185 mg;
2290 kJ (545 cal)

Place a sprig of each herb into the cavity of each fish, with the lime and garlic.

Lightly brush the skin of the fish with olive oil so that it becomes crisp.

Cook the fish until the flesh flakes when tested with a fork.

PRAWNS WITH MANGO SALSA

Preparation time: 25 minutes +
  1 hour marinating
Total cooking time: 5 minutes
Serves 4–6

1 kg (2 lb) raw prawns
1/3 cup (80 ml/2³/4 fl oz) lemon juice
1/3 cup (80 ml/2³/4 fl oz) olive oil
1/4 cup (15 g/¹/2 oz) chopped fresh dill
450 g (14 oz) mango, cubed

1 onion, finely diced
1 red chilli, seeded and finely chopped
1 tablespoon grated lemon rind

1 Peel and devein the raw prawns, keeping the tails intact.
2 Combine the lemon juice, olive oil, dill and a teaspoon of salt in a shallow, non-metallic dish, add the prawns and toss. Cover and refrigerate for 1 hour.
3 Drain the prawns, reserving the marinade, and cook on a very hot, lightly oiled barbecue flatplate for 3 minutes, or until they change colour.

4 Put the reserved marinade in a pan on the stovetop or barbecue and boil for 5 minutes. Mix with the prawns.
5 Mix together the mango, onion, chilli, lemon rind and some salt and pepper. Add the prawns and toss together gently.

NUTRITION PER SERVE (6)
Protein 35 g; Fat 15 g; Carbohydrate 10 g;
Dietary Fibre 2 g; Cholesterol 250 mg;
1320 kJ (315 cal)

Peel the prawns and remove the veins from the prawn backs, leaving the tails intact.

Cook the prawns on the very hot barbecue until they change colour.

Mix together the mango, onion, chilli, lemon rind and salt and pepper.

SALMON WITH GREMOLATA AND POTATO GRIDDLE CAKES

Preparation time: 25 minutes
Total cooking time: 15 minutes
Serves 4

GREMOLATA
30 g (1 oz) fresh parsley, finely
  chopped
grated rind of 1 lemon
grated rind of 1 orange
2 cloves garlic, crushed

POTATO GRIDDLE CAKES
250 g (8 oz) potatoes
250 g (8 oz) sweet potatoes, peeled
1/3 cup (20 g/³/4 oz) chopped fresh
  chives
2 tablespoons plain flour
1 egg, lightly beaten
4 salmon fillets, about 200 g (6¹/2 oz)
  each
2–3 teaspoons baby capers, drained

1 For the gremolata, mix the parsley, lemon and orange rind and garlic.
2 To make the potato griddle cake, coarsely grate the peeled potatoes and sweet potatoes and squeeze to remove

any excess moisture. Mix with the chives, flour, egg and salt and pepper. Preheat a barbecue flatplate and drizzle with olive oil. Use a heaped tablespoon of mixture to make each patty, flattening slightly. Cook, turning once, for 5 minutes, or until golden.
3 Cook the salmon on the lightly oiled hot plate for 2–3 minutes each side, or until just tender. Serve with the gremolata, griddle cakes and capers.

NUTRITION PER SERVE
Protein 40 g; Fat 30 g; Carbohydrate 20 g;
Dietary Fibre 3 g; Cholesterol 185 mg;
2215 kJ (525 cal)

To make the gremolata, mix together the parsley, lemon and orange rind and garlic.

Coarsely grate the potato and sweet potato and then squeeze out any excess moisture.

As you cook the griddle cakes, flatten them slightly with the spatula.

128

SCALLOPS WITH GREEN PEPPERCORNS

Preparation time: 20 minutes +
  20 minutes marinating
Total cooking time: 5 minutes
Serves 4

1/4 cup (60 ml/2 fl oz) olive oil
2 teaspoons green peppercorns,
  chopped
2 teaspoons finely grated lime rind
1 teaspoon finely grated fresh ginger
500 g (1 lb) scallops with corals,
  deveined
salad leaves and pickled ginger, to
  serve

1 Combine the oil, peppercorns, rind and fresh ginger. Add the scallops and refrigerate for 20 minutes.
2 Cook the scallops on a very hot, lightly oiled barbecue flatplate, in batches, stirring gently, for about 2 minutes, or until they become lightly golden brown.
3 Serve the scallops on salad leaves and topped with ginger strips.

NUTRITION PER SERVE
Protein 15 g; Fat 15 g; Carbohydrate 1 g;
Dietary Fibre 0 g; Cholesterol 40 mg;
820 kJ (195 cal)

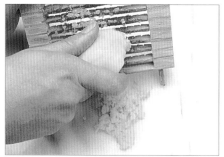

Peel the skin from the fresh ginger and finely grate the flesh.

Mix together the oil, peppercorns, lime rind and ginger to make a marinade.

Cook the scallops on a very hot barbecue flatplate until they are lightly golden brown.

SCALLOPS WITH SESAME BOK CHOY

Preparation time: 10 minutes +
    15 minutes marinating
Total cooking time: 10 minutes
Serves 4

24 large scallops with corals
2 tablespoons light soy sauce
1 tablespoon fish sauce
1 tablespoon honey
1 tablespoon kecap manis
grated rind and juice of 1 lime
2 teaspoons grated fresh ginger
lime wedges, to serve

SESAME BOK CHOY
1 tablespoon sesame oil
1 tablespoon sesame seeds
1 clove garlic, crushed
8 baby bok choy, halved lengthways

1 Rinse the scallops, remove the dark vein and dry with paper towels. Mix the soy and fish sauce, honey, kecap manis, lime rind and juice and ginger. Pour over the scallops, cover and refrigerate for 15 minutes. Drain, keeping the marinade.
2 To make the sesame bok choy, pour the oil onto a hot barbecue flatplate and add the sesame seeds and garlic. Cook, stirring, for 1 minute, or until

the seeds are golden. Arrange the bok choy in a single layer on the hot plate and pour over the reserved marinade. Cook for 3–4 minutes, turning once, until tender. Remove and keep warm.
3 Wipe clean the flatplate, brush with oil and reheat. Add the scallops and cook, turning, for about 2 minutes, or until they become opaque. Serve on top of the bok choy, with the lime wedges.

NUTRITION PER SERVE
Protein 15 g; Fat 5 g; Carbohydrate 10 g;
Dietary Fibre 1 g; Cholesterol 25 mg;
670 kJ (160 cal)

Rinse the scallops and then remove their dark veins and dry with paper towels.

Arrange the halved bok choy in a single layer on the flatplate.

Cook the scallops for about 2 minutes, turning often, until they are opaque.

BARBECUED SARDINES

Preparation time: 25 minutes + 2 hours
  marinating
Total cooking time: 10 minutes
Serves 4

8 large fresh sardines
8 sprigs fresh lemon thyme
3 tablespoons extra virgin olive oil
2 cloves garlic, crushed
1 teaspoon finely grated lemon rind
2 tablespoons lemon juice

1 teaspoon ground cumin
lemon wedges, for serving

1 Carefully slit the sardines from head to tail and remove the gut. Rinse, then pat dry inside and out with paper towels. Place a sprig of fresh lemon thyme in each fish cavity and arrange the fish in a shallow non-metallic dish.
2 Combine the olive oil, garlic, lemon rind, lemon juice and cumin and pour over the fish. Cover and refrigerate for 2 hours.
3 Cook on a hot, lightly oiled

barbecue flatplate for 2–3 minutes each side, basting frequently with the marinade, or until the flesh flakes easily when tested with a fork. Alternatively, barbecue in a sardine cooking rack until tender. Serve with lemon wedges.

NUTRITION PER SERVE
Protein 46 g; Fat 12 g; Carbohydrate 0 g;
Dietary Fibre 1 g; Cholesterol 180 mg;
1200 kJ (245 cal)

Slit the sardine from head to tail with a sharp knife and then remove the gut.

Place a sprig of lemon thyme in the cavity of each fish and put in a shallow dish to marinate.

Cook the sardines until the flesh flakes easily when tested with a fork.

SALMON WITH DILL CREAM

Preparation time: 25 minutes
Total cooking time: 25 minutes
Serves 4

4 small salmon
4 cloves garlic, peeled
2 lemons, sliced
8 fresh bay leaves
8 sprigs fresh flat-leaf parsley
8 sprigs fresh thyme
olive oil, for brushing

DILL CREAM
90 g (3 oz) butter
1 cup (250 ml/8 fl oz) fish stock
1 1/2 teaspoons wholegrain mustard
1 cup (250 ml/8 fl oz) cream
2 tablespoons lemon juice
3 tablespoons chopped fresh dill

1 Wash the fish and pat dry inside and out with paper towels. Place a clove of garlic, a few slices of lemon and a bay leaf in the cavity of each fish. Bundle together a sprig of parsley and thyme and tie a bundle with string onto each fish, near the tail. Reserve the other sprigs. Brush both sides of the fish with a little of the olive oil.
2 For the dill cream, melt the butter in a pan and add the fish stock, mustard and cream. Bring to the boil, then reduce the heat and simmer for 15 minutes, or until the sauce is slightly thickened. Stir in the lemon juice and dill. Season and keep warm.
3 While the dill cream is cooking, cook the fish on a hot, lightly oiled barbecue grill or flatplate for 3–6 minutes on each side, turning carefully, or until cooked through. Discard the herbs. For serving, bundle together a fresh parsley sprig, a thyme sprig and a bay leaf, and tie a bundle near each fish tail. Serve warm with the dill cream.

NUTRITION PER SERVE
Protein 52 g; Fat 78 g; Carbohydrate 1 g; Dietary Fibre 0 g; Cholesterol 350 mg; 3860 kJ (920 cal)

NOTE: Rainbow trout is also a suitable fish for this recipe.

Wash the fish and pat dry inside and out with paper towels.

Tie together a sprig of parsley and a sprig of thyme and tie to the tail of the fish.

BARBECUED TUNA AND WHITE BEAN SALAD

Preparation time: 25 minutes
Total cooking time: 5 minutes
Serves 4–6

400 g (13 oz) tuna steaks
1 small red onion, thinly sliced
1 tomato, seeded and chopped
1 small red capsicum, thinly sliced
2 x 400 g (13 oz) cans cannellini
    beans
2 cloves garlic, crushed
1 teaspoon chopped fresh thyme
4 tablespoons finely chopped fresh
    flat-leaf parsley

1¹/₂ tablespoons lemon juice
¹/₃ cup (80 ml/2³/₄ fl oz) extra virgin
    olive oil
1 teaspoon honey
100 g (3¹/₂ oz) rocket leaves

1 Place the tuna steaks on a plate, sprinkle with cracked black pepper on both sides, cover with plastic and refrigerate until needed.
2 Combine the onion, tomato and capsicum in a large bowl. Rinse the cannellini beans under cold running water for 30 seconds, drain and add to the bowl with the garlic, thyme and 3 tablespoons of the parsley.
3 Place the lemon juice, oil and honey in a small pan, bring to the boil, then

simmer, stirring, for 1 minute, or until the honey dissolves. Remove from the heat.
4 Cook the tuna on a hot, lightly oiled barbecue grill or flatplate for 1 minute on each side. The meat should still be pink in the middle. Slice into small cubes and combine with the salad. Toss with the warm dressing.
5 Arrange the rocket on a platter. Top with the salad, season well and toss with the remaining parsley.

NUTRITION PER SERVE (6)
Protein 30 g; Fat 20 g; Carbohydrate 17 g;
Dietary Fibre 10 g; Cholesterol 0 mg;
1656 kJ (394 cal)

Add the beans, garlic, thyme and parsley to the bowl and mix well.

Heat the lemon juice, honey and oil in a saucepan until the honey dissolves.

Cook the tuna until still pink in the middle and cut into small cubes.

TUNA WITH CAPONATA

Preparation time: 25 minutes + 1 hour
standing
Total cooking time: 50 minutes
Serves 6

CAPONATA
500 g (1 lb) ripe tomatoes
750 g (1¹/₂ lb) eggplant, diced
¹/₃ cup (80 ml/2³/₄ fl oz) olive oil
2 tablespoons olive oil, extra
1 onion, chopped
3 celery sticks, chopped
2 tablespoons drained capers
¹/₂ cup (90 g/3 oz) green olives, pitted
1 tablespoon sugar
¹/₂ cup (125 ml/4 fl oz) red wine
vinegar

6 x 200 g (6¹/₂ oz) tuna steaks

1 To make the caponata, score a cross in the base of each tomato. Place in a bowl of boiling water for 1 minute, then plunge into cold water and peel the skin away from the cross. Cut into small cubes.
2 Sprinkle the eggplant with salt and leave for 1 hour. Place in a colander, rinse under cold running water and pat dry. Heat the oil in a frying pan and cook the eggplant, in batches, for 4–5 minutes, or until golden and soft. Remove from the pan.
3 Heat the extra oil in the pan, add the onion and celery, and cook for 3–4 minutes, or until golden. Reduce the heat to low, add the tomato and simmer for 15 minutes, stirring occasionally. Stir in the capers, olives, sugar and vinegar, season and simmer, stirring occasionally, for 10 minutes, or until slightly reduced. Stir in the

eggplant. Allow to cool.
4 Cook the tuna on a hot, lightly oiled barbecue grill or flatplate for 2–3 minutes each side, or until cooked to your liking. Serve immediately with the caponata.

NUTRITION PER SERVE
Protein 45 g; Fat 30 g; Carbohydrate 7 g;
Dietary Fibre 5 g; Cholesterol 140 mg;
1963 kJ (470 cal)

Cook the eggplant, in batches if your pan is small, until golden and soft.

Add the capers, olives, sugar and vinegar to the tomato mixture.

Cook the tuna on a hot barbecue until cooked to your taste.

BAY BUGS WITH LIME BUTTER

Preparation time: 10 minutes +
 1 hour freezing
Total cooking time: 10 minutes
Serves 6

90 g (3 oz) butter, softened
2 teaspoons finely grated lime
 rind
2 tablespoons lime juice
3 tablespoons chopped fresh
 coriander
1 teaspoon cracked black pepper
1 kg (2 lb) raw Balmain bugs (see
 NOTE)
3 cloves garlic, crushed
2 tablespoons oil

1 Mix the butter, lime rind and juice, coriander and pepper in a bowl. Put in the centre of a piece of foil and roll into a log shape. Twist the ends tightly, then refrigerate until firm.
2 Put the Balmain bugs in the freezer for 1 hour to immobilise.
3 Cook the bugs, garlic and oil on a hot barbecue flatplate for 5–6 minutes, tossing regularly, or until the bugs turn deep orange and the flesh turns white and starts to come away from the shell. Serve with rounds of flavoured butter.

NUTRITION PER SERVE
Protein 33 g; Fat 28 g; Carbohydrate 1 g;
Dietary Fibre 0 g; Cholesterol 190 mg;
2270 kJ (540 cal)

NOTE: Balmain bugs, or Moreton Bay bugs, are also known as slipper lobsters. Recipes for Balmain bugs, such as this one, are also usually suitable for Dublin Bay prawns or king prawns.

Spoon the lime and coriander butter onto a piece of foil.

Wrap the butter, roll into a log and twist the ends tightly to seal.

CALAMARI RINGS WITH SALSA VERDE

Preparation time: 30 minutes +
  30 minutes marinating
Total cooking time: 15 minutes
Serves 4

1 kg (2 lb) calamari
1 cup (250 ml/8 fl oz) olive oil
2 tablespoons lemon juice
2 cloves garlic, crushed
2 tablespoons chopped fresh oregano
2 tablespoons chopped fresh
  flat-leaf parsley
lemon wedges, to serve

SALSA VERDE
2 anchovy fillets, drained
1 tablespoon capers
1 clove garlic, crushed
2 tablespoons chopped fresh
  flat-leaf parsley
2 tablespoons olive oil

1 To clean the calamari, hold onto the hood and gently pull the tentacles away from the head. Cut out the beak and discard with any intestines still attached to the tentacles. Rinse the tentacles in cold running water, pat dry and cut into 5 cm (2 inch) lengths. Place in a bowl. Clean out the hood cavity and remove the transparent backbone. Under cold running water, pull away the skin, rinse and dry well. Cut into rings and place in the bowl with the tentacles. Add the oil, lemon juice, garlic and oregano and toss to coat. Refrigerate for 30 minutes.
2 To make the salsa verde, crush the anchovy fillets in a mortar and pestle. Rinse and chop the capers very finely and mix with the anchovies. Add the garlic and parsley, then slowly stir in the olive oil. Season and mix well.
3 Drain the calamari and cook on a hot, lightly oiled barbecue grill or flatplate in batches for 1–2 minutes each side, basting with the marinade. To serve, sprinkle the calamari with salt, pepper and fresh parsley, and serve with the salsa verde and lemon wedges.

NUTRITION PER SERVE
Protein 42.5 g; Fat 72 g; Carbohydrate 0.5 g;
Dietary Fibre 0.5 g; Cholesterol 499 mg;
3404 kJ (813 cal)

Hold the calamari and gently pull the tentacles away from the head.

Mix together the crushed anchovies, capers, garlic and parsley.

Cook the calamari in batches on a hot barbecue grill or flatplate.

137

CAJUN BLACKENED FISH WITH PINEAPPLE SALSA

Preparation time: 15 minutes +
  20 minutes refrigeration
Total cooking time: 10 minutes
Serves 6

8 cm (3 inch) piece fresh pineapple,
  finely diced
6 spring onions, thinly sliced
2 tablespoons finely shredded fresh
  mint
1/4 cup (60 ml/ 2 fl oz) coconut vinegar
2 tablespoons olive oil

6 tablespoons ready-made Cajun
  spices
6 ling fillets
1/4 cup (60 g/2 oz) Greek-style plain
  yoghurt

1 Place the pineapple, spring onion and mint in a bowl. Season with pepper and mix together well. Just before serving, stir in the vinegar and olive oil.
2 Place the Cajun spices in a dry frying pan and dry-fry over medium heat for 1 minute, or until fragrant. Transfer the spices to a sheet of baking paper and lightly coat each side of the

fish fillets, patting off any excess. Refrigerate for 20 minutes.
3 Cook the fish on a hot, lightly oiled barbecue grill or flatplate for 2–3 minutes on each side, depending on the thickness of the fish. Serve with a little yoghurt spooned over the top and the salsa on the side.

NUTRITION PER SERVE
Protein 15 g; Fat 12 g; Carbohydrate 8 g;
Dietary Fibre 2 g; Cholesterol 47 mg;
883 kJ (199 cal)

Mix together the pineapple, spring onion and mint and season with pepper.

Put the spices on a sheet of baking paper and lightly coat both sides of the fish.

Cook the fish for 2–3 minutes on each side, depending on its thickness.

GARLIC SCALLOPS WITH ANGEL HAIR PASTA

Preparation time: 10 minutes
Total cooking time: 15 minutes
Serves 4

20 large scallops with corals
250 g (8 oz) angel hair pasta
150 ml (5 fl oz) extra virgin olive oil
2 cloves garlic, finely chopped
1/4 cup (60 ml/2 fl oz) white wine
1 tablespoon lemon juice
100 g (3 1/2 oz) baby rocket leaves
30 g (1 oz) chopped fresh coriander

1 Pull or trim any veins, membrane or hard white muscle from the scallops. Pat dry with paper towels. Cook the pasta in boiling water until *al dente*. Drain and toss with 1 tablespoon oil to keep it from sticking.
2 Meanwhile, heat 1 tablespoon oil in a frying pan, add the garlic and cook for a few seconds. Add the combined wine and lemon juice and remove from the heat.
3 Season the scallops with salt and pepper and cook on a hot, lightly oiled barbecue grill or flatplate for 1 minute each side, or until just cooked. Gently reheat the garlic

mixture, add the rocket and stir over medium heat for 1–2 minutes, or until wilted. Toss through the pasta with the remaining oil, coriander and scallops.

NUTRITION PER SERVE
Protein 15 g; Fat 37 g; Carbohydrate 45 g; Dietary Fibre 4 g; Cholesterol 20 mg; 2425 kJ (580 cal)

VARIATION: Add 1/2 teaspoon dried chilli flakes just before the wine and lemon juice for an added kick.

Drain the pasta and toss with a tablespoon of oil to prevent it sticking.

Cook the garlic for a few seconds and then add the wine and lemon juice.

Cook the scallops for just 1 minute on each side until they are cooked through.

JUMBO PRAWNS

Preparation time: 15 minutes +
  30 minutes marinating
Total cooking time: 5 minutes
Serves 4

8 (800 g) large raw king prawns
1/3 cup (80 ml/2³/4 fl oz) olive oil
3 cloves garlic, crushed
1 tablespoon sweet chilli sauce
2 tablespoons lime juice
1/4 cup (60 ml/2 fl oz) olive oil, extra
2 tablespoons lime juice, extra

1 Remove the heads from the prawns and, using a sharp knife, cut through the centre of the prawns lengthways to form two halves, leaving the tails and shells intact.
2 Place the olive oil, 2 crushed garlic cloves, sweet chilli sauce and lime juice in a shallow, non-metallic dish and mix together well. Add the prawns, toss to coat and marinate for 30 minutes. Meanwhile, combine the extra oil and lime juice and remaining garlic to make a dressing.
3 Drain the prawns and cook on a hot barbecue grill or flatplate, cut-side-down first, for 1–2 minutes each side, brushing with the leftover marinade. Serve the prawns with the dressing spooned over the top of them.

NUTRITION PER SERVE
Protein 40 g; Fat 35 g; Carbohydrate 1.5 g;
Dietary Fibre 0.5 g; Cholesterol 298 mg;
2025 kJ (484 cal)

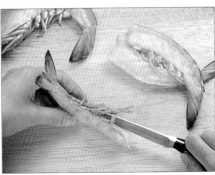
Remove the heads from the prawns and then cut in half lengthways.

While the prawns are cooking, cut-side-down, brush with the marinade.

TERIYAKI TUNA WITH WASABI MAYONNAISE AND PICKLED GINGER

Preparation time: 10 minutes +
10 minutes marinating
Total cooking time: 10 minutes
Serves 4

1/2 cup (125 ml/4 fl oz) teriyaki
marinade
1/2 teaspoon five-spice powder
1 tablespoon grated fresh ginger

3 tuna steaks, each cut into 4 strips
1/4 cup (60 g/2 oz) mayonnaise
1 teaspoon wasabi paste
2 tablespoons pickled ginger, to serve

1 Combine the teriyaki marinade, five-spice powder and ginger. Place the tuna in a non-metallic dish, pour over the marinade, cover and leave to marinate for 10 minutes. Drain and discard the marinade.
2 Cook the tuna, in batches if necessary, on a very hot, lightly oiled barbecue flatplate for 1–2 minutes

each side, or until cooked to your taste. Cooking time will vary depending on the thickness of the tuna steaks.
3 Mix together the mayonnaise and wasabi paste and serve with the tuna steaks, garnished with pickled ginger.

NUTRITION PER SERVE
Protein 27 g; Fat 17 g; Carbohydrate 4 g;
Dietary Fibre 0 g; Cholesterol 50 mg;
1196 kJ (284 cal)

Put the pieces of tuna in a shallow, non-metallic dish and add the marinade.

Cook the tuna on a very hot flatplate until it is cooked to your taste.

Mix together the mayonnaise and wasabi paste to serve with the tuna.

SWEET CHILLI OCTOPUS

Preparation time: 15 minutes
Total cooking time: 5 minutes
Serves 4

1.5 kg (3 lb) baby octopus
1 cup (250 ml/8 fl oz) sweet chilli
    sauce
1/3 cup (80 ml/2³/4 fl oz) lime juice
1/3 cup (80 ml/2³/4 fl oz) fish sauce
1/3 cup (60 g/2 oz) soft brown sugar
lime wedges, to serve

1 Cut off the octopus heads, below the eyes, with a sharp knife. Discard the heads and guts. Push the beaks out with your index finger, remove and discard. Wash the octopus thoroughly under running water and drain on crumpled paper towels. If the octopus tentacles are large, cut into quarters.
2 Mix together the sweet chilli sauce, lime juice, fish sauce and sugar.
3 Cook the octopus on a very hot, lightly oiled barbecue grill or flatplate, turning often, for 3–4 minutes, or until it just changes colour. Brush with a

quarter of the sauce during cooking. Do not overcook the octopus or it will toughen. Serve immediately with the remaining sauce and lime wedges.

NUTRITION PER SERVE
Protein 43 g; Fat 11 g; Carbohydrate 25 g;
Dietary Fibre 2.5 g; Cholesterol 500 mg;
1543 kJ (370 cal)

Push the beak upwards with your index finger to remove it.

Mix together the sweet chilli sauce, lime juice, fish sauce and sugar.

Cook the octopus just until it changes colour, otherwise it will be tough.

GARLIC PRAWNS

Preparation time: 10 minutes + 2 hours
 marinating
Total cooking time: 5 minutes
Serves 4

500 g (1 lb) raw king prawns

MARINADE
2 tablespoons lemon juice
2 tablespoons sesame oil
2 cloves garlic, crushed
2 teaspoons grated fresh ginger

1 Peel and devein the prawns, leaving the tails intact. Make a cut in the prawn body, slicing three-quarters of the way through the flesh from head to tail. Put the prawns in a non-metallic dish or bowl.
2 To make the marinade, mix together the lemon juice, oil, garlic and ginger and pour over the prawns. Cover and refrigerate for 2 hours.
3 Cook the prawns on a hot, lightly oiled barbecue flatplate for 3–5 minutes or until pink and cooked through. Brush frequently with the marinade while cooking and then serve immediately.

NUTRITION PER SERVE
Protein 26 g; Fat 10 g; Carbohydrate 0.5 g;
Dietary Fibre 0 g; Cholesterol 186 mg;
834 kJ (199 cal)

STORAGE: Prawns should always be cooked and eaten within 24 hours of purchase.

VARIATION: For a stronger flavour, double the quantity of garlic and omit the ginger.

Peel and devein the prawns, leaving their tails intact. Then make cuts in the bodies.

Put the prawns in a non-metallic dish to marinate so that the lemon juice doesn't react.

Cook the prawns on a hot, lightly greased barbecue until they are pink.

Marinades for Seafood

Add a little extra zest to your seafood by using one of these tangy mixtures for marinating before cooking or a spicy baste for brushing over the seafood on the barbecue.

LIME AND PEPPERCORN MARINADE

(For prawns, fish steaks and cutlets—tuna, swordfish, blue-eye, salmon.) Stir-fry 1 cup (60 g/2 oz) Szechwan or black peppercorns in a wok until fragrant. Transfer to a mortar and pestle or spice grinder, add 4 chopped Asian shallots and crush together. Transfer to a shallow non-metallic dish and add 1/3 cup (80 ml/2 3/4 fl oz) lime juice, 1 tablespoon salt, 1 teaspoon sesame oil and 1/4 cup (60 ml/2 fl oz) peanut oil. Add 1 kg (2 lb) firm white fish fillets or 1 kg (2 lb) peeled, deveined prawns with tails intact. Cover; chill for 3 hours.

Cook on a hot , lightly oiled barbecue flatplate in batches until the seafood is cooked through. If you are using tuna or salmon, don't overcook it or it will be dry. Serves 4–6

TEXAN BARBECUE BASTING SAUCE

(For all shellfish.) Combine 1 cup (250 ml/8 fl oz) tomato sauce, 6 splashes of Tabasco, 3 chopped rehydrated chipotle chillies, 1 tablespoon each of vinegar and oil in a bowl. Use to baste while cooking 1 kg (2 lb) prawns, bugs or yabbies. Serves 4–6

SPICED YOGHURT MARINADE

(For firm-fleshed fish—snapper, bream, ocean perch, flake.) Combine 400 g (13 oz) yoghurt, 1 tablespoon each of grated fresh ginger, ground cumin, ground cinnamon, ground coriander and ground mace, 1–2 tablespoons each of grated lime rind and juice and 2 tablespoons chopped fresh mint. Add 1 kg (2 lb) fish fillets, cover and refrigerate for 3 hours. Cook on a hot barbecue flatplate until tender. Serves 4–6

GARLIC MARINADE

(For prawns and fish.) Crush 6 cloves of garlic and mix with 1 cup (250 ml/8 fl oz) extra virgin olive oil, 1 tablespoon lemon juice and 1 tablespoon chopped fresh dill in a shallow, non-metallic dish. Add 1 kg (2 lb) cubed firm white fish or 1 kg (2 lb) peeled, deveined prawns. Cover and chill overnight. Return to room temperature, thread onto skewers and cook on a hot barbecue grill or flatplate until cooked through. Serves 4–6

THAI MARINADE

(For octopus.) Combine 1/2 cup (125 ml/4 fl oz) fish sauce, 4 finely shredded kaffir lime leaves, 2–3 tablespoons grated palm sugar or brown sugar, the juice and rind of 2 limes and 1 teaspoon sesame oil. Add 1 kg (2 lb) cleaned octopus and marinate overnight. Drain well. Cook over very high heat on a barbecue grill, turning frequently, for 3 minutes or until cooked. Serves 4–6

SWEET AND SPICY BASTING SAUCE

(For yabbies, bugs and scampi.) Combine 1 cup (250 ml/ 8 fl oz) sweet chilli sauce, 2 crushed cloves garlic, 1–2 tablespoons lemon juice, 1 tablespoon peanut oil, 50 g (1 3/4 oz) melted butter and 2 tablespoons chopped fresh coriander in a large jug. Toss 1 kg (2 lb) seafood in 1 tablespoon oil and cook in batches on a hot barbecue flatplate, turning and basting frequently with the sauce. Serve with any leftover sauce. Serves 4–6

Clockwise, from top left: Spiced Yoghurt Marinade; Lime and Peppercorn Marinade; Thai Marinade; Texan Barbecue Basting Sauce; Garlic Marinade; Sweet and Spicy Basting Sauce

Butters for Seafood

These butters melt into simple barbecued seafood. All can be stored, wrapped tightly, in the fridge for up to 1 week, or frozen for 2–3 months.

OLIVE, ANCHOVY AND CAPER BUTTER

Beat 125 g (4 oz) butter with electric beaters until smooth. Beat in 2 teaspoons chopped capers, 3–4 chopped anchovy fillets and 1 tablespoon finely chopped green olives. Spoon onto greaseproof paper, shape into a log, roll up and twist the ends to seal. Refrigerate until firm, then cut into thick slices. Serves 6

SEMI-DRIED TOMATO AND WHITE COSTELLO BUTTER

Beat 90 g (3 oz) butter with electric beaters until smooth. Fold in 60 g (2 oz) finely chopped semi-dried tomatoes and 60 g (2 oz) chopped white costello cheese. Spoon onto greaseproof paper, shape into a log, roll up and twist the ends to seal. Refrigerate until firm, then cut into thick slices. Serves 6

LEMON AND DILL BUTTER

Beat 90 g (3 oz) butter with electric beaters until smooth. Beat in 2 teaspoons finely chopped fresh dill, $1/2$ teaspoon finely grated lemon rind and 2 tablespoons lemon juice until well combined. Spoon onto greaseproof paper, shape into a log, roll up and twist the ends to seal. Refrigerate until firm, then cut into thick slices. Serves 6

ROASTED CAPSICUM AND ROCKET BUTTER

Beat 125 g (4 oz) butter with electric beaters until smooth. Fold through 1 large crushed garlic clove, 2 tablespoons finely chopped rocket leaves, $1^{1}/_{2}$ tablespoons finely chopped fresh basil and $1/2$ red capsicum, roasted, peeled and chopped. Spoon onto greaseproof paper, shape into a log, roll up and twist the ends to seal. Refrigerate until firm, then cut into thick slices. Serves 6

PESTO BUTTER

Place 4 tablespoons fresh basil leaves, 1 tablespoon each of pine nuts and grated Parmesan and 1 crushed garlic clove in a food processor or blender and process until smooth. Transfer to a bowl, add 125 g (4 oz) butter and beat with a wooden spoon until combined. Spoon onto greaseproof paper, shape into a log, roll up and twist the ends to seal. Refrigerate until firm, then cut into thick slices. Serves 6

WASABI AND SEAWEED BUTTER

Beat 125 g (4 oz) butter with electric beaters until smooth. Fold through 2 teaspoons wasabi paste, 1 teaspoon rice vinegar and 1 sheet finely sliced nori (dried seaweed). Spoon onto greaseproof paper, shape into a log, roll up and twist the ends to seal. Refrigerate until firm, then cut into thick slices. Serves 6

SAFFRON AND PARSLEY BUTTER

Grind $1/4$ teaspoon saffron threads in a mortar and pestle or spice grinder until powdery. Transfer to a small bowl, add 1 tablespoon hot water and soak for 2 minutes. Beat 125 g (4 oz) butter with electric beaters until smooth. Beat in 2 teaspoons finely chopped fresh parsley and the saffron and water. Spoon onto greaseproof paper, shape into a log, roll up and twist the ends to seal. Refrigerate until firm, then cut into thick slices. Serves 6

SWEET CHILLI AND CORIANDER BUTTER

Beat 125 g (4 oz) butter with electric beaters until smooth. Beat in 2 tablespoons sweet chilli sauce, 1 tablespoon chopped fresh coriander, $1/2$ teaspoon grated fresh ginger and 1–2 teaspoons fish sauce. Spoon onto greaseproof paper, shape into a log, roll up and twist the ends to seal. Refrigerate until firm, then cut into thick slices. Serves 6

Opposite page, from top: Olive, Anchovy and Caper Butter; Semi-dried Tomato and White Costello Butter; Lemon and Dill Butter; Roasted Capsicum and Rocket Butter
This page, from top: Pesto Butter; Wasabi and Seaweed Butter; Saffron and Parsley Butter; Sweet Chilli and Coriander Butter

Sauces for Seafood

These sauces and salsas are a perfect accompaniment for plain barbecued fish or seafood. Leftovers can be refrigerated in an airtight container for up to 3 days.

SALSA VERDE

Place 1 cup (30 g/1 oz) tightly packed fresh flat-leaf parsley, 1 crushed clove garlic, 3 tablespoons fresh dill, 2 tablespoons chopped chives and 4 tablespoons fresh mint in a food processor and process for 30 seconds, or until combined. Add 1 tablespoon lemon juice, 5 anchovy fillets and 3 tablespoons drained, bottled capers and process until mixed. With the motor running, slowly add 1/2 cup (125 ml/ 4 fl oz) olive oil in a thin stream and process until all the oil is added and the mixture is smooth. Ideal with prawns or fish kebabs (e.g. swordfish or salmon). Serves 4

BUTTER SAUCE

Finely chop two French shallots and place in a small saucepan with 1/4 cup (60 ml/2 fl oz) each of white wine vinegar and water. Bring to the boil, then reduce the heat and simmer until reduced to 2 tablespoons. Remove from the heat and strain into a clean saucepan. Return to the heat and whisk in 220 g (7 oz) cubed unsalted butter, a few pieces at a time. The sauce will thicken as the butter is added. Season, to taste, with salt, pepper and lemon juice. Ideal with barbecued lobster tail. Serves 4–6

Clockwise, from bottom left: Salsa Verde; Cannellini Bean and Semi-dried Tomato Salsa; Creamy Tarragon Sauce; Mango Avocado Salsa; Roasted Capsicum and Basil Sauce; Butter Sauce

CANNELLINI BEAN AND SEMI-DRIED TOMATO SALSA

Drain a 400 g (13 oz) can cannellini beans and rinse the beans. Put in a bowl and stir with 1/2 cup (75 g/2 1/2 oz) chopped semi-dried tomatoes, 1/4 cup (30 g/1 oz) sliced pitted black olives and 1/4 red onion, chopped. Stir in 1 tablespoon olive oil, 3 teaspoons white wine vinegar and 1 tablespoon finely chopped fresh flat-leaf parsley. Cover and refrigerate for 30 minutes, or until required. Serve with fish such as red mullet or snapper. Serves 6

ROASTED CAPSICUM AND BASIL SAUCE

Preheat the oven to hot 210°C (415°F/Gas 6–7). Halve two red capsicums and place skin-side-up on a greased baking tray with two cloves unpeeled garlic. Brush with olive oil and bake for 20 minutes, or until the capsicum is soft and the skin is blackened and blistered. Remove and cool the capsicums in a plastic bag. Peel the capsicums and garlic and mix in a food processor or blender for 30 seconds, or until combined. With the motor running, slowly add 100 ml (3 1/2 fl oz) olive oil in a thin stream and blend until all the oil is added and the mixture is smooth. Add 1 tablespoon finely chopped fresh basil, 1/4 teaspoon salt and black pepper. Serve warm or cold with barbecued sardines, swordfish or tuna. Serves 4

CREAMY TARRAGON SAUCE

Combine 1/2 cup (125 ml/4 fl oz) fish stock in a small saucepan with 1 crushed clove garlic, 1 teaspoon dried tarragon leaves and 1 thinly sliced spring onion. Bring to the boil, then reduce the heat and simmer for 3 minutes, or until reduced by half. Add 1 cup (250 ml/8 fl oz) thick cream or mascarpone. Reduce the heat to very low and stir until the cream has fully melted. Add 1/2 teaspoon lemon juice, 2 tablespoons grated Parmesan and salt and black pepper, to taste. Simmer for 1 minute, then serve with firm white fish such as blue-eyed cod. Serves 4–6

MANGO AVOCADO SALSA

Cut 1 mango and 1 avocado into small cubes and place in a small bowl with 1 diced small red capsicum. Mix 2 tablespoons lime juice with 1 teaspoon caster sugar and pour over the mango. Stir in 3 tablespoons chopped fresh coriander leaves. Delicious with barbecued prawns. Serves 6

Kettle Barbecues

ORANGE AND GINGER GLAZED HAM

Preparation time: 25 minutes
Total cooking time: 1 hour 30 minutes
Serves 20

6 kg (12 lb) ham on the bone
3 tablespoons orange juice
3/4 cup (250 g/8 oz) orange
    marmalade
1 tablespoon grated fresh ginger
2 teaspoons mustard powder
2 tablespoons soft brown sugar
whole cloves (about 30)

1 Prepare a covered barbecue for indirect cooking at moderate heat (normal fire), see page 7. Run your thumb around the edge of the ham, under the rind to remove the rind. Begin pulling from the widest edge. When you've removed the rind to within 10 cm (4 inches) of the shank end, cut through the rind around the shank. Using a sharp knife, remove the excess fat from the ham. (If you like crackling, rub the rind with salt and barbecue for 40 minutes.)

2 Using a sharp knife, score the top of the ham with deep diagonal cuts. Score diagonally the other way, forming a diamond pattern. Place the ham on the barbecue; put the lid on the barbecue and cook for 45 minutes.
3 Put the juice, marmalade, ginger, mustard and sugar in a small pan. Stir over medium heat until combined and then cool. Carefully press the cloves into the top of the ham, one clove per diamond, and brush all over with the marmalade mixture. Cover the barbecue and cook for a further 45 minutes. Serve warm or cold.

NUTRITION PER SERVE
Protein 38 g; Fat 7 g; Carbohydrate 8 g;
Dietary Fibre 0 g; Cholesterol 102 mg;
1030 kJ (250 cal)

STORAGE: Cover the ham with a clean, dry cloth and it will keep in the fridge for up to 1 month. Change the cloth every 2–3 days.

Pull away the ham rind to within 10 cm of the thin shank end.

Score the thin layer of fat on top of the ham with a diagonal pattern.

SPICED SWEET POTATOES

Preparation time: 20 minutes
Total cooking time: 20 minutes
Serves 4–6

500 g (1 lb) orange sweet potatoes
3 tablespoons demerara sugar
3/4 teaspoon mixed spice
30 g (1 oz) butter, chopped
1/3 cup (80 ml/2 3/4 fl oz) orange juice

1 Prepare a covered barbecue for indirect cooking at moderate heat (normal fire), see page 7. Peel the sweet potatoes and cut into thick slices. Arrange in layers in a shallow greased tray.
2 Sprinkle the sweet potato with the combined sugar and mixed spice and then dot with butter and sprinkle with the orange juice.
3 Cover the tray with foil, place on the top grill of the barbecue, cover and cook for 20 minutes, or until tender

(remove the foil and test with a sharp knife; cook a few more minutes, if necessary). Sprinkle over a little more orange juice if drying out.

NUTRITION PER SERVE (6)
Protein 1 g; Fat 5 g; Carbohydrate 24 g;
Dietary Fibre 2 g; Cholesterol 13 mg;
566 kJ (135 cal)

Peel and thickly slice the sweet potato and arrange in a tray.

Sprinkle with the combined sugar and mixed spice, then dot with butter and orange juice.

Test the sweet potato with the point of a sharp knife and cook a little longer if not tender.

LAMB SHANKS

Preparation time: 5 minutes +
   overnight marinating
Total cooking time: 45 minutes
Serves 6

2 cloves garlic, halved
1/3 cup (80 ml/2¾ fl oz) olive oil
6 lamb shanks

1 Combine the garlic and oil in a small bowl, cover and marinate at room temperature overnight. Prepare the covered barbecue for indirect cooking at moderate heat (normal fire), see page 7. Place a drip tray under the top grill. Trim the shanks of excess fat and sinew.
2 Brush the garlic oil generously over the shanks and sprinkle with salt and pepper.
3 Place the shanks on the top grill of the barbecue, cover and roast for 35–45 minutes or until the meat is tender when pierced with a fork.

NUTRITION PER SERVE
Protein 30 g; Fat 16 g; Carbohydrate 0 g;
Dietary Fibre 0 g; Cholesterol 84 mg;
1095 kJ (260 cal)

HINT: For a more intense flavour, double the quantity of garlic in the oil and brush over the lamb several hours before cooking. Pour the remaining oil over the shanks before serving.

VARIATION: Try this recipe with other cuts of meat on the bone, such as lamb neck chops, osso buco, pieces of ox tail and chicken drumsticks.

Trim the lamb shanks of any excess fat and sinew with a sharp knife.

Brush the marinated garlic oil generously over the shanks to add flavour.

Cook the shanks in the barbecue until the meat is tender when pierced.

LEG OF LAMB

Preparation time: 15 minutes
Total cooking time: 1 hour 30 minutes
Serves 6

2 kg (4 lb) leg of lamb
4 cloves garlic, cut in
    half lengthways
6–8 sprigs fresh rosemary
2 tablespoons olive oil
2 tablespoons freshly
    ground black pepper

1 Prepare a covered barbecue for indirect cooking at moderate heat (normal fire), see page 7. Place a drip tray on the bottom grill. Trim the meat of excess fat and sinew. Cut narrow, deep slits all over the top and sides of the meat.
2 Push the halved garlic cloves and the rosemary sprigs into the cuts on the meat. Brush all over with oil and sprinkle with black pepper.
3 Put the lamb on the barbecue grill over the drip tray, cover and cook for 1 hour 30 minutes for medium-rare

meat. Brush with olive oil occasionally. Leave in a warm place, covered with foil, for 10–15 minutes before carving.

NUTRITION PER SERVE
Protein 41 g; Fat 10 g; Carbohydrate 0 g;
Dietary Fibre 0 g; Cholesterol 120 mg;
1085 kJ (260 cal)

Trim the lamb of excess fat and sinew before making small cuts all over it.

Push the halved cloves of garlic and the rosemary sprigs into the cuts.

Brush the lamb with olive oil occasionally while it is cooking.

BAKED VEGETABLES

Preparation time: 20 minutes
Total cooking time: 1 hour 15 minutes
Serves 6

6 potatoes
60 g (2 oz) butter, melted
1/4 teaspoon paprika
750 g (11/2 lb) pumpkin
6 small onions
150 g (5 oz) green beans, topped and
    tailed
150 g (5 oz) broccoli, cut into
    florets
30 g (1 oz) butter, chopped, extra

1 Prepare a covered barbecue for indirect cooking at moderate heat (normal fire), see page 7. Peel the potatoes and cut in half. Using a small, sharp knife, make deep, fine cuts in the potatoes, taking care not to cut all the way through. Take two large sheets of foil, fold in half and brush liberally with melted butter. Place the potatoes, unscored-side-down, on the foil and fold up the edges of the foil to create a tray. Brush the potatoes generously with melted butter and sprinkle with paprika.
2 Cut the pumpkin into 3 wedges and cut each wedge in half. Peel the onions and trim the bases slightly, so they will sit flat on the grill. Brush the

pumpkin and onions with melted butter. Place the pumpkin, onions and the tray of potatoes on the barbecue grill. Cover the barbecue and cook for 1 hour.
3 Put the beans and broccoli on a sheet of foil brushed with melted butter. Dot with the extra butter and wrap completely in the foil. Add to the other vegetables on the grill and cook for a further 15 minutes.

NUTRITION PER SERVE
Protein 8 g; Fat 4 g; Carbohydrate 26 g;
Dietary Fibre 6 g; Cholesterol 34 mg;
1020 kJ (240 cal)

Make deep fine cuts in the potatoes and then brush with butter and sprinkle with paprika.

Put the pumpkin, onions and tray of potatoes on the barbecue grill.

Put the beans and broccoli on a sheet of foil and dot with the extra butter.

SMOKED CHICKEN FILLETS

Preparation time: 5 minutes
Total cooking time: 25 minutes
Serves 4

4 chicken breast fillets
1 tablespoon olive oil
seasoned pepper, to taste
hickory or mesquite chips, for smoking

1 Prepare a covered barbecue for indirect cooking at moderate heat (normal fire), see page 7. Trim the chicken of excess fat and sinew. Brush with oil and sprinkle with the seasoned pepper.
2 Spoon a pile of smoking chips (about 25) over the coals in each charcoal rail.
3 Cover the barbecue and cook the chicken for 15 minutes. Test with a sharp knife. If the juices do not run clear, cook for another 5–10 minutes until cooked through.

NUTRITION PER SERVE
Protein 56 g; Fat 10 g; Carbohydrate 0 g;
Dietary Fibre 0 g; Cholesterol 125 mg;
1350 kJ (320 cal)

Brush the chicken with oil and then sprinkle with seasoned pepper.

Spoon a pile of about 25 smoking chips over the coals in each charcoal rail.

Test the chicken with a sharp knife—if it is cooked through the juices should run clear.

WHOLE FISH WITH LEMON HERB BUTTER

Preparation time: 15 minutes
Total cooking time: 1 hour
Serves 4

2 kg (4 lb) whole white-fleshed fish,
    washed and scaled
1 small lemon, sliced

HERB BUTTER
90 g (3 oz) butter, softened
1 tablespoon chopped fresh parsley
3 teaspoons fresh thyme leaves
1 tablespoon chopped chives
2 teaspoons grated lemon rind

1 Prepare a covered barbecue for indirect cooking at moderate heat (normal fire), see page 7. Put the fish on a large sheet of oiled foil.
2 To make the herb butter, blend the butter, herbs and lemon rind in a small bowl and beat until smooth. Spread half of the butter inside the cavity of the fish. Put the remaining butter in a serving bowl.
3 Lay the lemon slices over the fish, wrap the fish in the foil and place on the barbecue grill. Cover and cook for 1 hour, or until the flesh flakes easily with a fork. Serve with the small bowl of herb butter.

NUTRITION PER SERVE
Protein 52 g; Fat 23 g; Carbohydrate 0 g;
Dietary Fibre 0 g; Cholesterol 226 mg;
1753 kJ (420 cal)

NOTE: Leftover herb butter can be spread on hot bread, or served with cooked vegetables or meats.

The fish should be washed and scaled—your fishmonger will do this for you.

Spread half of the herb butter into the cavity of the fish.

Lay the lemon slices over the fish and then wrap in the foil.

FILLET OF BEEF WITH MUSTARD COATING

Preparation time: 1 hour + 1 hour
  standing
Total cooking time: 40 minutes
Serves 8

2 kg (4 lb) scotch fillet of beef
3 tablespoons brandy
4 tablespoons wholegrain mustard
3 tablespoons cream
3/4 teaspoon coarsely ground black
  pepper

1 Prepare a covered barbecue for
indirect cooking at moderate heat
(normal fire), see page 7. Trim the
meat of excess fat and sinew and tie
securely with string at regular intervals
to retain its shape. Brush all over with
the brandy and leave for 1 hour.
2 Mix together the mustard, cream
and pepper and spread evenly over
the fillet.
3 Place the meat on a large greased
sheet of foil. Pinch the corners
securely to form a tray to hold in the
juices. Cover the barbecue and cook
for 30–40 minutes for medium-rare
meat. Leave for 10–15 minutes before
carving into thick slices. If you like, stir
a tablespoon of mustard into the pan
juices to make a gravy.

NUTRITION PER SERVE
Protein 54 g; Fat 14 g; Carbohydrate 0 g;
Dietary Fibre 0 g; Cholesterol 130 mg;
1480 kJ (350 cal)

STORAGE: The beef can be marinated
in brandy for up to a day. Keep,
covered, in the fridge.

Tie the meat at intervals with string so that it keeps
its shape.

Mix together the mustard, cream and pepper and
spread over the meat.

Pinch up the corners of the foil to make a tray
that will hold the meat juices.

GARLIC ROAST CHICKEN

Preparation time: 10 minutes
Total cooking time: 1 hour
Serves 6

1.8 kg (3 lb 10 oz) chicken
1/2 teaspoon cracked peppercorns
1 whole head garlic
small bunch fresh oregano
3 tablespoons olive oil

1 Prepare a covered barbecue for indirect cooking at moderate heat (normal fire), see page 7. Place a drip tray under the top grill. Wipe the chicken and pat dry with paper towel.

Season the cavity with salt and pepper. Using a sharp knife, cut the top off the head of garlic. Push the whole head of garlic, unpeeled, into the cavity. Follow with the whole bunch of oregano. Close the cavity with several toothpicks or a skewer.
2 Rub the chicken skin with salt and brush with oil. Place on the barbecue over the drip tray. Cover and cook for 1 hour, brushing occasionally with olive oil to keep the skin moist. Test the chicken by poking a skewer into the thigh—if the juices run clear the chicken is cooked through. Leave the chicken for 5 minutes before carving.
3 Carefully separate the garlic cloves and serve 1 or 2 cloves with each

serving of chicken. (The soft flesh can be squeezed from the clove and eaten with the chicken.)

NUTRITION PER SERVE
Protein 21 g; Fat 14 g; Carbohydrate 0 g; Dietary Fibre 0 g; Cholesterol 70 mg; 875 kJ (210 cal)

STORAGE: The chicken can be kept warm in the barbecue with the top and bottom vents open.

HINT: Toast slices of French bread and spread with the soft, cooked garlic. Add a drizzle of olive oil and season with salt and pepper.

Cut the top off the head of garlic and then cook in the cavity of the chicken.

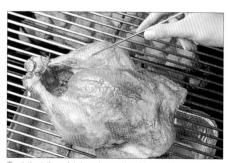
Test that the chicken is cooked by poking the thickest part of the thigh with a skewer.

Separate the cooked cloves of garlic and serve a couple with each portion of chicken.

Smoked Seafood

Smoked seafood is delicious and can often be found in fishmongers and supermarkets. However, with a covered barbecue, it is easy to make your own. Smoked fish can be kept for 3–5 days.

There are two types of smoking: hot and cold. Cold smoking is the commercial method used to produce smoked salmon. The fish is smoked at a low temperature and is not actually cooked during the smoking process.

Hot smoking is the method described here, using a covered barbecue. This method is particularly suitable for whole trout and mackerel. The fish is simultaneously smoked and cooked on the hot barbecue.

BRINING

All fish for smoking must first be soaked in a brine solution (salted water), or salted by rubbing generous quantities of salt into the skin. This helps preservation and improves the flavour. To determine the strength of the brine solution, see if a potato will float. If it doesn't, keep adding and dissolving more salt until the potato floats. Once the brine solution is

the right strength, add the whole fish and leave it for 3 hours, or 2 hours if the fish is gutted. Fish fillets will only need 30 minutes. Next, clean the fish and gut, if necessary. If you don't have time to brine the fish, you can leave this step out, but the fish won't keep after smoking and you will have to eat it straight away. Ungutted fish are the most suitable to use for hot smoking, so ask your fishmonger for advice on types.

TYPE OF WOOD TO USE

The recommended smoking woodchips are hickory, oak, apple, red gum, or any hardwood, available from barbecue and related speciality stores. Resinous woods, including pine, should never be used as they taint the fish with an antiseptic flavour. Adding herbs such as thyme, rosemary or bay leaves will infuse aromatic flavours into the fish.

TO SMOKE WHOLE FISH

The first thing you will need if you want to smoke fish at home is a covered kettle barbecue or a smoke box. We have given a recipe for use with a covered barbecue as these are more popular.

1 Place a cupful of smoking chips (apple, hickory or oak) in a non-reactive bowl, add ¹/₂ cup (125 ml/4 fl oz) white wine or water and leave to stand for 1 hour. Drain well.

2 Meanwhile, light your coals and leave them until they turn white.

3 Fill the cavities of 4 whole rainbow trout with thin slices of lime and red onion. Tie a small bunch of fresh herbs around each tail. Suitable fresh herbs include bay leaves, sprigs of dill, lemon thyme and parsley.

4 Carefully lift the sides of the rack and scatter the chips over the coals.

5 Place the rainbow trout directly on the lightly greased rack or a double layer of foil. Spray lightly with olive oil, and season generously with sea salt and cracked black pepper. Cover and smoke for 7–15 minutes, or until the fish flakes easily when tested with the tip of a knife. The cooking time will vary, depending on the size of the fish.

TO SMOKE FISH FILLETS

Fish fillets or butterflied fish can be smoked in the same way, but the cooking time will depend on the size of the fillet. Oily fish, including salmon, mackerel, tailor or warehou, are best.

TO SMOKE MUSSELS

Mussels do not require soaking. Thoroughly scrub the mussels and pull out the hairy beards. Discard any that do not close when tapped on the bench. Put the mussels in a baking dish in the prepared barbecue. Cover and cook for 3–5 minutes.

From left: Rainbow trout soaking in a brine solution; Trout filled with lime and red onion, ready for the barbecue; Trout being smoked on a kettle barbecue

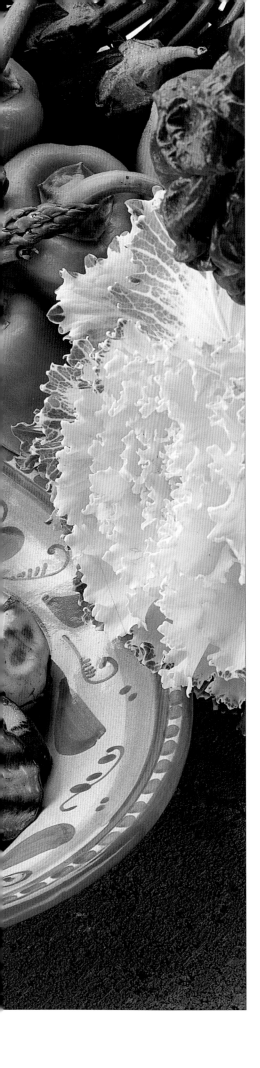

Vegetables & Salads

MARINATED GRILLED VEGETABLES

Preparation time: 30 minutes + 1 hour
  marinating
Total cooking time: 5 minutes
Serves 6

3 small slender eggplants
2 small red capsicums
3 zucchini
6 mushrooms

MARINADE
3 tablespoons olive oil
3 tablespoons lemon juice
3 tablespoons shredded basil leaves
1 clove garlic, crushed

1 Cut the eggplant into diagonal slices. Place on a tray in a single layer, sprinkle with salt and leave for 15 minutes. Rinse thoroughly and pat dry with paper towels. Trim the capsicum, remove the seeds and membrane and cut into long, wide pieces. Cut the zucchini into diagonal slices. Trim each mushroom stalk so that it is level with the cap. Place all the vegetables in a large, shallow non-metallic dish.

2 To make the marinade, put the oil, juice, basil and garlic in a small screw-top jar. Shake vigorously to combine. Pour over the vegetables and toss well. Store, covered with plastic wrap, in the fridge for 1 hour, stirring occasionally.
3 Cook the vegetables on a hot, lightly oiled barbecue grill or flatplate. Cook each vegetable piece over the hottest part of the fire for 2 minutes on each side, brushing frequently with any remaining marinade.

NUTRITION PER SERVE
Protein 1 g; Fat 10 g; Carbohydrate 2 g;
Dietary Fibre 2 g; Cholesterol 0 mg;
445 kJ (110 cal)

STORAGE: The vegetables can be marinated for up to 2 hours before cooking. Take the vegetables out of the fridge 15 minutes before cooking to allow the oil in the marinade to soften. Once cooked, they can be served warm or cold. The marinade can also be used as a salad dressing. Make up extra and store in the fridge, in a screw-top jar, for up to 2 weeks.

Put the vegetables in a shallow, non-metallic dish and pour over the marinade.

Cook the vegetables over the hottest part of the fire for 2 minutes on each side.

GRILLED HALOUMI AND ROAST VEGETABLE SALAD

Preparation time: 15 minutes
Total cooking time: 30 minutes
Serves 4

4 slender eggplants, cut in half and
    then halved lengthways
1 red capsicum, halved, thickly sliced
4 small zucchini, cut in half and then
    halved lengthways
1/3 cup (80 ml/2 3/4 fl oz) olive oil
2 cloves garlic, crushed

200 g (6 1/2 oz) haloumi cheese, thinly
    sliced
150 g (5 oz) baby English spinach
    leaves, trimmed
1 tablespoon balsamic vinegar

1 Preheat the oven to hot 220°C
(425°F/Gas 7). Place the vegetables in
a large bowl, add 1/4 cup (60 ml/
2 fl oz) of the olive oil and the garlic,
season and toss well to combine. Place
the vegetables in an ovenproof dish in
a single layer. Roast for 20–30 minutes,
or until tender and browned around
the edges.
2 Meanwhile, cook the haloumi slices

on a hot, lightly oiled barbecue grill
for 1–2 minutes each side.
3 Top the spinach with the roast
vegetables and haloumi. Whisk
together the remaining oil and vinegar
to make a dressing.

NUTRITION PER SERVE
Protein 14 g; Fat 28 g; Carbohydrate 6 g;
Dietary Fibre 5 g; Cholesterol 26 mg;
1383 kJ (330 cal)

VARIATION: You can use any
roasted vegetable for this recipe. Try
orange sweet potatoes, leeks and
Roma tomatoes.

Roast the vegetables in a single layer until they
are tender and browned at the edges.

Cook the haloumi on a lightly oiled barbecue grill
for 1–2 minutes on each side.

Mix the remaining oil with the vinegar to make a
dressing for the salad.

CHARGRILLED POTATOES WITH PISTACHIO SALSA

Preparation time: 25 minutes
Total cooking time: 20 minutes
Serves 4

PISTACHIO SALSA
150 g (5 oz) pistachio nuts, toasted
2 ripe tomatoes, chopped
2 cloves garlic, finely chopped
1 small red chilli, finely chopped
2 tablespoons chopped fresh parsley
1 tablespoon chopped fresh mint
1 teaspoon finely grated lemon rind

750 g (1¹/₂ lb) potatoes
3 tablespoons plain flour
2 tablespoons olive oil
sour cream, to serve

1 To make the pistachio salsa, roughly chop the nuts and combine with the tomato, garlic, chilli, herbs and lemon rind. Season with salt and pepper.
2 Peel the potatoes and cut into large wedges. Place in a pan and cover with water, bring to the boil and cook for 5 minutes. Transfer to a colander and rinse under running water to stop the cooking. Pat the wedges dry with paper towels.

3 Sprinkle the flour over the potatoes in a bowl and toss to lightly coat. Cook the potato wedges in a single layer on a hot, lightly oiled barbecue flatplate or grill for 5–10 minutes, or until golden brown and tender. Drizzle with the olive oil and turn the potatoes regularly during cooking. Serve with the salsa and a bowl of sour cream.

NUTRITION PER SERVE
Protein 10 g; Fat 30 g; Carbohydrate 30 g;
Dietary Fibre 5 g; Cholesterol 0 mg;
1755 kJ (415 cal)

To make the salsa, simply mix together all the ingredients and season well.

Cut the potatoes into wedges and then boil for 5 minutes.

Cook the pototo wedges on the barbecue until they are golden brown.

165

WARM MARINATED MUSHROOM SALAD

Preparation time: 25 minutes +
  20 minutes marinating
Total cooking time: 5 minutes
Serves 4

750 g (1¹/₂ lb) mixed mushrooms
  (such as baby button, oyster,
  Swiss brown, shiitake and enoki)
2 cloves garlic, finely chopped
¹/₂ teaspoon green peppercorns,
  crushed
¹/₃ cup (80 ml/2³/₄ fl oz) olive oil

¹/₃ cup (80 ml/2³/₄ fl oz) orange juice
250 g (8 oz) salad leaves, watercress
  or baby spinach leaves
1 teaspoon finely grated orange rind

1 Trim the mushroom stems and wipe the mushrooms with a damp paper towel. Cut any large mushrooms in half. Mix together the garlic, peppercorns, olive oil and orange juice. Pour over the mushrooms and marinate for about 20 minutes.
2 Arrange the salad leaves in a serving dish.
3 Drain the mushrooms, reserving the marinade. Cook the flat and button

mushrooms on a hot, lightly oiled barbecue grill or flatplate for about 2 minutes. Add the softer mushrooms and cook for 1 minute, or until they just soften.
4 Scatter the mushrooms over the salad leaves and drizzle with the marinade. Sprinkle with orange rind and season well.

NUTRITION PER SERVE
Protein 10 g; Fat 15 g; Carbohydrate 5 g;
Dietary Fibre 5 g; Cholesterol 0 mg;
790 kJ (190 cal)

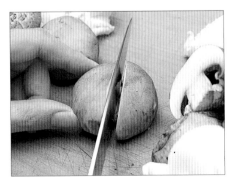

Trim the mushroom stems and wipe clean with paper towel. Cut any large mushrooms in half.

Mix together the garlic, peppercorns, olive oil and orange juice and pour over the mushrooms.

Add the softer mushrooms to the barbecue and just cook for 1 minute.

TABBOULEH

Preparation time: 20 minutes + 2 hours
   soaking and drying
Total cooking time: Nil
Serves 6

$^{3}/_{4}$ cup (120 g/4 oz) burghul
3 ripe tomatoes
1 telegraph cucumber
4 spring onions, sliced
4 cups (120 g/4 oz) chopped fresh
   flat-leaf parsley
$^{1}/_{2}$ cup (15 g/$^{1}/_{2}$ oz) fresh mint,
   chopped

DRESSING
$^{1}/_{3}$ cup (80 ml/2$^{3}/_{4}$ fl oz) lemon juice
3 tablespoons olive oil
1 tablespoon extra virgin olive oil

1 Place the burghul in a bowl, cover
with 2 cups (500 ml/16 fl oz) water
and leave for 1 hour 30 minutes.
2 Cut the tomatoes in half, squeeze
gently to remove the seeds and dice
the flesh. Cut the cucumber in half
lengthways, remove the seeds with a
teaspoon and dice the flesh.
3 To make the dressing, whisk the
lemon juice and 1$^{1}/_{2}$ teaspoons salt.
Slowly whisk in the olive oil and extra
virgin olive oil. Season with pepper.
4 Drain the burghul and squeeze out
any excess water. Spread on paper
towels and leave to dry for 30 minutes.
Mix with the tomato, cucumber, spring
onion and herbs. Add the dressing and
toss together well.

NUTRITION PER SERVE
Protein 4 g; Fat 13 g; Carbohydrate 22 g;
Dietary Fibre 3.5 g; Cholesterol 0 mg;
950 kJ (227 cal)

Whisk the olive oil and extra virgin olive oil into the
lemon juice.

Drain the burghul and squeeze out any excess
water, then spread on paper towel to dry.

Toss the salad ingredients together before adding
the dressing.

LENTIL SALAD

Preparation time: 15 minutes +
  30 minutes standing
Total cooking time: 30 minutes
Serves 4–6

1/2 onion
2 cloves
1 1/2 cups (300 g/10 oz) puy lentils (see
  NOTE)
1 strip lemon rind
2 cloves garlic, peeled
1 fresh bay leaf
2 teaspoons ground cumin

2 tablespoons red wine vinegar
3 tablespoons olive oil
1 tablespoon lemon juice
2 tablespoons fresh mint leaves,
  finely chopped
3 spring onions, finely chopped

1 Stud the onion with the cloves and
place in a saucepan with the lentils,
rind, garlic, bay leaf, 1 teaspoon cumin
and 3 1/2 cups (875 ml/28 fl oz) water.
Bring to the boil and cook over
medium heat for 25–30 minutes, or
until the water has been absorbed.
Discard the onion, rind and bay leaf.
Reserve the garlic and finely chop.

2 Whisk together the vinegar, oil,
juice, garlic and remaining cumin. Stir
through the lentils with the mint and
spring onion. Season well. Leave for
30 minutes to let the flavours absorb.
Serve at room temperature.

NUTRITION PER SERVE (6)
Protein 13 g; Fat 11 g; Carbohydrate 20 g;
Dietary Fibre 7.5 g; Cholesterol 0 mg;
930 kJ (222 cal)

NOTE: Puy lentils are small, green
lentils from France. They are available
dried from gourmet food stores.

Stud the onion half with the cloves so that they
are easy to remove after cooking.

Cook the lentils, then discard the onion, lemon
rind and bay leaf.

Whisk together the vinegar, oil, lemon juice, garlic
and cumin.

TOMATO AND BOCCONCINI SALAD

Preparation time: 10 minutes
Total cooking time: Nil
Serves 4

3 large vine-ripened tomatoes
250 g (8 oz) bocconcini or mozzarella
12 fresh basil leaves
3 tablespoons extra virgin olive oil

1 Slice the tomatoes thickly (you will need roughly 12 slices). Slice the bocconcini into about 24 slices.
2 Arrange the tomato slices on a serving plate, alternating them with 2 slices of bocconcini. Place the basil leaves between the bocconcini slices.
3 Drizzle with the oil and season well with salt and ground black pepper.

NUTRITION PER SERVE
Protein 14 g; Fat 25 g; Carbohydrate 3 g;
Dietary Fibre 1 g; Cholesterol 33 mg;
1221 kJ (292 cal)

Slice the bocconcini or mozzarella into about 24 fairly thick slices.

Arrange the tomato slices on a serving plate, alternating with the bocconcini.

169

CARAMELISED ONION AND POTATO SALAD

Preparation time: 20 minutes
Total cooking time: 1 hour
Serves 10

oil, for cooking
6 red onions, thinly sliced
1 kg (2 lb) small waxy potatoes, unpeeled
4 rashers bacon, rind removed
2/3 cup (30 g/1 oz) fresh chives, snipped
1 cup (250 g/8 oz) mayonnaise

1 tablespoon Dijon mustard
juice of 1 lemon
2 tablespoons sour cream

1 Heat 2 tablespoons of oil in a large heavy-based frying pan, add the onion and cook over medium-low heat for 40 minutes, or until very soft.
2 Cut the potatoes into large chunks (if they are small enough, leave them whole). Cook in boiling water for 10 minutes, or until just tender, then drain and cool slightly. (Do not overcook the potatoes or they will fall apart.)
3 Grill the bacon until crisp, drain on paper towels and cool slightly before coarsely chopping.
4 Put the potato, onion and chives in a large bowl, reserving a few chives for a garnish, and mix well.
5 Put the mayonnaise, mustard, lemon juice and sour cream in a bowl and whisk together. Pour over the salad and toss to coat. Sprinkle with the bacon and garnish with the reserved chives.

NUTRITION PER SERVE
Protein 9 g; Fat 13 g; Carbohydrate 35 g; Dietary Fibre 4.5 g; Cholesterol 20 mg; 1221 kJ (292 cal)

Cook the sliced onion over medium-low heat until soft and caramelised.

Wash the potatoes and cut them into large chunks or leave whole if they are small enough.

Whisk together the mayonnaise, mustard, lemon juice and sour ceam.

ROASTED BALSAMIC ONIONS

Preparation time: 15 minutes +
 overnight refrigeration
Total cooking time: 1 hour 30 minutes
Serves 8

1 kg (2 lb) pickling onions, unpeeled
 (see NOTE)
3/4 cup (185 ml/6 fl oz) balsamic
 vinegar
2 tablespoons soft brown sugar
3/4 cup (185 ml/6 fl oz) olive oil

1 Preheat the oven to warm 160°C
(315°F/Gas 2–3). Place the unpeeled
onions in a baking dish and roast for
1¹/₂ hours. Leave until cool enough to
handle. Trim the stems from the
onions and peel away the skin (the
outer part of the root should come
away but the onions will remain
intact). Rinse a 1-litre wide-necked jar
with boiling water and dry in a warm
oven (do not dry with a tea towel). Put
the onions in the jar.
2 Combine the vinegar and sugar in a
small screw-top jar and stir to dissolve
the sugar. Add the oil, seal the jar and
shake vigorously until combined—the
mixture will be paler and may separate
on standing.
3 Pour the vinegar mixture over the
onions, seal, and turn upside down to
coat. Marinate overnight in the
refrigerator, turning occasionally.
Return to room temperature and shake
before serving.

NUTRITION PER SERVE
Protein 0.5 g; Fat 7.5 g; Carbohydrate 20 g;
Dietary Fibre 2 g; Cholesterol 0 mg;
677 kJ (162 cal)

NOTE: Pickling onions are very small,
usually packed in 1 kg (2 lb) bags. The
ideal size is around 35 g (1¹/₄ oz) each.
The sizes in the bag will probably
range from 20 g (³/₄ oz) up to 40 g
(1¹/₄ oz). The cooking time given is
suitable for this range and there is no
need to cook the larger ones for any
longer. The marinating time given is a
minimum time and the onions may be
marinated for up to 3 days in the
refrigerator. The marinade may
separate after a few hours, which is
fine—simply stir occasionally.

When cool, trim the stems from the onions and
peel away the skin.

Add the oil to the vinegar and sugar and shake
vigorously to combine.

Pour the vinegar mixture over the onions, turning
the jar to coat thoroughly.

CHARGRILLED VEGETABLES

Preparation time: 15 minutes +
  40 minutes standing
Total cooking time: 1 hour
Serves 6

2 eggplants
900 g (1³/₄ lb) orange sweet potato
4 zucchini
2 red capsicums
600 g (1¹/₄ lb) button mushrooms
¹/₃ cup (80 ml/2³/₄ fl oz) olive oil

BASIL DRESSING
¹/₂ cup (125 ml/4 fl oz) olive oil
2 cloves garlic, crushed
2 tablespoons balsamic vinegar
¹/₂ teaspoon sugar
¹/₃ cup (20 g/³/₄ oz) fresh basil leaves

1 Cut the eggplant into 1 cm (¹/₂ inch) thick slices. Place on a wire rack and sprinkle liberally with salt. Leave for 30 minutes, then rinse under cold water and pat dry with paper towels.
2 Cut the sweet potato into 5 mm (¹/₄ inch) slices and the zucchini into 1 cm (¹/₂ inch) slices lengthways. Quarter the capsicums, remove the seeds and membranes and put on a hot, lightly oiled barbecue grill, skin-side-down, until the skin blackens and blisters. Place in a plastic bag and leave to cool. Peel away the skin.
3 Brush the eggplant, sweet potato, zucchini and mushrooms with oil. Cook on a hot, lightly oiled barbecue grill or flatplate in batches until lightly browned and cooked through.
4 To make the basil dressing, put the oil, garlic, vinegar, sugar and basil in a food processor or blender and process until smooth.
5 Toss the vegetables with the basil dressing. Allow to cool, then cover and refrigerate until ready to use. Return to room temperature before serving.

NUTRITION PER SERVE
Protein 9 g; Fat 20 g; Carbohydrate 28 g;
Dietary Fibre 9 g; Cholesterol 0 mg;
1495 kJ (355 cal)

Put the slices of eggplant on a wire rack and sprinkle with salt.

Use a sharp knife to cut the sweet potato into thin slices.

Once cooled, gently peel the blackened skin off the capsicums.

Brush the vegetables with oil and barbecue until lightly browned.

VEGETABLE PLATTER

Preparation time: 25 minutes
Total cooking time: 1 hour
Serves 8

HERB VINAIGRETTE
1/2 cup (125 ml/4 fl oz) olive oil
2 tablespoons balsamic vinegar
2 cloves garlic, crushed
2 tablespoons fresh lime juice
1/3 cup (20 g/3/4 oz) chopped fresh
    mint, basil and coriander, mixed

4 potatoes, unpeeled and halved
400 g (13 oz) pumpkin, unpeeled, cut
    into large pieces
300 g (10 oz) sweet potatoes,
    unpeeled and cut into large pieces
4 slender eggplants, halved
2 red onions, cut into wedges
1 yellow capsicum, quartered
1 red capsicum, quartered
1 green capsicum, quartered
8 large flat mushrooms, trimmed

BASIL MAYONNAISE
4 egg yolks
2 teaspoons mustard
1/4 cup (60 ml/2 fl oz) lemon juice
12/3 cups (410 ml/13 fl oz) olive oil
1/3 cup (20 g/3/4 oz) fresh basil leaves

1 To make the herb vinaigrette, whisk together the ingredients. Brush over the potato, pumpkin and sweet potato and wrap in foil. Cook on a hot, lightly oiled barbecue grill for 40–50 minutes, or until tender.
2 Brush the eggplant, onion, capsicum and mushrooms with the vinaigrette. Place on the barbecue for 10 minutes, or until golden brown.
3 To make the mayonnaise, process the yolks, mustard and lemon juice in a food processor for 1 minute, or until pale and creamy. Slowly add the oil with the motor running. When thick, add the basil and mix for 20 seconds.
4 Drizzle the vegetables with the remaining vinaigrette and serve with the mayonnaise.

NUTRITION PER SERVE
Protein 5 g; Fat 65 g; Carbohydrate 15 g;
Dietary Fibre 5 g; Cholesterol 90 mg;
2840 kJ (675 cal)

Cut the pumpkin, sweet potato, capsicum and onion into large pieces.

Brush the potato, pumpkin and sweet potato with vinaigrette and wrap in foil.

Barbecue the eggplant, onion, capsicum and mushrooms on a grill.

Add the basil to the mayonnaise and process for 20 seconds.

CHARGRILLED ASPARAGUS

Preparation time: 5 minutes
Total cooking time: 3 minutes
Serves 4

500 g (1 lb) asparagus
2 cloves garlic, crushed
2 tablespoons balsamic vinegar
2 tablespoons olive oil
50 g (1¾ oz) Parmesan shavings

1 Break off the woody ends from the asparagus by gently bending the stems until the tough end snaps away. Cook the asparagus on a hot, lightly oiled grill or flatplate for 3 minutes, or until bright green and tender.

2 To make the dressing, whisk the garlic, vinegar and olive oil.
3 Pour the dressing over the warm asparagus and top with the Parmesan shavings and lots of black pepper.

NUTRITION PER SERVE
Protein 8 g; Fat 15 g; Carbohydrate 2 g;
Dietary Fibre 2 g; Cholesterol 10 mg;
700 kJ (165 cal)

To break the woody ends from the asparagus, hold both ends and bend gently.

Cook the asparagus on a hot barbecue grill until it is bright green and tender.

The easiest way to make Parmesan shavings is to run a potato peeler over the block of cheese.

HAM AND HERB MUSHROOMS

Preparation time: 15 minutes
Total cooking time: 5 minutes
Serves 8

8 large flat field mushrooms
3 spring onions, finely chopped
150 g (5 oz) smoked ham, finely
    chopped
3/4 cup (60 g/2 oz) fresh breadcrumbs
2 tablespoons finely grated Parmesan
1 tablespoon chopped fresh parsley
2 teaspoons chopped fresh oregano
2 tablespoons olive oil

1 Remove the stalks from the mushrooms and finely chop them. Mix the mushroom stalks with the spring onion, ham, breadcrumbs, Parmesan, parsley and oregano. Season with salt and black pepper and add a little water to bring the mixture together.
2 Divide the mixture among the mushroom caps and brush lightly with the olive oil.

3 Cook on a hot, lightly oiled barbecue flatplate, filling-side-up, for about 3 minutes. Cover loosely with foil and steam for another 2 minutes.

NUTRITION PER SERVE
Protein 7 g; Fat 5 g; Carbohydrate 6 g;
Dietary Fibre 1 g; Cholesterol 10 mg;
415 kJ (98 cal)

NOTE: Serve as a main course with bread or as a side dish with barbecued meats. For vegetarian mushrooms, use feta cheese instead of ham.

Remove the stalks from the mushrooms and leave the mushroom caps for filling.

Finely chop the mushroom stalks to mix with the other filling ingredients.

Spoon the filling into the mushroom caps and then brush lightly with oil.

HERBED FETA SALAD

Preparation time: 20 minutes +
  30 minutes marinating
Total cooking time: 10 minutes
Serves 8

2 slices thick white bread
200 g (6¹/2 oz) feta cheese
1 clove garlic, crushed
1 tablespoon chopped fresh marjoram
1 tablespoon snipped chives
1 tablespoon chopped fresh basil

2 tablespoons white wine vinegar
¹/3 cup (80 ml/2³/4 fl oz) olive oil
1 red coral lettuce
1 green mignonette or oak leaf lettuce

1 Preheat the oven to 180°C (350°F/Gas 4). Remove the crusts from the bread and cut the bread into small cubes. Place on an oven tray in a single layer and bake for 10 minutes, until crisp and lightly golden. Transfer to a bowl and cool completely.
2 Cut the feta into small cubes and put in a bowl. Put the garlic, marjoram,

chives, basil, vinegar and oil in a screw-top jar and shake well. Pour over the feta and cover with plastic wrap. Leave for at least 30 minutes, stirring occasionally.
3 Tear the lettuce into large pieces and put in a serving bowl. Add the feta with the dressing and bread cubes and toss the salad well.

NUTRITION PER SERVE
Protein 6 g; Fat 16 g; Carbohydrate 4 g;
Dietary Fibre 1 g; Cholesterol 17 mg;
750 kJ (180 cal)

Remove the crusts from the bread and then cut it into small cubes.

Cut the feta into cubes and then pour the dressing over and leave to marinate.

Add the bread cubes to the salad leaves and marinated feta.

SUMMER SALAD WITH BASIL DRESSING

Preparation time: 15 minutes
Total cooking time: 5 minutes
Serves 8

2 carrots
6 radishes
150 g (5 oz) snow peas
250 g (8 oz) asparagus
1 cup (30 g/1 oz) fresh basil leaves
1/2 cup (125 ml/4 fl oz) olive oil
1 tablespoon white wine vinegar
1/2 teaspoon French mustard
1/4 teaspoon sugar

1 Thinly slice the carrots and radishes. Trim the ends from the snow peas and cut into short lengths. Snap the woody ends from the asparagus and put in a pan with a small amount of water.
2 Cook the asparagus over low heat until just tender. Plunge into cold water and then drain and pat dry with paper towels.
3 Put the basil in a food processor and blend until finely chopped. Add the oil, vinegar, mustard and sugar and process until smooth. Store in a screw-top jar until required. Put the vegetables in a large serving bowl and toss together. Add the dressing and toss well.

NUTRITION PER SERVE
Protein 2 g; Fat 15 g; Carbohydrate 4 g; Dietary Fibre 2 g; Cholesterol 0 mg; 650 kJ (156 cal)

STORAGE: The dressing can be kept in the fridge for up to 2 days.

VARIATION: Make the dressing with fresh coriander instead of basil.

Cut the radishes and carrots into thin slices and cut the snow peas into short lengths.

Plunge the asparagus into cold water to stop the cooking and dry with paper towels.

Blend the basil leaves until finely chopped, then add the other dressing ingredients.

MARINATED CUCUMBER AND CARROT SALAD

Preparation time: 20 minutes + 2 hours 15 minutes marinating
Total cooking time: Nil
Serves 8

2 Lebanese cucumbers
1 teaspoon salt
1 large onion, finely sliced
3 tablespoons white vinegar
2 1/2 teaspoons sugar
2 teaspoons salt, extra
2 large carrots, peeled and cut into thin matchsticks
1 teaspoon sugar, extra
1 tablespoon white vinegar, extra

1 Peel the cucumbers and slice in half, horizontally. Remove the seeds and slice into thin sticks. Toss with the salt and leave for 30 minutes. Toss the onion, vinegar, sugar and half the extra salt with 1/2 cup (125 ml/4 fl oz) water. Leave for 1 hour.
2 Mix together the carrot, remaining salt, extra sugar and extra vinegar in a third bowl and leave for 30 minutes.

Rinse the cucumber well and add to the onions. Leave for 1 hour.
3 Toss together all the vegetables in a serving bowl. Leave to stand for another 15 minutes before serving.

NUTRITION PER SERVE
Protein 1 g; Fat 0 g; Carbohydrate 6 g; Dietary Fibre 2 g; Cholesterol 0 mg; 125 kJ (30 cal)

STORAGE: Unused marinated vegetables will keep for several weeks in a sealed container in the fridge, if completely covered by the marinade.

Peel the cucumber and slice in half horizontally. Scoop out the seeds with a teaspoon.

After the cucumber has been salted, add it to the bowl of onions.

Mix together all the marinated vegetables in one bowl and leave for another 15 minutes.

SCALLOPED POTATO AND TOMATO GRATIN

Preparation time: 15 minutes
Total cooking time: 1 hour 15 minutes
Serves 8

1.5 kg (3 lb) potatoes
45 g (1 1/2 oz) butter, melted
1 tablespoon chopped fresh herbs (such as thyme, marjoram, parsley, rosemary and oregano)
1/2 teaspoon cracked black pepper
1/2 teaspoon salt
1 1/4 cups (310 ml/10 fl oz) cream
2 ripe tomatoes, thinly sliced
1/2 cup (45 g/1 1/2 oz) fresh breadcrumbs
1 cup (125 g/4 oz) grated Cheddar cheese
1 tablespoon chopped chives

1 Preheat the oven to 180°C (350°F/ Gas 4). Peel and thinly slice the potatoes. Brush a shallow baking dish with butter and arrange the potatoes in an overlapping layer.
2 Scatter on the herbs, pepper and salt and pour the cream into the centre of the dish. Cover with foil and bake for 1 hour. (The dish can now be removed from the oven, allowed to cool, then refrigerated for later.)

3 Increase the oven to 210°C (415°F/ Gas 6–7). Arrange the tomato over the potato. Scatter evenly with the combined breadcrumbs and cheese and return to the oven. Bake, uncovered, for 15 minutes until golden on top. Sprinkle with chives and serve immediately.

NUTRITION PER SERVE
Protein 14 g; Fat 32 g; Carbohydrate 30 g; Dietary Fibre 4 g; Cholesterol 99 mg; 1960 kJ (468 cal)

VARIATION: Thinly slice an onion and layer alternately with the potato.

Scatter the herbs, pepper and salt over the potato and pour the cream in the centre.

Arrange the tomato slices over the cooked potato and sprinkle with crumbs and cheese.

Peel the potatoes and thinly slice them, then arrange in the dish.

CURLY ENDIVE SALAD WITH CRISP PROSCIUTTO AND GARLIC CROUTONS

Preparation time: 20 minutes
Total cooking time: 5 minutes
Serves 6

1 large bunch curly endive
1/2 red oak leaf lettuce
2 red onions
4 slices white or brown bread
2 large cloves garlic, crushed
60 g (2 oz) butter, softened
30 g (1 oz) feta cheese, mashed
4–6 thin slices prosciutto
1 large avocado

DRESSING
2 tablespoons olive oil
3 tablespoons sugar
3 tablespoons spicy tomato sauce
1 tablespoon soy sauce
1/3 cup (80 ml/2 3/4 fl oz) red wine
   vinegar

1 Tear the endive and lettuce into pieces. Peel and slice the onions and separate into rings. Toss the endive, lettuce and onion in a salad bowl.
2 Toast the bread on one side only. Mash the garlic, butter and feta cheese into a paste and spread over the untoasted side of the bread. Remove the crusts and toast the buttered side of the bread until crisp and golden. Cut into small cubes.
3 Crisp the prosciutto under a very hot grill for a few seconds. Remove and cut into pieces. Cut the avocado into thin wedges.
4 To make the dressing, whisk the oil, sugar, tomato sauce, soy sauce and vinegar together. Add the prosciutto and avocado to the salad and pour over half the dressing. Arrange the croutons on top and serve the remaining dressing in a jug.

NUTRITION PER SERVE
Protein 5 g; Fat 24 g; Carbohydrate 22 g;
Dietary Fibre 2 g; Cholesterol 27 mg;
1356 kJ (324 cal)

STORAGE: The dressing will keep for a day in a screw-top jar.

Peel the red onion, slice it thinly and then separate into rings.

Spread the feta, butter and garlic paste over the untoasted side of the bread.

Crisp the prosciutto under a hot grill and then cut it into pieces.

Whisk together the oil, sugar, tomato sauce, soy sauce and vinegar.

CHICKPEA SALAD

Preparation time: 20 minutes
Total cooking time: Nil
Serves 8

2 large cans chickpeas
   (see NOTE)
3 tomatoes
1 red onion, thinly sliced
1 small red capsicum, cut into thin
   strips
4 spring onions, cut into thin strips
1 cup (60 g/2 oz) chopped fresh
   parsley
2–3 tablespoons chopped fresh mint
   leaves

DRESSING
2 tablespoons tahini (sesame paste)
2 tablespoons fresh lemon juice
3 tablespoons olive oil
2 cloves garlic, crushed
1/2 teaspoon ground cumin

1 Drain the chickpeas and rinse well.
Cut the tomatoes in half and remove
the seeds with a spoon. Dice the flesh.
Mix the onion, tomato, capsicum and
spring onion in a bowl. Add the
chickpeas, parsley and mint.
2 To make the dressing, put all the
ingredients in a screw-top jar with
2 tablespoons water, season well and
shake vigorously to make a creamy
liquid. Pour over the salad and toss.

NUTRITION PER SERVE
Protein 4 g; Fat 2 g; Carbohydrate 8 g;
Dietary Fibre 3 g; Cholesterol 0 mg;
877 kJ (210 cal)

STORAGE: Can be kept, covered, in
the fridge for up to 3 hours.

NOTE: You can also use dried
chickpeas, but they will need to be
soaked and cooked first. Use 13/4 cups
(380 g/12 oz) dried chickpeas and
put in a pan with 3.5 litres water and
3 tablespoons olive oil. Partially cover
and boil for 21/2 hours, or until tender.
Rinse, drain well and allow to cool a
little before making the salad.

Both canned and dried chickpeas should be
rinsed and drained well.

Cut the tomatoes in half and scoop out the
seeds with a teaspoon.

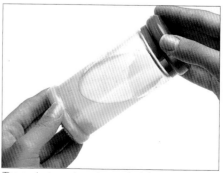

The easiest way to make a salad dressing is by
shaking the ingredients in a screw-top jar.

BARBECUED CORN IN THE HUSK

Preparation time: 15 minutes
Total cooking time: 40 minutes
Serves 8

8 fresh young corn cobs
1/2 cup (125 ml/4 fl oz) olive oil
6 cloves garlic, chopped
4 tablespoons chopped fresh parsley

1 Peel back the corn husks, leaving them intact. Pull off the white silks and discard. Wash the corn and pat dry with paper towels.
2 Combine the olive oil, garlic, parsley and some salt and black pepper and brush over each cob. Pull up the husks and tie together at the top with string. Steam over boiling water for 20 minutes, then pat dry.
3 Cook on a hot, lightly oiled barbecue grill or flatplate for

20 minutes, turning regularly. Spray with water during the cooking to keep the corn moist.

NUTRITION PER SERVE
Protein 3 g; Fat 15 g; Carbohydrate 15 g;
Dietary Fibre 3 g; Cholesterol 0 mg;
860 kJ (205 cal)

Carefully peel back the corn husks, then pull away the white silks (threads) and wash the corn.

Brush the oil, garlic, parsley and seasoning over the corn, then pull up the husk.

Tie the tops of the husks in place with kitchen string so they are secure.

CORN ON THE COB WITH TOMATO RELISH

Preparation time: 15 minutes
Total cooking time: 1 hour
Serves 6

TOMATO RELISH
400 g (13 oz) can peeled tomatoes
2/3 cup (170 ml/5¹/2 fl oz) white vinegar
1/2 cup (125 g/4 oz) sugar
1 clove garlic, finely chopped
2 spring onions, finely chopped
4 sun-dried tomatoes, finely chopped
1 small fresh red chilli, finely chopped
1/2 teaspoon salt
1/2 teaspoon cracked black pepper

6 large fresh cobs corn
1–2 tablespoons olive or vegetable oil
60 g (2 oz) butter
salt, to serve

1 To make the tomato relish, roughly chop the tomatoes by hand or in a food processor. Put the vinegar and sugar in a pan and stir over heat until the sugar dissolves. Bring to the boil, then reduce the heat and simmer for 2 minutes.
2 Add the tomatoes, garlic, spring onions, sun-dried tomatoes and chilli. Bring to the boil, reduce the heat and simmer, stirring often, for 35 minutes or until thickened. Season, remove from the heat and allow to cool.
3 Brush the corn with oil and cook on a hot, lightly oiled barbecue grill for 10 minutes, or until the corn is soft and flecked with brown in places. Transfer to the flatplate and add a knob of butter and salt to each cob. Serve at once with the relish.

NUTRITION PER SERVE
Protein 6 g; Fat 16 g; Carbohydrate 58 g; Dietary Fibre 7 g; Cholesterol 26 mg; 1683 kJ (400 cal)

STORAGE: The relish will keep for several weeks in an airtight container in the fridge.

HINT: The relish is also delicious with barbecued sausages.

Add the tomatoes, garlic, spring onions, sun-dried tomatoes and chilli to the pan.

Simmer the relish until thickened, then season well with salt and pepper.

Once the corn is cooked and tender, transfer to the flatplate and add butter and salt.

183

BARBECUED FIELD MUSHROOMS

Preparation time: 10 minutes
Total cooking time: 10 minutes
Serves 6

6 large field mushrooms
50 g (1³/₄ oz) butter, melted
2 cloves garlic, crushed
2 tablespoons finely chopped fresh
    chives
1 tablespoon fresh thyme leaves
¹/₂ cup (50 g/1³/₄ oz) shredded
    Parmesan

1 Peel the skin from the mushroom caps and remove the stalks. Mix together the butter and garlic in a small bowl.
2 Brush the mushroom tops with garlic butter and cook, brushed-side-down, on a very hot barbecue flatplate for 2 minutes or until that side is browned. Turn over, brush the other side of the mushrooms with garlic butter and cook for 2 minutes.
3 Sprinkle the mushrooms with the combined chives and thyme, then the cheese, and cook for 3 minutes, until the cheese begins to melt.

NUTRITION PER SERVE
Protein 6 g; Fat 10 g; Carbohydrate 1 g;
Dietary Fibre 1 g; Cholesterol 31 mg;
499 kJ (119 cal)

STORAGE: The mushrooms should be served immediately they are cooked.

NOTE: Any type of mushroom can be used in this recipe. Larger types such as flat or field mushrooms will take longer to cook than button or cup. Mushrooms should remain firm and chewy after cooking.

Carefully peel the skin away from the mushrooms before brushing with garlic butter.

Cook one side of the mushrooms, then turn over and brush the other side.

Sprinkle with the combined herbs and the grated Parmesan cheese.

STIR-FRIED SALAD

Preparation time: 20 minutes
Total cooking time: 5 minutes
Serves 6

1 red capsicum
100 g (3¹/₂ oz) oyster mushrooms
425 g (14 oz) can baby corn
500 g (1 lb) Chinese cabbage
1 tablespoon olive oil
250 g (8 oz) bean sprouts
5 spring onions, cut into short pieces
2 cloves garlic, crushed
1 tablespoon olive oil
2 teaspoons sesame oil
2 tablespoons teriyaki marinade
¹/₂ teaspoon sugar
sweet chilli sauce, to taste

1 Cut the capsicum in half and remove the seeds and membrane. Cut into thin strips. Slice the mushrooms in half. Cut any large baby corn in half. Cut the cabbage into thick slices, then into squares.
2 Brush a hot barbecue flatplate with oil. Toss the capsicum, mushrooms, corn, cabbage, sprouts, spring onions and garlic onto the flatplate and cook for 4 minutes, tossing and stirring to prevent burning or sticking.
3 Mix together the olive oil, sesame oil, teriyaki marinade and sugar and pour over the vegetables. Stir thoroughly to coat and cook for 1 minute longer. Serve immediately, drizzled with sweet chilli sauce.

NUTRITION PER SERVE
Protein 5 g; Fat 8 g; Carbohydrate 8 g;
Dietary Fibre 8 g; Cholesterol 0 mg;
520 kJ (124 cal)

NOTE: All the vegetables should be cut to about the same size to ensure even cooking.

Cut the capsicum into thin strips, the spring onions into lengths and the cabbage into squares.

Brush the barbecue flatplate with oil and then stir-fry the vegetables directly on the barbecue.

Pour the dressing over the stir-fried vegetables, toss and cook for a minute longer.

SNOW PEA SALAD

Preparation time: 10 minutes
Total cooking time: Nil
Serves 8

150 g (5 oz) snow peas
250 g (8 oz) fresh asparagus
2 carrots, peeled
425 g (14 oz) can baby corn, drained
230 g (7¹/₂ oz) can bamboo shoots,
    drained

DRESSING
3 tablespoons vegetable oil
3 teaspoons sesame oil
1 tablespoon soy sauce

1 Trim the snow peas and cut in half.
Snap the woody ends from the
asparagus and cut into short lengths.
Cut the carrots into matchsticks.
2 Put the snow peas and asparagus in
a heatproof bowl and cover with
boiling water. Leave for 1 minute, then
drain and plunge into iced water.
Drain and dry on paper towels.
3 Combine the snow peas, asparagus,
carrots, corn and bamboo shoots in a
serving bowl. To make the dressing,
put the oils and sauce in a small screw-
top jar and shake well to combine.
Pour over the salad and toss well.

NUTRITION PER SERVE
Protein 3 g; Fat 10 g; Carbohydrate 12 g;
Dietary Fibre 4 g; Cholesterol 0 mg;
603 kJ (144 cal)

NOTE: Sesame oil is a very strongly
flavoured oil and should be used
sparingly as its flavour tends to
dominate. The darker the oil, the
stronger the flavour.

Cut all the vegetables into similar-sized strips and
pieces so the salad is balanced.

Drain the snow peas and asparagus and then pat
dry on paper towels.

Combine all the dressing ingredients in a screw-
top jar, then pour over the salad.

BARBECUED BABY POTATOES

Preparation time: 20 minutes + 1 hour
  standing
Total cooking time: 20 minutes
Serves 6

750 g (1¹/₂ lb) baby potatoes,
    unpeeled
2 tablespoons olive oil
2 tablespoons fresh thyme leaves
2 teaspoons crushed sea salt

1 Cut any large potatoes in half so that they are all the same size for even cooking. Boil, steam or microwave the potatoes until just tender. Drain and lightly dry with paper towels.
2 Put the potatoes in a large bowl and add the oil and thyme. Toss gently and leave for 1 hour.
3 Cook the potatoes on a hot, lightly oiled barbecue flatplate for 15 minutes, turning frequently and brushing with the remaining oil and thyme mixture, until golden brown. Sprinkle with salt to serve.

NUTRITION PER SERVE
Protein 3 g; Fat 7 g; Carbohydrate 16 g;
Dietary Fibre 2 g; Cholesterol 0 mg;
576 kJ (138 cal)

NOTE: The potatoes can be left in the marinade for up to 2 hours before barbecuing, but should be served immediately they are cooked.

Boil, steam or microwave the potatoes until they are just tender but still whole and intact.

Toss the potatoes with the oil and thyme and then leave for an hour.

While the potatoes are cooking, turn and brush them frequently with the oil and thyme.

187

Side Salads

When you're catering for a crowd at a barbecue, the easiest way to manage is to just prepare a couple of large side salads for everyone to dip into. These salads will all serve 6 and can be multiplied for feeding larger numbers.

COUSCOUS SALAD

Prepare 500 g (1 lb) couscous according to the packet. Place in a large bowl with 1 chopped red onion, 200 g (6¹/₂ oz) diced feta cheese, ¹/₂ cup (60 g/2 oz) sliced black olives, 2 peeled, seeded and chopped Lebanese cucumbers and 1 cup (60 g/2 oz) chopped fresh mint. Whisk together ¹/₂ cup (125 ml/4 fl oz) olive oil and ¹/₂ cup (125 ml/ 4 fl oz) lemon juice and toss through. Serves 6

FETA, BEETROOT AND ROCKET SALAD

Drain two 340 g (11 oz) jars baby beetroot and cut into quarters. Place in a large serving bowl with 200 g (6¹/₂ oz) baby rocket leaves and 300 g (10 oz) drained and cubed marinated feta. Whisk together 3 tablespoons olive oil and 1 tablespoon balsamic vinegar, then pour over the salad and toss well. Season with black pepper. Serves 6

SEMI-DRIED TOMATO AND BABY SPINACH SALAD

Remove and discard the pith and flesh from 2 quarters preserved lemon (this is bought in a jar and only the rind is used). Wash the rind and thinly slice. Place 150 g (5 oz) baby English spinach leaves in a bowl with 200 g (6¹/₂ oz) sliced semi-dried tomatoes, a 225 g (7 oz) jar drained and sliced marinated artichoke hearts, ¹/₂ cup (90 g/3 oz) small black olives and the preserved lemon. Whisk together 2 tablespoons lemon juice, 3 tablespoons olive oil and 1 large crushed garlic clove, season and pour over the salad. Toss and serve immediately. Serves 6

BEAN SALAD

Bring a saucepan of lightly salted water to the boil. Add 250 g (8 oz) green beans and 250 g (8 oz) yellow beans and cook for 2 minutes, or until just tender. Plunge into cold water and drain. Whisk together 3 tablespoons olive oil, 1 tablespoon lemon juice and 1 crushed garlic clove and season well. Place the beans in a serving bowl, pour on the dressing and toss to coat. Top with Parmesan shavings and serve immediately. Serves 6

ROAST TOMATO SALAD

Cut 6 Roma tomatoes into quarters lengthways. Cook, skin-side-down, on a hot barbecue grill or under a kitchen grill for 4–5 minutes, or until golden. Cool to room temperature. Combine 2 teaspoons capers, 6 torn fresh basil leaves, 1 tablespoon olive oil, 1 tablespoon balsamic vinegar, 2 crushed garlic cloves and $1/2$ teaspoon honey in a bowl, season with salt and freshly ground black pepper, and pour over the tomatoes. Toss gently. Serves 6

KIPFLER POTATO SALAD

Boil 1 kg (2 lb) washed kipfler potatoes, or other waxy potatoes, for 20 minutes, or until tender. Cut into thick slices on the diagonal. Cook 125 g (4 oz) chopped bacon in a little oil until crispy and golden. Add to the potatoes with 2 chopped spring onions. Whisk together $1/2$ cup (125 g/4 oz) sour cream, 2 tablespoons each olive oil and red wine vinegar and 2 teaspoons each Dijon and wholegrain mustard. Pour the dressing over the potatoes and gently toss. Season with black pepper. Serves 6

This page, from top: Bean Salad; Roast Tomato Salad; Kipfler Potato Salad
Opposite, from top: Couscous Salad; Feta, Beetroot and Rocket Salad; Semi-dried Tomato and Baby Spinach Salad

Dressings

Mayonnaise is something that most of us expect to buy in a jar in the supermarket and take a chance as to whether it's rich and creamy or, as if often the case, rather gluey and oversweet. Try making your own—it's actually very easy and you'll get a good-quality result every time.

MAYONNAISE

Whisk together 2 egg yolks, 1 teaspoon Dijon mustard and 1 tablespoon lemon juice for 30 seconds, or until light and creamy. Add $3/4$ cup (185 ml/6 fl oz) olive oil, about a teaspoon at a time, whisking continuously. You can add the oil more quickly as the mayonnaise thickens. Season, to taste, with salt and white pepper.

Alternatively, place the egg yolks, mustard and lemon juice in a food processor and mix for 10 seconds. With the motor running, add the oil in a thin stream. Season, to taste.
Makes about 1 cup (250 ml/8 fl oz)

THOUSAND ISLAND DRESSING

Mix together $1^1/2$ cups (375 ml/12 fl oz) mayonnaise, 1 tablespoon sweet chilli sauce, 1–2 tablespoons tomato sauce, $1/4$ red capsicum and $1/4$ green capsicum, finely chopped, 1 tablespoon chopped chives and $1/2$ teaspoon sweet paprika. Stir well and season. Cover and refrigerate for up to 3 days. Thousand Island dressing is traditionally served on lettuce leaves.
Makes $1^2/3$ cups (410 ml/13 fl oz)

GREEN GODDESS DRESSING

Mix together $1^1/2$ cups (375 ml/12 fl oz) mayonnaise, 4 mashed anchovy fillets, 4 finely chopped spring onions, 1 crushed clove garlic, $1/4$ cup (7 g/$1/4$ oz) chopped fresh flat-leaf parsley, $1/4$ cup (15 g/$1/2$ oz) finely chopped chives and 1 teaspoon tarragon vinegar. Serve on salad or with barbecued seafood.
Makes about $1^2/3$ cups (410 ml/13 fl oz)

AIOLI (GARLIC MAYONNAISE)

Mix together 1 cup (250 ml/8 fl oz) mayonnaise with 3 crushed cloves of garlic. Season, to taste, with salt and pepper. Serve with barbecued seafood, such as prawns.
Makes about 1 cup (250 ml/8 fl oz)

TARTARE SAUCE

Mix together 1$^{1}/_{2}$ cups (375 ml/12 fl oz) mayonnaise, 1 tablespoon finely chopped onion, 1 teaspoon lemon juice, 1 tablespoon chopped gherkins, 1 teaspoon chopped capers, $^{1}/_{4}$ teaspoon Dijon mustard and 1 tablespoon finely chopped fresh parsley. Mix and season with salt and pepper. Top with a few capers and serve with barbecued seafood.
Makes about 1$^{2}/_{3}$ cups (410 ml/13 fl oz)

COCKTAIL SAUCE

Mix together 1 cup (250 ml/8 fl oz) mayonnaise, 3 tablespoons tomato sauce, 2 teaspoons Worcestershire sauce, $^{1}/_{2}$ teaspoon lemon juice and 1 drop of Tabasco sauce. Season with salt and pepper. Keep, covered, in the fridge for up to 2 days.
Makes about 1$^{1}/_{4}$ cups (315 ml/10 fl oz)

BLUE CHEESE DRESSING

Mix together $^{1}/_{2}$ cup (125 ml/4 fl oz) mayonnaise, $^{1}/_{4}$ cup (60 ml/2 fl oz) thick cream, 1 teaspoon white wine vinegar and 1 tablespoon finely chopped chives. Crumble 50 g (1$^{3}/_{4}$ oz) blue cheese into the mixture and gently stir through. Season with salt and white pepper. Can be kept refrigerated, covered, for up to 2 days. Serve as a salad dressing or with barbecued asparagus.
Makes about 1 cup (250 ml/8 fl oz)

CAESAR DRESSING

Cook an egg in boiling water for 1 minute. Break the egg into a small bowl and add 2 tablespoons white wine or tarragon vinegar, 2 teaspoons Dijon mustard, 2 chopped anchovy fillets and 1 crushed clove garlic. Mix together with a small wire whisk. Add $^{1}/_{2}$ cup (125 ml/4 fl oz) oil in a thin stream, whisking continuously until the mixture is smooth and creamy. Keep, covered, in the fridge for up to 2 days. Serve over crisp salad.
Makes about $^{3}/_{4}$ cup (185 ml/6 fl oz)

Top, from left: Tartare Sauce; Blue Cheese; Thousand Island; Mayonnaise
Bottom, from left: Aioli; Green Goddess; Caesar Dressing; Cocktail Sauce

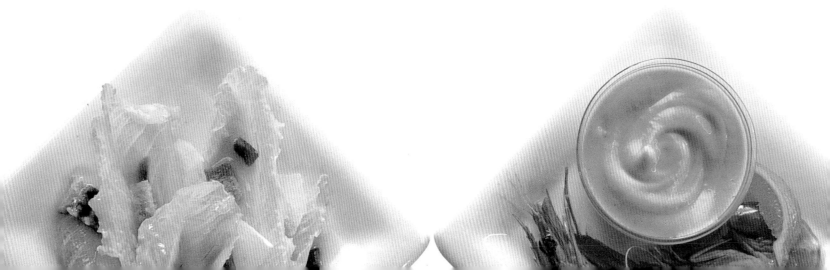

Breads

ROSEMARY BREAD TRIOS

Preparation time: 40 minutes +
  1 hour 30 minutes rising
Total cooking time: 15 minutes
Makes 10 trios

7 g (¹/4 oz) sachet dried yeast
1 teaspoon caster sugar
4 cups (500 g/1 lb) plain flour
1 tablespoon caster sugar, extra
1 teaspoon salt
1 cup (250 ml/8 fl oz) warm milk
¹/4 cup (60 ml/2 fl oz) vegetable oil
10 small sprigs of rosemary
1 egg yolk
sea salt flakes, to sprinkle

1 Combine the yeast, caster sugar and ¹/2 cup (125 ml/4 fl oz) of warm water in a small bowl. Cover and set aside in a warm place for 10 minutes, or until frothy.
2 Sift the flour into a large bowl and stir in the extra caster sugar and salt. Make a well in the centre and pour in the warm milk, oil and frothy yeast. Mix to a soft dough, gather into a ball then turn out onto a lightly floured surface and knead for 10 minutes, or until smooth and elastic. Add a little extra flour if the dough becomes too sticky. Place in a large, oiled bowl, cover loosely with greased plastic wrap and leave in a warm place for

1 hour, or until doubled in size.
3 Punch down the dough, then turn out onto a lightly floured surface and knead for 1 minute. Lightly grease 2 large baking trays. Divide the dough into 10 pieces. Form each piece into three balls—keeping the remaining pieces covered—and place close together on the prepared baking tray; add a sprig of rosemary to the centre of each trio. Repeat with the remaining pieces of dough, and lay each set separately on the baking tray.
4 Cover the trios with a damp tea towel and set aside for 20 minutes, or until well risen. Preheat the oven to moderate 180°C (350°F/Gas 4). Brush the trios lightly with the combined egg yolk and 1 teaspoon of water and sprinkle with the sea salt flakes. Bake for 15 minutes, or until golden brown. Allow to cool on a wire rack and replace the rosemary sprigs with fresh ones, if you want.

NUTRITION PER TRIO
Protein 7 g; Fat 8 g; Carbohydrate 40 g;
Dietary Fibre 2 g; Cholesterol 20 mg;
1080 kJ (260 cal)

NOTE: 'Punching down' is when you knock the dough with your fist to expel the air.

Knead the dough on a lightly floured surface until smooth and elastic.

Arrange the trio of balls together on a lightly greased baking tray.

PARMESAN AND PROSCIUTTO LOAF

Preparation time: 30 minutes + 2 hours rising
Total cooking time: 25 minutes
Serves 6

7 g (¹/₄ oz) dried yeast
1 teaspoon caster sugar
¹/₂ cup (125 ml/4 fl oz) warm milk
2 cups (250 g/8 oz) plain flour
1 teaspoon salt
1 egg, lightly beaten
30 g (1 oz) butter, melted and cooled slightly
1 tablespoon milk, extra

60 g (2 oz) sliced prosciutto, finely chopped
¹/₂ cup (50 g/1³/₄ oz) grated Parmesan

1 Mix the yeast, sugar and milk in a bowl. Cover and set aside in a warm place for 10 minutes, or until frothy.
2 Mix the flour and salt in a bowl. Make a well in the centre and add the egg, butter and frothy yeast. Mix to a soft dough and gather into a ball; turn out onto a floured surface and knead for 8 minutes, or until elastic.
3 Put in an oiled bowl, cover loosely with greased plastic wrap and leave in a warm place for 1¹/₄ hours, or until doubled in size.

4 Punch down the dough, turn out onto a floured surface and knead for 30 seconds, or until smooth. Roll out to a rectangle, 30 x 20 cm (12 x 8 inches), and brush with some extra milk. Sprinkle with the prosciutto and Parmesan, leaving a border. Roll lengthways into a log shape.
5 Lay on a greased baking tray and brush with the remaining milk. Slash the loaf at intervals. Leave to rise in a warm place for 30 minutes. Bake at 220°C (425°F/Gas 7) for 25 minutes.

NUTRITION PER SERVE
Protein 10 g; Fat 9 g; Carbohydrate 30 g;
Dietary Fibre 2 g; Cholesterol 60 mg;
1060 kJ (250 cal)

Sprinkle the prosciutto and Parmesan on the dough, leaving a clear border.

Roll up the dough tightly lengthways into a log shape for baking.

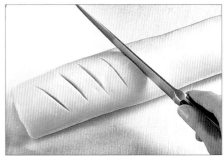
Using a sharp knife, slash the loaf diagonally at intervals.

OLIVE SPIRALS

Preparation time: 25 minutes +
  1 hour 40 minutes rising
Total cooking time: 35 minutes
Makes 12 spirals

7 g (^{1}/$_4$ oz) dried yeast
1 teaspoon sugar
4 cups (500 g/1 lb) plain flour
1 teaspoon salt
2 tablespoons olive oil
2 cups (250 g/8 oz) pitted black olives
^{1}/$_2$ cup (50 g/1^3/$_4$ oz) finely grated
  Parmesan
3 cloves garlic, chopped
1 tablespoon oil

1 Mix the yeast, sugar and ^{1}/$_2$ cup (125 ml/4 fl oz) warm water in a bowl. Cover and set aside in a warm place for 10 minutes, or until frothy.
2 Sift the flour and salt into a bowl and make a well in the centre. Add the frothy yeast, oil and 1 cup (250 ml/ 8 fl oz) of warm water. Mix to a soft dough and gather into a ball. Turn out onto a floured surface and knead for 10 minutes, or until smooth. Cover loosely with greased plastic wrap and set aside for 1 hour, or until well risen.
3 Process the olives, Parmesan and garlic in a food processor until chopped. With the motor running, add the tablespoon of oil and process to a paste.

4 Punch down the dough and knead for 1 minute. Roll out to a rectangle 42 x 35 cm (18 x 14 inches). Spread with the olive paste, leaving a border along one long side. Roll up length- ways, ending with the clear long side.
5 Cut into 12 slices and place close together on a greased baking tray. Cover with a damp tea towel and set aside for 30 minutes, or until well risen. Preheat the oven to moderately hot 200°C (400°F/Gas 6). Bake for 35 minutes, or until golden brown.

NUTRITION PER SPIRAL
Protein 8 g; Fat 8 g; Carbohydrate 40 g; Dietary Fibre 3 g; Cholesterol 4 mg; 1050 kJ (250 cal)

Spread the rectangle of dough with olive paste and roll up lengthways.

Using a serrated knife, cut the rolled log into 12 equal slices.

Place the spirals close together on the baking tray so that they touch while cooking.

CHEESE AND HERB PULL-APART LOAF

Preparation time: 25 minutes +
    1 hour 40 minutes rising
Total cooking time: 30 minutes
Serves 8

7 g (¹/4 oz) dried yeast
1 teaspoon sugar
4 cups (500 g/1 lb) plain flour
1¹/2 teaspoons salt
2 tablespoons chopped fresh parsley
2 tablespoons chopped chives
1 tablespoon chopped fresh thyme
60 g (2 oz) Cheddar cheese, grated
milk, to glaze

1 Combine the yeast, sugar and ¹/2 cup (125 ml/4 fl oz) of warm water in a small bowl. Cover and set aside in a warm place for 10 minutes, or until frothy.
2 Sift the flour and salt into a bowl. Make a well in the centre and pour in 1 cup (250 ml/8 fl oz) warm water and the frothy yeast. Mix to a soft dough. Knead on a lightly floured surface for 10 minutes, or until smooth. Put the dough in an oiled bowl, cover loosely with greased plastic wrap and leave for 1 hour, or until doubled in size.
3 Punch down and knead for 1 minute. Divide the dough in half and shape each half into 10 flat discs, 6 cm (2¹/2 inches) in diameter. Mix the fresh herbs with the Cheddar and put

2 teaspoons on a disc. Press another disc on top. Repeat with the remaining discs and herb mixture.
4 Grease a 21 x 10.5 x 6.5 cm (8¹/2 x 4¹/4 x 2¹/2 inch) loaf tin. Stand the filled discs upright in the prepared tin, squashing them together. Cover the tin with a damp tea towel and set aside in a warm place for 30 minutes, or until well risen. Preheat the oven to hot 210°C (415°F/Gas 6–7).
5 Glaze with a little milk and bake for 30 minutes, or until brown and crusty.

NUTRITION PER SERVE
Protein 10 g; Fat 4 g; Carbohydrate 60 g; Dietary Fibre 3 g; Cholesterol 8 mg; 1255 kJ (300 cal)

Working on a lightly floured surface, flatten the dough into flat discs.

Spoon the filling onto one disc and top with another, pressing down firmly.

Stand the discs upright in the loaf tin, squashing them together.

CARAMELISED ONION BRAIDS

Preparation time: 1 hour +
    1 hour 45 minutes rising
Total cooking time: 1 hour 35 minutes
Serves 10

2¹/2 cups (310 g/10 oz) plain flour
1 cup (125 g/4 oz) buckwheat flour
1 teaspoon salt
15 g (¹/2 oz) fresh yeast or
    7 g (¹/4 oz) dried yeast
1¹/4 cups (315 ml/10 fl oz) warm milk
30 g (1 oz) butter
1 tablespoon oil
1 kg (2 lb) onions, thinly sliced into
    rings
1 egg, lightly beaten
2 teaspoons fennel seeds

1 Sift the flours and salt into a large bowl and make a well in the centre. Dissolve the yeast in ¹/2 cup (125 ml/4 fl oz) of the warm milk in a small bowl. Then add the remaining warm milk. Pour into the well and mix to a dough. Turn out onto a floured surface and knead for 8 minutes, or until smooth. Place in a large oiled bowl, cover loosely with greased plastic wrap and leave in a warm place for 45 minutes–1 hour, or until doubled in size.
2 Melt the butter and oil in a frying pan, add the onion and cook over medium-low heat for 40–50 minutes, or until the onion is golden.
3 Punch down the dough, turn out onto a lightly floured surface and knead for 10 minutes, or until smooth and elastic.
4 Lightly grease 2 baking trays. Divide the dough in half. Working with

1 piece at a time, divide it into 3 pieces. Roll each piece out to a 30 x 10 cm (12 x 4 inch) rectangle. Divide the onion mixture into 6 portions and spread a portion along the middle of each rectangle, leaving a 2 cm (3/4 inch) border. Brush the edge with some of the beaten egg and roll over lengthways to enclose the filling.
5 Plait the 3 pieces together and place seam-side-down on a baking tray. Pinch the ends together. Repeat with the remaining dough and caramelised onion. Cover with a damp tea towel

and leave in a warm place for 45 minutes, or until well risen.
6 Preheat the oven to moderate 180°C (350°F/Gas 4). Brush the top with the beaten egg and sprinkle with the fennel seeds. Bake for 35–45 minutes, or until well browned. Transfer to a wire rack to cool.

NUTRITION PER SERVE
Protein 8 g; Fat 7 g; Carbohydrate 40 g; Dietary Fibre 3 g; Cholesterol 30 mg; 1030 kJ (250 cal)

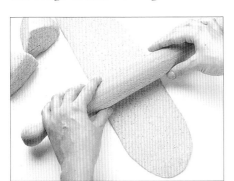
On a lightly floured surface, roll each portion out into a rough rectangle.

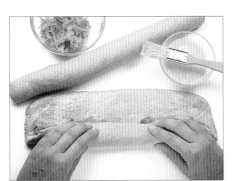
Brush the edge with the beaten egg and roll over to enclose the filling.

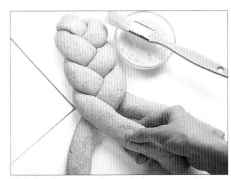
Plait the pieces together and place seam-side-down on a baking tray

197

BEER BREAD WITH SUN-DRIED TOMATO AND HERBS

Preparation time: 20 minutes
Total cooking time: 45 minutes
Serves 8

1 tablespoon finely chopped fresh oregano, or 1¹/₂ teaspoons dried
3 tablespoons finely chopped fresh parsley
2 tablespoons finely chopped fresh basil
3 tablespoons chopped sun-dried tomato

1 teaspoon cracked black pepper
3 tablespoons grated Parmesan
2 cloves garlic, crushed
3 cups (375 g/12 oz) self-raising flour
1 teaspoon salt
2 teaspoons sugar
1¹/₂ cups (375 ml/12 fl oz) beer (not bitter), at room temperature
2 teaspoons olive oil

1 Preheat the oven to 210°C (415°C/ Gas 6–7). Brush a 25 x 15 cm (10 x 6 inch) loaf tin with melted butter. Mix the oregano, parsley, basil, sun-dried tomato, pepper, cheese and garlic.
2 Sift the flour, salt and sugar into a large mixing bowl. Make a well in the centre and add the herb mixture and beer. Stir with a wooden spoon for 1 minute. (It should be very moist— add a little more beer if necessary.)
3 Spoon into the tin and smooth the surface. Bake for 10 minutes, then reduce to 180°C (350°F/Gas 4) and bake for 30 more minutes. Brush the top with oil and cook for 5 more minutes or until well browned and cooked through. Turn out onto a wire rack to cool.

NUTRITION PER SERVE
Protein 7 g; Fat 3 g; Carbohydrate 45 g; Dietary Fibre 2 g; Cholesterol 4 mg; 800 kJ (210 cal)

Mix together the oregano, parsley, basil, sun-dried tomato, pepper, cheese and garlic.

Make a well in the centre of the dry ingredients and add the herbs and beer.

Cook the loaf until it is well browned, then turn out onto a wire rack to cool.

LEMON PEPPER DAMPER

Preparation time: 18 minutes
Total cooking time: 25 minutes
Serves 8

2 cups (250 g/8 oz) self-raising flour
1 teaspoon salt (see NOTE)
2 teaspoons lemon pepper, or
    1 teaspoon grated lemon rind
    and 2 teaspoons black pepper
45 g (1½ oz) butter, chopped
1 tablespoon snipped chives
90 g (3 oz) Cheddar cheese, grated
2 teaspoons white vinegar
¾ cup (185 ml/6 fl oz) milk

1 Preheat the oven to 210°C (415°F/Gas 6–7). Brush a baking tray with melted butter or oil. Sift the flour into a large bowl and add the salt and lemon pepper. Rub in the butter with your fingertips until the mixture resembles coarse breadcrumbs. Stir in the chives and grated cheese.
2 Stir the vinegar into the milk (it should look slightly curdled). Make a well in the middle of the flour, add the milk and mix to a soft dough, adding a little more milk if the dough is too stiff.
3 Turn out onto a lightly floured surface and knead until smooth. Place on the baking tray and press out into a circle approximately 2.5 cm (1 inch)

thick. Mark with a knife into 8 wedges, cutting lightly into the top of damper. Dust the top lightly with flour. Bake for 25 minutes, or until the damper is deep golden and sounds hollow when tapped on the base.

NUTRITION PER SERVE
Protein 10 g; Fat 14 g; Carbohydrate 26 g;
Dietary Fibre 1 g; Cholesterol 41 mg;
1118 kJ (267 cal)

NOTE: If you are using commercial lemon pepper, omit the salt.

Rub the butter into the flour until it forms coarse crumbs then add the chives and cheese.

Make a well in the centre of the flour and then add the milk and vinegar mixture.

Mark the loaf into 8 wedges, cutting lightly into the top with a knife.

ROASTED RED CAPSICUM BUNS

Preparation time: 40 minutes +
  1 hour 40 minutes rising
Total cooking time: 1 hour
Makes 8 buns

2 red capsicums, cut into large flat
  pieces
7 g (1/4 oz) dried yeast
2 teaspoons sugar
4 cups (500 g/1 lb) plain flour
1 teaspoon salt
1 tablespoon olive oil
1 egg, lightly beaten

1 Place the capsicum skin-side-up under a hot grill, until the skins blacken. Cool in a plastic bag, then peel away the skin and dice the flesh.
2 Combine the dried yeast, sugar and 1/2 cup (125 ml/4 fl oz) of warm water in a bowl and leave in a warm place for 10 minutes, or until frothy.
3 Sift the flour and salt into a bowl, make a well in the centre and pour in the oil, the frothy yeast and 1 1/4 cups (315 ml/10 fl oz) of warm water. Mix to a soft dough, gather into a ball and knead on a floured surface until smooth. Add a little extra flour if needed. Place in a lightly oiled bowl, cover loosely with greased plastic wrap and leave in a warm place for

1 hour, or until doubled.
4 Punch down the dough, turn out onto a floured surface and knead for 10 minutes, adding the capsicum half-way through. Divide the dough into eight and form into rounds. Lay apart on a greased baking tray. Cover with a damp tea towel and leave for 30 minutes, or until well risen. Preheat the oven to 180°C (350°F/Gas 4). Brush the buns with beaten egg. Bake for 40–45 minutes, or until the bases sound hollow when tapped.

NUTRITION PER BUN
Protein 9 g; Fat 4 g; Carbohydrate 50 g;
Dietary Fibre 3 g; Cholesterol 20 mg;
1125 kJ (270 cal)

Sift the flour and salt together into a large bowl, then make a well in the centre.

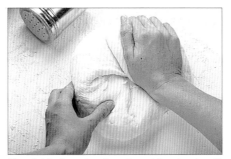
On a lightly floured surface, knead the dough until it is smooth.

Knead the dough for 5 minutes, then add the capsicum and knead for another 5 minutes.

TOMATO HERB ROLLS

Preparation time: 30 minutes
 + 1 hour 25 minutes rising
Total cooking time: 35 minutes
Makes 12 rolls

7 g (1/4 oz) dried yeast
1 teaspoon sugar
4 cups (500 g/l lb) plain flour
1 teaspoon salt
2 cloves garlic, finely chopped
1/2 cup (75 g/21/2 oz) sun-dried
    tomatoes, finely chopped
1 tablespoon chopped fresh oregano
1 tablespoon chopped fresh marjoram
1 tablespoon chopped fresh thyme
2 tablespoons chopped fresh flat-leaf
    parsley
30 g (1 oz) butter, melted
1/2 cup (125 ml/4 fl oz) milk, plus
    extra, to glaze

1 Mix the yeast, sugar and 1/2 cup
(125 ml/4 fl oz) of warm water in a
bowl. Set aside for 10 minutes, or until
frothy. Sift the flour and salt into a
bowl and make a well in the centre.
2 Mix in the garlic, sun-dried tomato
and herbs. Pour in the melted butter,
frothy yeast and milk and mix to a soft
dough. Knead on a lightly floured
surface for 10 minutes, or until
smooth. Cover loosely with greased
plastic wrap and leave for 45 minutes,
or until well risen.
3 Punch down and knead for
5 minutes. Divide into twelve and roll
into balls. Lay apart on a greased
baking tray. Leave for 30 minutes, or
until well risen. Preheat the oven to
hot 210°C (415°F/Gas 6–7). Brush
the rolls with milk and bake for
10 minutes. Reduce the oven to
180°C (350°F/Gas 4) and bake for
20–25 minutes, or until golden.

NUTRITION PER ROLL
Protein 5 g; Fat 3 g; Carbohydrate 30 g;
Dietary Fibre 2 g; Cholesterol 8 mg;
730 kJ (175 cal)

Add the garlic, sun-dried tomato and herbs to the
flour mixture.

Using a sharp floured knife, divide the dough into
12 equal portions.

The rolls are cooked when the bases sound
hollow when tapped.

Dips

HUMMUS

Preparation time: 20 minutes +
  overnight soaking
Total cooking time: 1 hour 15 minutes
Serves 20

1 cup (220 g/7 oz) dried chickpeas
2 tablespoons tahini (sesame paste)
4 cloves garlic, crushed
2 teaspoons ground cumin
1/3 cup (80 ml/2³/₄ fl oz) lemon juice
3 tablespoons olive oil
large pinch cayenne pepper
extra lemon juice, optional
extra olive oil, to garnish
paprika, to garnish
chopped fresh parsley, to garnish

1 Soak the chickpeas in 1 litre water overnight. Drain and place in a large saucepan with 2 litres fresh water (enough to cover the chickpeas by 5 cm/2 inches). Bring to the boil, then reduce the heat and simmer for 1 hour 15 minutes, or until the chickpeas are very tender. Skim any froth from the surface. Drain well, reserve the cooking liquid and leave until cool enough to handle. Pick over for any loose skins and discard.

2 Process the chickpeas, tahini, garlic, cumin, lemon juice, olive oil, cayenne pepper and 1¹/₂ teaspoons salt in a food processor until thick and smooth. With the motor still running, gradually add about ³/₄ cup (185 ml/6 fl oz) reserved cooking liquid to form a smooth creamy purée. Season with salt or extra lemon juice.
3 Spread onto a flat bowl or plate, drizzle with oil, sprinkle with paprika and scatter the parsley over the top. Serve with pitta or pide breads that have been warmed on the barbecue.

NUTRITION PER SERVE
Protein 1.2 g; Fat 4.7 g; Carbohydrate 1.6 g;
Dietary Fibre 0.9 g; Cholesterol 0 mg;
228 kJ (54 cal)

Pick through the cooled chickpeas to remove any loose skins.

Process the chickpea mixture with the reserved cooking liquid until creamy.

GUACAMOLE

Preparation time: 30 minutes
Total cooking time: Nil
Serves 6

3 ripe avocados
1 tablespoon lime or lemon juice (see
    HINT)
1 tomato
1–2 red chillies, finely chopped
1 small red onion, finely chopped
1 tablespoon finely chopped fresh
    coriander leaves
2 tablespoons sour cream
1–2 drops Tabasco or habanero sauce

1 Roughly chop the avocado flesh
and place in a bowl. Mash lightly with
a fork and sprinkle with the lime or
lemon juice to prevent the avocado
discolouring.
2 Cut the tomato in half horizontally
and use a teaspoon to scoop out the
seeds. Finely dice the flesh and add to
the avocado.
3 Stir in the chilli, onion, coriander,
sour cream and Tabasco or habanero
sauce. Season with freshly cracked
black pepper.
4 Serve immediately or cover the
surface with plastic wrap and
refrigerate for 1–2 hours. If
refrigerated, allow to come to room
temperature before serving.

NUTRITION PER SERVE
Protein 3 g; Fat 30 g; Carbohydrate 2 g;
Dietary Fibre 3 g; Cholesterol 9 mg;
1200 kJ (290 cal)

HINT: You will need 1–2 limes to
produce 1 tablespoon of juice,
depending on the lime. A heavier lime
will probably be more juicy. To get
more juice from a citrus fruit, prick it
all over with a fork and then heat on
High (100%) in the microwave for
1 minute. Don't forget to prick it or the
fruit may burst.

Use disposable gloves when chopping chilli to avoid skin irritation.

Remove the avocado stone by chopping into it with a sharp knife and lifting up.

Cut the tomato in half horizontally and scoop out the seeds with a teaspoon.

You will only need a couple of drops of Tabasco or habanero—they are very hot.

PRAWN, CORN AND SWEET CHILLI DIP

Preparation time: 1 hour + 2 hours refrigeration
Total cooking time: 5 minutes
Serves 8

1 kg (2 lb) cooked prawns
juice and grated rind of 3 limes
100 g (3½ oz) frozen corn kernels
250 g (8 oz) soft cream cheese
¼ cup (15 g/½ oz) finely chopped chives
1 tablespoon sweet chilli sauce
4 cooked king prawns, to garnish

1 Peel, devein and rinse the prawns; pat them dry and place in a bowl. Add the lime juice to the prawns, cover and refrigerate for 10 minutes.
2 Cook the frozen corn kernels in boiling water for 2–3 minutes, or until tender. Drain and plunge the kernels into iced water to prevent further cooking, then drain and pat dry with paper towel.
3 Place the prawns and lime juice in a food processor and process in short bursts for 2–3 seconds until the prawns are chopped into small pieces but not minced.
4 Transfer the chopped prawns to a bowl and mix in the cream cheese, corn kernels, lime rind and chives. Add the chilli sauce and mix well. Cover the dip with plastic wrap and refrigerate for at least 2 hours. Just before serving, peel and devein the king prawns, leaving the tails intact. Transfer the dip to a serving bowl and garnish with the peeled prawns. Delicious served with a bowl of barbecued king prawns, for dipping.

NUTRITION PER SERVE
Protein 35 g; Fat 12 g; Carbohydrate 5 g; Dietary Fibre 0 g; Cholesterol 280 mg; 1090 kJ (260 cal)

Finely grate the rind and squeeze the juice from the fresh limes.

Cook the corn kernels briefly, then plunge into iced water, drain and pat dry.

Process the marinated prawns in short bursts until roughly chopped.

Mix together all the ingredients and leave in the fridge for 2 hours before serving.

TARAMASALATA

Preparation time: 10 minutes +
10 minutes soaking
Total cooking time: Nil
Serves 10

5 slices white bread, crusts removed
1/3 cup (80 ml/2³/4 fl oz) milk
100 g (3¹/2 oz) can tarama (mullet roe)
1 egg yolk

1/2 small onion, grated
1 clove garlic, crushed
2 tablespoons lemon juice
1/3 cup (80 ml/2³/4 fl oz) olive oil
pinch ground white pepper

1 Soak the bread in the milk for
10 minutes. Press in a strainer to
extract any excess milk, then place in a
food processor with the tarama, egg
yolk, onion and garlic. Process for
30 seconds, or until smooth, then add

1 tablespoon lemon juice.
2 With the motor running, slowly
pour in the olive oil. The mixture
should be smooth and of a dipping
consistency. Add the remaining lemon
juice and a pinch of white pepper. If
too salty, add another piece of bread.

NUTRITION PER SERVE
Protein 3.8 g; Fat 10.4 g; Carbohydrate 8.3 g;
Dietary Fibre 0.6 g; Cholesterol 57 mg;
596 kJ (142 cal)

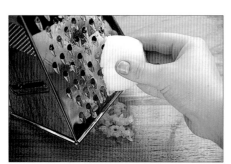

Using a cheese grater, grate half a small onion so
that the pieces are small and even.

Press the soaked bread pieces in a strainer to
extract any excess milk.

Process the bread, tarama, egg yolk, onion and
garlic until smooth.

GARLIC DIP WITH CRUDITES

Preparation time: 15 minutes
Total cooking time: 15 minutes
Serves 4

4 cloves garlic, crushed
2 egg yolks
300 ml (10 fl oz) light olive or
    vegetable oil
1 tablespoon lemon juice
pinch ground white pepper
12 asparagus spears, trimmed
26 radishes, trimmed
1/2 telegraph cucumber, seeded,
    halved and cut into batons
1 head witlof, leaves separated

1 Place the garlic, egg yolks and a pinch of salt in the bowl of a food processor. Process for 10 seconds.
2 With the motor running, add the oil in a thin, slow stream. The mixture will start to thicken. When this happens you can add the oil a little faster. Process until all the oil is incorporated and the mayonnaise is thick and creamy. Transfer to a bowl and stir in the lemon juice and a pinch of pepper.
3 Bring a saucepan of water to the boil, add the asparagus and cook for 1 minute. Remove and plunge into a bowl of iced water. Arrange the asparagus, radish, cucumber and witlof on a platter and place the garlic dip in a bowl on the platter.

NUTRITION PER SERVE
Protein 3 g; Fat 74 g; Carbohydrate 1.5 g;
Dietary Fibre 2 g; Cholesterol 90 mg;
28807 kJ (670 cal)

NOTE: Should the mayonnaise start to curdle as the oil is added, beat in

1–2 teaspoons boiling water. If this fails, put another egg yolk in a clean bowl and very slowly whisk in the curdled mixture, one drop at a time, then continue as above.

HINT: For best results when making mayonnaise, make sure all the ingredients are at room temperature before you start.

Seed the cucumbers, then halve widthways and cut into batons.

Stir the lemon juice into the thick and creamy mayonnaise.

Refresh the asparagus spears by plunging into a bowl of iced water.

WHITE BEAN, CHICKPEA AND HERB DIP

Preparation time: 20 minutes +
  overnight soaking
Total cooking time: 1 hour
Serves 12

180 g (6 oz) dried cannellini beans
100 g (3¹/₂ oz) dried chickpeas
3 slices white bread
3 tablespoons milk
2 spring onions, finely chopped
4 tablespoons thick plain yoghurt

1 tablespoon lemon juice
2 teaspoons finely grated lemon rind
1 tablespoon chopped fresh parsley
2 teaspoons chopped fresh oregano
2 tablespoons olive oil

1 Soak the beans and chickpeas in cold water overnight. Rinse well and transfer to a pan. Cover with cold water and bring to the boil. Reduce the heat and simmer for 1 hour, or until very tender, adding more water if needed. Skim any froth from the surface. Drain well, cool and mash.
2 Remove the crusts from the bread,

place in a bowl and drizzle with the milk. Leave for 2 minutes, then mash with your fingertips until very soft. Mix together with the beans.
3 Add the spring onion, yoghurt, lemon juice, rind, fresh herbs and oil and season well. Mix together well and serve at room temperature.

NUTRITION PER SERVE
Protein 4 g; Fat 4 g; Carbohydrate 12 g;
Dietary Fibre 2 g; Cholesterol 2 mg;
416 kJ (99 cal)

Simmer the beans and chickpeas for an hour, skimming froth from the surface.

Soak the bread in the milk for 2 minutes, then mash up with your fingertips.

Add the spring onion, yoghurt, herbs, oil, lemon juice, rind and seasoning.

TZATZIKI

Preparation time: 10 minutes +
    15 minutes standing
Total cooking time: Nil
Serves 12

2 Lebanese cucumbers
400 g (13 oz) Greek-style plain
    yoghurt
4 cloves garlic, crushed
3 tablespoons finely chopped fresh
    mint, plus extra to garnish
1 tablespoon lemon juice

1 Cut the cucumbers in half lengthways, scoop out the seeds and discard. Leave the skin on and coarsely grate the cucumber into a small colander. Sprinkle with salt and leave over a large bowl for 15 minutes to drain off any bitter juices.
2 Meanwhile, stir together the yoghurt, crushed garlic, mint and lemon juice.
3 Rinse the cucumber under cold water then, taking small handfuls, squeeze out any excess moisture. Combine the grated cucumber with the yoghurt mixture and season well.

Serve immediately with pitta or pide bread or as a sauce with chicken.

NUTRITION PER SERVE
Protein 1.6 g; Fat 1.2 g; Carbohydrate 2.3 g; Dietary Fibre 0.5 g; Cholesterol 5.3 mg; 119 kJ (28 cal)

STORAGE: Will keep in an airtight container in the fridge for 2–3 days.

Cut the cucumbers in half and scoop out the seeds with a teaspoon.

Mix the yoghurt, crushed garlic, mint and lemon juice together.

Squeeze the grated cucumber to remove any excess moisture.

TAPENADE

Preparation time: 10 minutes
Total cooking time: Nil
Serves 10

400 g (13 oz) Kalamata olives, pitted
2 cloves garlic, crushed
2 anchovy fillets in oil, drained
2 tablespoons capers in brine, rinsed,
    squeezed dry
2 teaspoons chopped fresh thyme
2 teaspoons Dijon mustard
1 tablespoon lemon juice
3 tablespoons olive oil
1 tablespoon brandy, optional

1 Place the kalamata olives, crushed garlic, anchovies, capers, chopped thyme, Dijon mustard, lemon juice, olive oil and brandy in a food processor and process until smooth. Season with salt and black pepper. Spoon into a clean, warm jar, cover with a layer of olive oil, seal and refrigerate for up to 1 week. Serve as a dip with bruschetta and olives.

NUTRITION PER SERVE
Protein 1.3 g; Fat 2.4 g; Carbohydrate 2 g;
Dietary Fibre 8.5 g; Cholesterol 0.6 mg;
376 kJ (90 cal)

NOTE: When refrigerated, the olive oil may solidify, turning it opaque white. This is a property of olive oil and will not affect the flavour of the dish. Simply bring to room temperature before serving and the olive oil will return to a liquid state. The word 'tapenade' comes from the French word tapéno, meaning capers. Tapenade is the famous olive, anchovy and caper spread from Provence.

HINT: To make sure your storage jar is very clean, preheat the oven to very slow 120°C (250°F/Gas 1/2). Wash the jar and lid thoroughly in hot soapy water (or preferably in a dishwasher) and rinse well with hot water. Put the jar on a baking tray and place in the oven for 20 minutes, or until fully dry and you are ready to use it. Do not dry the jar or lid with a tea towel.

Use an olive pitter or small sharp knife to remove the stones from the olives.

Process all the ingredients in a food processor until smooth.

PESTO

Preparation time: 10 minutes
Total cooking time: 5 minutes
Serves 6

50 g (1³/₄ oz) pine nuts
50 g (1³/₄ oz) small fresh basil leaves
2 cloves garlic, crushed
¹/₂ teaspoon sea salt

¹/₂ cup (125 ml/4 fl oz) olive oil
30 g (1 oz) Parmesan, finely grated
20 g (³/₄ oz) pecorino cheese, finely grated

1 Preheat the oven to 180°C (350°F/Gas 4). Spread the pine nuts on a baking tray and bake for 2 minutes, or until lightly golden. Cool.
2 Chop the pine nuts, basil, garlic, salt and oil in a food processor until

smooth. Transfer to a bowl and stir in the cheeses. Serve as a dip with bread, crackers or crudités, or as a sauce for barbecued meat, chicken or seafood.

NUTRITION PER SERVE
Protein 4 g; Fat 28 g; Carbohydrate 0.5 g; Dietary Fibre 0.6 g; Cholesterol 7.6 mg; 1118 kJ (267 cal)

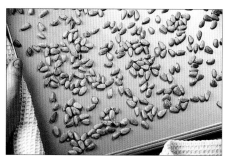

Spread the pine nuts on a baking tray and toast until lightly golden.

Process the pine nuts, basil, garlic, sea salt and oil until smooth.

Transfer to a bowl and stir the Parmesan and pecorino into the basil mixture.

ARTICHOKE DIP

Preparation time: 10 minutes
Total cooking time: 15 minutes
Serves 8

2 x 400 g (13 oz) cans artichoke
    hearts, drained
1 cup (250 g/8 oz) mayonnaise
$^3/_4$ cup (75 g/2$^1/_2$ oz) grated
    Parmesan
2 teaspoons onion flakes
2 tablespoons grated Parmesan, extra
paprika, to sprinkle

1 Preheat the oven to 180°C (350°F/
Gas 4). Gently squeeze the artichokes
to remove any remaining liquid. Chop
and place in a bowl. Stir through the
mayonnaise, Parmesan and the
onion flakes.
2 Spread into a 1-litre capacity
shallow ovenproof dish. Sprinkle with
the extra Parmesan and a little paprika.
Bake for 15 minutes, or until heated
through and lightly browned on top.
Serve with crusty bread.

NUTRITION PER SERVE
Protein 7 g; Fat 14 g; Carbohydrate 8 g;
Dietary Fibre 3 g; Cholesterol 21 mg;
773 kJ (185 cal)

Gently squeeze the artichoke hearts to remove
any remaining liquid.

Mix the chopped artichoke with the mayonnaise,
Parmesan and onion flakes.

Spread the dip in a shallow dish and sprinkle
with Parmesan and paprika.

BABA GHANNOUJ

Preparation time: 20 minutes +
   30 minutes cooling
Total cooking time: 50 minutes
Serves 10

2 eggplants
3 cloves garlic, crushed
1/2 teaspoon ground cumin
1/3 cup (80 ml/2³/4 fl oz) lemon juice
2 tablespoons tahini
pinch cayenne pepper
1¹/2 tablespoons olive oil
1 tablespoon finely chopped
   fresh flat-leaf parsley
black olives, to garnish

1 Preheat the oven to 200°C (400°F/Gas 6). Pierce the eggplants several times with a fork, then cook over an open flame for about 5 minutes, or until the skin is black and blistering, then place in a roasting tin and bake for 40–45 minutes, or until the eggplants are very soft and wrinkled. Place in a colander over a bowl to drain off any bitter juices and leave to stand for 30 minutes, or until cool.
2 Carefully peel the skin from the eggplant, chop the flesh and place in a food processor with the garlic, cumin, lemon, tahini, cayenne and olive oil. Process until smooth and creamy. Alternatively, use a potato masher or fork. Season with salt and stir in the parsley. Spread onto a flat bowl or plate and garnish with the olives. Serve with flatbread or pide.

NUTRITION PER SERVE
Protein 1.8 g; Fat 5 g; Carbohydrate 3 g; Dietary Fibre 3 g; Cholesterol 0 mg; 269 kJ (64 cal)

NOTE: If you prefer, you can simply roast the eggplant in a roasting tin in a 200°C (400°F/Gas 6) oven for 1 hour, or until very soft and wrinkled. Eggplants are also known as aubergines. The name baba ghannouj can be roughly translated as 'poor man's caviar'.

Carefully peel the black and blistered skin away from the baked eggplant.

Process the eggplant, garlic, cumin, lemon, tahini, cayenne and olive oil.

CREAMY BLUE CHEESE DIP WITH PEARS

Preparation time: 25 minutes +
  20 minutes refrigeration
Total cooking time: Nil
Serves 4

150 g (5 oz) creamy blue cheese (see
  NOTE)
200 ml (6¹/₂ fl oz) thick cream
3 tablespoons thick plain yoghurt
2 tablespoons finely chopped chives
4 ripe pears, cored and cut into
  wedges

1 Mash the blue cheese with a fork to soften it slightly. Add the cream and yoghurt and season with black pepper, mixing until smooth and well blended—do not overmix or it will become grainy and curdled. Spoon into a serving bowl, cover and refrigerate for 20 minutes, or until firm.
2 Scatter the chives over the dip. Serve with the pear wedges.

NUTRITION PER SERVE
Protein 10 g; Fat 30 g; Carbohydrate 45 g;
Dietary Fibre 8 g; Cholesterol 100 mg;
2042 kJ (488 cal)

NOTE: A creamy cheese such as Dolcelatte, Gorgonzola or King Island Blue will give the best result.

Use ripe pears for dipping. Any variety will suit—we used beurre bosc.

Mash the blue cheese with a fork to soften it slightly.

Add the cream and yoghurt and season to taste with ground black pepper.

CHILLI CRAB AND TOMATO DIP

Preparation time: 25 minutes
Total cooking time: Nil
Serves 6

2 x 170 g (5^1/$_2$ oz) cans crab meat, drained
200 g (6^1/$_2$ oz) neufchatel cheese (see NOTE)
2 tablespoons chilli sauce

2 teaspoons tomato paste
1 teaspoon grated lemon rind
2 teaspoons lemon juice
1 small onion, finely grated
3 spring onions, finely sliced
1 tomato, seeded and finely chopped

1 Squeeze any remaining liquid from the crab meat. Beat the neufchatel cheese until smooth, then add the crab meat, chilli sauce, tomato paste, lemon rind, lemon juice and onion. Season well with salt and pepper. Mix well and spoon into a serving bowl.

2 Scatter the spring onion and chopped tomato over the top and chill before serving.

NUTRITION PER SERVE
Protein 11 g; Fat 11 g; Carbohydrate 6 g;
Dietary Fibre 1 g; Cholesterol 79 mg;
682 kJ (163 cal)

NOTE: Neufchatel is a smooth, mild, good-quality cream cheese available from delicatessens.

Squeeze any remaining liquid from the crab or the dip will be watery.

Beat the neufchatel cheese with a wooden spoon until it is smooth.

Add the crab meat, chilli sauce, tomato paste, lemon rind and juice, and onion.

Quick Dips

Dips are an excellent way to keep friends happy while the barbecue is heating up or cooking larger pieces of meat. These recipes make great use of pantry staples and fridge leftovers, in a truly imaginative manner.

SWEET CHILLI AND SOUR CREAM DIP

Mix 250 g (8 oz) sour cream with 3 tablespoons sweet chilli sauce. Swirl another teaspoon of sweet chilli sauce on top to decorate. Serve with herb and garlic pitta chips, goujons or sweet potato chips. Serves 4

RED PESTO DIP

Mix together 250 g (8 oz) soft cream cheese, 2 tablespoons ready-made red pesto, 1 teaspoon lemon juice and 2 teaspoons chopped fresh flat-leaf parsley. Season with black pepper and serve with herb and garlic pitta chips or savoury biscuits. Serves 4

MUSTARD DIP

Mix together $^1/_2$ cup (125 g/4 oz) mayonnaise, $^1/_2$ cup (125 g/4 oz) plain yoghurt, 2 teaspoons Dijon mustard and 3 tablespoons wholegrain mustard. Season well and serve with potato wedges or strips of barbecued chicken. Serves 4

HUMMUS AND ORANGE DIP

Mix together 250 g (8 oz) hummus, 2 tablespoons orange juice, $^1/_4$ teaspoon ground cumin and 2 teaspoons chopped fresh coriander. Season with pepper and cover with plastic wrap. Refrigerate for 2–3 hours. Serve with sweet potato chips, crisp lavash bread or pitta chips. Serves 4

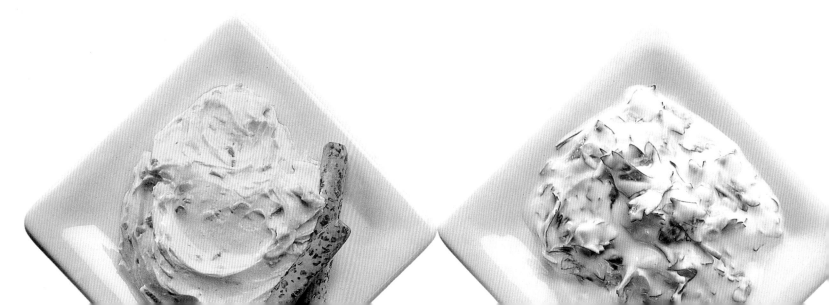

ROSEMARY AND CANNELLINI BEAN DIP

Mix a 400 g (13 oz) can rinsed and drained cannellini beans in a food processor with 1 crushed clove garlic, 2 teaspoons chopped fresh rosemary and 1 tablespoon lemon juice for 1 minute. With the motor running, add 2 tablespoons extra virgin olive oil in a thin stream. Season and serve with crisp lavash bread or pitta chips. Serves 4

FRENCH ONION DIP

Use a fork to blend 250 g (8 oz) sour cream with a 30 g (1 oz) packet French onion soup mix. Cover and refrigerate for 1–2 hours. Serve with potato wedges, sweet potato chips or savoury biscuits. Serves 4

CREAMY TOMATO TUNA DIP

Mix 250 g (8 oz) soft cream cheese with a 100 g (3¹/₂ oz) can tuna with tomato and onion (including the oil). Add black pepper, cover and refrigerate for 1–2 hours. Serve with sweet chilli chips, lavash bread or potato wedges. Serves 4

MIXED HERB DIP

Chop 15 g (¹/₂ oz) chives and mix with 1¹/₄ cups (315 g/ 10 oz) plain yoghurt. Add ¹/₄ cup (7 g/¹/₄ oz) fresh marjoram leaves, ¹/₄ cup (5 g/¹/₄ oz) fresh mint leaves and ¹/₂ cup (10 g/¹/₄ oz) fresh flat-leaf parsley leaves. Season with black pepper. Serve with lavash bread, pitta or sweet chilli chips. Can also be made with thyme, oregano, garlic chives or dill. Serves 6

Top, from left: Mustard Dip; Sweet Chilli and Sour Cream Dip; Creamy Tomato Tuna Dip; Rosemary and Cannellini Bean Dip
Bottom, from left: French Onion Dip; Mixed Herb Dip; Red Pesto Dip; Hummus and Orange Dip

Sauces & Salsas

SKORDALIA

Preparation time: 15 minutes
Total cooking time: 10 minutes
Serves 12

500 g (1 lb) floury potatoes (see NOTE)
5 cloves garlic, crushed
ground white pepper
3/4 cup (185 ml/6 fl oz) olive oil
2 tablespoons white vinegar

1 Peel the potatoes and cut into small cubes. Cook in boiling water for 10 minutes, or until very soft.
2 Drain the potato and mash until smooth. Stir in the garlic, 1 teaspoon salt and a pinch of white pepper. Gradually pour in the olive oil, mixing well with a wooden spoon. Add the vinegar and season with additional salt and ground white pepper, if needed. Serve as a sauce with barbecued meat, seafood or chicken or as a dip with crusty bread or crackers.

NUTRITION PER SERVE
Protein 1 g; Fat 14.8 g; Carbohydrate 5.6 g; Dietary Fibre 0.9 g; Cholesterol 0 mg; 662 kJ (158 cal)

NOTE: Use King Edward, russet or pontiac potatoes. Do not make skordalia with a food processor—the processing will turn the potato into a gluey mess.

STORAGE: Skordalia will keep in an airtight container for up to 2–3 days in the fridge. The potato will absorb the salt so check the seasoning before serving.

Drain the potato and then mash with a potato masher until smooth.

Gradually add the oil to the potato mixture, mixing with a wooden spoon.

CHARGRILLED VEGETABLE SALSA

Preparation time: 30 minutes +
2 hours marinating
Total cooking time: 30 minutes
Serves 4

2 Roma tomatoes
1 small red capsicum
1 small green capsicum
2 small zucchini
2 slender eggplants
3 tablespoons olive oil
1 tablespoon chopped fresh flat-leaf
parsley
2 teaspoons chopped fresh marjoram
2 teaspoons chopped fresh oregano
2 tablespoons balsamic vinegar
1 tablespoon chopped fresh flat-leaf
parsley, extra
2 teaspoons chopped fresh marjoram,
extra

1 Halve the tomatoes, capsicums,
zucchini and eggplants lengthways.
Place in a large shallow dish and pour
over the combined olive oil and herbs.
Toss well and leave to marinate for at
least 2 hours or up to a day.
2 Cook the vegetables on a hot,
lightly oiled barbecue flatplate until
soft and a little blackened. Place the
capsicum in a plastic bag for a few
minutes, then peel away the skin. Cut
all the vegetables into small pieces and
mix with the vinegar and extra herbs.
Serve with barbecued meats.

NUTRITION PER SERVE
Protein 3 g; Fat 15 g; Carbohydrate 7 g;
Dietary Fibre 5 g; Cholesterol 0 mg;
733 kJ (175 cal)

Cut the tomatoes, capsicums, zucchini and
eggplants in half lengthways.

Barbecue the vegetables until they are soft and a
little blackened.

Cut the vegetables into small chunks and mix
with the herbs and vinegar.

BOCCONCINI, TOMATO AND SUN-DRIED CAPSICUM SALSA

Preparation time: 20 minutes
Total cooking time: Nil
Serves 6

180 g (6 oz) bocconcini, diced
200 g (6½ oz) tomatoes, diced
⅓ cup (50 g/1¾ oz) drained sun-
    dried capsicum in oil, chopped
1 spring onion, finely sliced

1 tablespoon extra virgin olive oil
2 teaspoons red wine vinegar
1 tablespoon shredded fresh basil
    leaves
1 tablespoon chopped fresh flat-leaf
    parsley

1 Mix together the bocconcini, tomato, sun-dried capsicum and spring onion in a large bowl.
2 Whisk together the oil and vinegar until thoroughly blended. Stir through the basil and parsley.
3 Toss the dressing through the bocconcini and tomato mixture and season well with salt and pepper. Serve at room temperature with barbecued steak or tuna.

NUTRITION PER SERVE
Protein 8 g; Fat 13 g; Carbohydrate 1 g;
Dietary Fibre 1 g; Cholesterol 19 mg;
644 kJ (154 cal)

NOTE: Bocconcini are small, fresh mozzarella cheeses.

Cut the bocconcini cheese and tomatoes into small dice.

Mix together the bocconcini, tomato, capsicum and spring onion.

Stir the basil and flat-leaf parsley into the vinaigrette dressing.

SMOKY TOMATO SAUCE

Preparation time: 15 minutes
Total cooking time: 50 minutes
Makes about 1 litre

SMOKING MIX
2 tablespoons Chinese or
   Ceylon tea leaves
2 star anise, crushed
1 strip orange rind
$1/2$ teaspoon five-spice powder
6 juniper berries, crushed

2 onions, quartered
2 red capsicums, cut into
   large pieces
2 red chillies, cut in half
3 tablespoons oil
3 cloves garlic, chopped
500 g (1 lb) tomatoes, chopped
2 tablespoons Worcestershire sauce
$1/2$ cup (125 ml/4 fl oz) barbecue
   sauce
2 tablespoons tamarind concentrate
1 tablespoon white vinegar
1 tablespoon soft brown sugar

1 Combine all the ingredients for the smoking mix in a small bowl. Pour the mix into the centre of a sheet of foil and fold the edges to prevent the mix from spreading. (This will form an open container to allow the mix to smoke.) Place the foil container on the bottom of a dry wok or wide frying pan. Place an open rack or steamer in the wok or frying pan, making sure it is elevated over the mix.
2 Place the onion, capsicum and chilli onto the rack and cover with a lid, or alternatively cover the entire wok or frying pan tightly with foil to prevent the smoke from escaping.

3 Smoke over medium heat for 10–15 minutes, or until the vegetables are tender. If you prefer a very smoky sauce cook the vegetables for longer, if you prefer it less so, reduce the time. Remove the container with the smoking mix.
4 Dice the onion, capsicum and chilli quite finely. Heat the oil in the wok and add the garlic and cooked vegetables. Fry over medium heat for 3 minutes, then add the tomato and cook until pulpy. Add the sauces, tamarind, vinegar and sugar. Simmer,

stirring occasionally, for 20–25 minutes, or until the sauce is quite thick. Serve with barbecued meat or seafood. Store in the refrigerator.

NUTRITION PER TABLESPOON
Protein 0.5 g; Fat 1.5 g; Carbohydrate 2.5 g; Dietary Fibre 0.5 g; Cholesterol 0 mg; 90 kJ (20 cal)

NOTE: For a smoother sauce, mix in a food processor for about 30 seconds.

Fold the edges of the foil to form an open container that allows the mix to smoke.

Place the open rack in the wok or frying pan then put on the onion, capsicum and chilli.

Add the tamarind concentrate to the sauce and simmer, stirring occasionally.

RED CAPSICUM RELISH

Preparation time: 40 minutes +
  a few weeks standing
Total cooking time: 1 hour 45 minutes
Fills three 250 ml (8 fl oz) jars

1 kg (2 lb) red capsicums
1 teaspoon black peppercorns
2 teaspoons black mustard seeds
2 red onions, thinly sliced
4 cloves garlic, chopped
1¹/₂ cups (375 ml/12 fl oz) red wine
  vinegar
2 apples, peeled, cored and grated
1 teaspoon grated fresh ginger
1 cup (230 g/7¹/₂ oz) soft brown sugar

1 Remove the capsicum seeds and membrane and thinly slice. Tie the peppercorns in a piece of muslin and secure with string. Combine the capsicum, peppercorns, mustard seeds, onion, garlic, vinegar, apple and ginger in a large pan. Simmer for 30 minutes until the capsicum is soft.
2 Add the sugar and stir over low heat until completely dissolved. Simmer, stirring occasionally, for 1¹/₄ hours, or until the relish has reduced and thickened. Remove the muslin bag.
3 Rinse the jars with boiling water then dry in a warm oven. Spoon the relish into the hot jars and seal. Turn the jars upside down for 2 minutes, then turn them the other way up and leave to cool. Label and date. Leave for a few weeks before using. Will keep in a cool dark place for 1 year. Refrigerate after opening.

NUTRITION PER TABLESPOON
Protein 0.5 g; Fat 0 g; Carbohydrate 85 g;
Dietary Fibre 0.5 g; Cholesterol 0 mg;
160 kJ (40 cal)

Put the peppercorns in the centre of a piece of muslin and tie with string.

Add the brown sugar to the capsicum mixture and stir over heat until dissolved.

Spoon the thickened relish into the sterilised jars and seal.

SATAY SAUCE

Preparation time: 10 minutes
Total cooking time: 15 minutes
Serves 8

1 tablespoon oil
1 large onion, finely chopped
2 cloves garlic, finely chopped
2 red chillies, finely chopped
1 teaspoon shrimp paste
1 cup (250 g/8 oz) peanut butter
1 cup (250 ml/8 fl oz) coconut milk
2 teaspoons kecap manis or thick soy
    sauce
1 tablespoon tomato sauce

1 Heat the oil in a pan and cook the onion and garlic for 8 minutes over low heat, stirring regularly. Add the chilli and shrimp paste, cook for 1 minute and remove from the heat.
2 Add the peanut butter, return to the heat and stir in the coconut milk and 1 cup (250 ml/8 fl oz) water. Bring to the boil over low heat, stirring so that it does not stick. Add the kecap manis and tomato sauce and simmer for 1 minute. Cool and serve with skewered meats or seafood.

NUTRITION PER SERVE
Protein 9 g; Fat 25 g; Carbohydrate 6 g;
Dietary Fibre 4 g; Cholesterol 0 mg;
1148 kJ (274 cal)

Chop the chillies very finely. If you prefer a milder taste, remove the seeds first.

Cook the onion and garlic over low heat, then add the chilli and shrimp paste.

Bring to the boil, stirring, then add the kecap manis and tomato sauce.

BARBECUE SAUCE

Preparation time: 15 minutes
Total cooking time: 10 minutes
Serves 4

2 teaspoons oil
1 small onion, finely chopped
1 tablespoon malt vinegar

1 tablespoon soft brown sugar
1/3 cup (80 ml/2¾ fl oz) tomato sauce
1 tablespoon Worcestershire sauce

1 Heat the oil in a small pan and cook the onion over low heat for 3 minutes, or until soft, stirring occasionally.
2 Add the remaining ingredients and bring to the boil. Reduce the heat and simmer for 3 minutes, stirring occasionally. Serve warm or at room temperature. Can be kept, covered and refrigerated, for up to a week. Serve with burgers or barbecued meat.

NUTRITION PER SERVE
Protein 1 g; Fat 1 g; Carbohydrate 17 g;
Dietary Fibre 1 g; Cholesterol 0 mg;
648 kJ (155 cal)

Chop the onion very finely so the sauce has a smooth texture.

Cook the onion over low heat, stirring occasionally, until soft.

Add the remaining ingredients to the pan and bring to the boil.

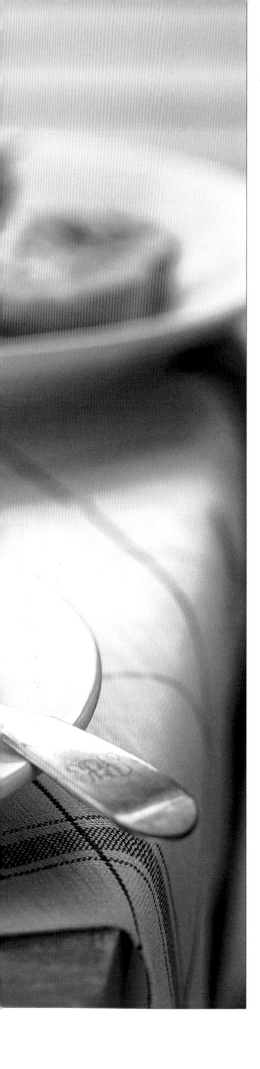

Desserts

PEACHES POACHED IN WINE

Preparation time: 20 minutes
Total cooking time: 20 minutes
Serves 4

4 just-ripe yellow-fleshed slipstone
    peaches (see NOTE)
2 cups (500 ml/16 fl oz) sweet white
    wine such as Sauternes
3 tablespoons orange liqueur
1 cup (250 g/8 oz) sugar
1 cinnamon stick
1 vanilla bean, split
8 fresh mint leaves
mascarpone or crème fraîche,
    to serve

1 Cut a small cross in the base of each peach. Immerse the peaches in boiling water for 30 seconds, then drain and cool slightly. Peel off the skin, cut in half and carefully remove the stones.
2 Place the wine, liqueur, sugar, cinnamon stick and vanilla bean in a deep-sided frying pan large enough to hold the peach halves in a single layer. Heat the mixture, stirring, until the sugar dissolves. Bring to the boil, then reduce the heat and simmer for

5 minutes. Add the peaches to the pan and simmer for 4 minutes, turning them over halfway through. Remove with a slotted spoon and leave to cool. Continue to simmer the syrup for 6–8 minutes, or until thick. Strain and set aside.
3 Arrange the peaches on a serving platter, cut-side-up. Spoon the syrup over the top and garnish each half with a mint leaf. Serve the peaches warm or chilled, with a dollop of mascarpone or crème fraîche.

NUTRITION PER SERVE
Protein 3 g; Fat 6.5 g; Carbohydrate 74 g;
Dietary Fibre 2 g; Cholesterol 19 mg;
1900 kJ (455 cal)

NOTE: There are two types of peach, the slipstone and the clingstone. As the names imply, clingstone indicates that the flesh will cling to the stone whereas the stones in slipstone or freestone peaches are easily removed without breaking up the flesh. Each has a variety with either yellow or white flesh, and all these peaches are equally delicious.

Peel the skin away from the cross cut in the base of the peaches.

Simmer the wine, liqueur, sugar, cinnamon and vanilla bean.

FIGS IN HONEY SYRUP

Preparation time: 15 minutes
Total cooking time: 1 hour
Serves 4

100 g (3¹/₂ oz) blanched whole
 almonds
12–16 whole fresh figs (see NOTE)
¹/₂ cup (125 g/4 oz) sugar
¹/₃ cup (115 g/4 oz) honey
2 tablespoons lemon juice
5 cm (2 inch) sliver of lemon rind
1 cinnamon stick
1 cup (250 g/8 oz) Greek-style plain
 yoghurt

1 Preheat the oven to 180°C (350°F/
Gas 4). Place the almonds on a baking
tray and bake for 5 minutes, or until
golden brown. Cool. Cut the tops off
the figs and make a small incision
down the top of each one. Push an
almond into the base of each fig.
Roughly chop the remaining almonds.
2 Place 3 cups (750 ml/24 fl oz) water
in a large saucepan, add the sugar and
stir over medium heat until the sugar
dissolves. Increase the heat and bring
to the boil. Stir in the honey, juice, rind
and cinnamon stick. Reduce the heat,
add the figs and cook for 30 minutes.
Remove with a slotted spoon.
3 Boil the liquid over high heat for
15–20 minutes, or until thick and
syrupy. Remove the cinnamon and
rind. Cool the syrup slightly and pour
over the figs. Sprinkle with the
remaining almonds. Serve warm or
cold with yoghurt.

NUTRITION PER SERVE
Protein 11 g; Fat 17 g; Carbohydrate 74 g;
Dietary Fibre 7 g; Cholesterol 10 mg;
2017 kJ (482 cal)

NOTE: You can also use 500 g dried
whole figs. Cover with 3 cups (750 ml)
cold water and soak for 8 hours.
Drain, reserving the liquid. Push a
blanched almond into the bottom of
each fig. Place the liquid in a large
saucepan, add the sugar and bring to
the boil, stirring as the sugar dissolves.
Add the honey, lemon juice, lemon
rind and cinnamon stick, and continue
the recipe as above.

Make a small crossways incision in the top of
each fig.

Push a blanched almond into the base of
each fig.

Using a slotted spoon, remove the figs from the
pan of syrup.

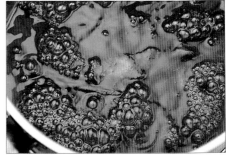
Continue to boil the liquid until it becomes thick
and syrupy.

LEMON GRANITA

Preparation time: 15 minutes + 2 hours
  freezing
Total cooking time: 5 minutes
Serves 6

1¼ cups (315 ml/10 fl oz) lemon juice
1 tablespoon lemon zest
200 g (6½ oz) caster sugar

1 Place the lemon juice, lemon zest and caster sugar in a small saucepan and stir over low heat for 5 minutes, or until the sugar is dissolved. Remove from the heat and leave to cool.
2 Add 2 cups (500 ml/16 fl oz) water to the juice mixture and mix together well. Pour the mixture into a shallow 30 x 20 cm (12 x 8 inch) metal container and place in the freezer until the mixture is beginning to freeze around the edges. Scrape the frozen sections back into the mixture with a fork. Repeat every 30 minutes until the mixture has even-size ice crystals. Beat the mixture with a fork just before serving. To serve, spoon the lemon granita into six chilled glasses.

NUTRITION PER SERVE
Protein 0 g; Fat 0 g; Carbohydrate 35 g;
Dietary Fibre 0 g; Cholesterol 0 mg;
592 kJ (140 cal)

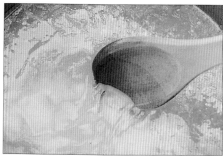
Stir the juice, zest and sugar over low heat until the sugar has dissolved.

Scrape the frozen edges of the mixture back into the centre.

Beat the granita mixture with a fork just prior to serving to break up the crystals.

RED FRUIT SALAD WITH BERRIES

Preparation time: 5 minutes +
  30 minutes cooling +
  1 hour 30 minutes refrigeration
Total cooking time: 5 minutes
Serves 6

SYRUP
1/4 cup (60 g/2 oz) caster sugar
1/2 cup (125 ml/4 fl oz) dry red wine
1 star anise
1 teaspoon finely chopped lemon rind

250 g (8 oz) strawberries, hulled and
    halved
150 g (5 oz) blueberries
150 g (5 oz) raspberries, mulberries or
    other red berries
250 g (8 oz) cherries
5 small red plums (about 250 g (8 oz)),
    stones removed and quartered
low-fat yoghurt, to serve

1 To make the syrup, place the sugar,
wine, star anise, lemon rind and
1/2 cup (125 ml/4 fl oz) water in a
small saucepan. Bring to the boil over
medium heat, stirring to dissolve the
sugar. Boil the syrup for 3 minutes,
then set aside to cool for 30 minutes.
When cool, strain the syrup.
2 Mix the fruit together in a large
bowl and pour on the red wine syrup.
Mix well to coat the fruit in the syrup
and refrigerate for 1 hour 30 minutes.
Serve the fruit dressed with a little
syrup and the yoghurt.

NUTRITION PER SERVE
Fat 0 g; Protein 2 g; Carbohydrate 24 g;
Dietary Fibre 5 g; Cholesterol 0 mg;
500 kJ (120 Cal)

Remove the stems to hull, then cut the
strawberries in half.

Boil the sugar, wine, star anise, lemon rind and
water for 3 minutes.

Mix together the strawberries, blueberries,
raspberries, cherries and plums.

STRAWBERRIES WITH BALSAMIC VINEGAR

Preparation time: 10 minutes +
  2 hours 30 minutes marinating
Total cooking time: Nil
Serves 4

750 g (1¹/₂ lb) small ripe strawberries
¹/₄ cup (60 g/2 oz) caster sugar
2 tablespoons balsamic vinegar
¹/₂ cup (125 g/4 oz) mascarpone

1 Wipe the strawberries with a clean damp cloth and carefully remove the green stalks. If the strawberries are large, cut each one in half.
2 Place all the strawberries in a large glass bowl, sprinkle the caster sugar evenly over the top and toss gently to coat. Set aside for 2 hours to macerate, then sprinkle the balsamic vinegar over the strawberries. Toss them again, then refrigerate for about 30 minutes.
3 Spoon the strawberries into four glasses, drizzle with the syrup and top with a dollop of mascarpone.

NUTRITION PER SERVE
Protein 6 g; Fat 11 g; Carbohydrate 20 g;
Dietary Fibre 4 g; Cholesterol 30 mg;
830 kJ (200 cal)

NOTE: If you leave the strawberries for more than 2 hours, it is best to refrigerate them.

Hull the strawberries after wiping clean with a damp cloth.

Sprinkle the caster sugar evenly over the strawberries and toss to coat.

Use good-quality balsamic vinegar to sprinkle over the strawberries.

MANDARIN ICE

Preparation time: 10 minutes +
  freezing
Total cooking time: 10 minutes
Serves 4–6

10 mandarins
1/2 cup (125 g/4 oz) caster sugar

1 Squeeze the mandarins to make
2 cups (500 ml/16 fl oz) juice.
2 Place the sugar and 1 cup (250 ml/
8 fl oz) water in a small saucepan. Stir
over low heat until the sugar has
dissolved, then simmer for 5 minutes.
Remove from the heat and leave to
cool slightly.
3 Stir the mandarin juice into the
sugar syrup, then pour into a shallow

metal tray. Freeze for 2 hours, or until
frozen. Transfer to a food processor
and blend until slushy. Return to the
freezer and repeat the process three
more times.

NUTRITION PER SERVE (6)
Fat 0 g; Protein 0.5 g; Carbohydrate 5 g;
Dietary Fibre 0 g; Cholesterol 0 mg;
105 kJ (25 Cal)

Squeeze the mandarins (as you would other
citrus fruits) to give 2 cups of juice.

Stir the mandarin juice into the saucepan of
sugar water.

Blend the frozen mixture in a food processor until
it is slushy.

BERRIES IN CHAMPAGNE JELLY

Preparation time: 10 minutes +
  overnight refrigeration
Total cooking time: 5 minutes
Serves 8

1 litre Champagne or sparkling white
  wine
1¹/₂ tablespoons gelatine
1 cup (250 g/8 oz) sugar
4 strips lemon rind
4 strips orange rind
250 g (8 oz) small hulled and halved
  strawberries
250 g (8 oz) blueberries

1 Pour 2 cups (500 ml) Champagne into a bowl and let the bubbles subside. Sprinkle the gelatine over the Champagne in an even layer. Leave until the gelatine is spongy—do not stir. Place the remaining Champagne in a large saucepan with the sugar, lemon and orange rind, and heat gently, stirring, for 3–4 minutes until all the sugar has dissolved.
2 Remove the pan from the heat, add the gelatine mixture and stir until thoroughly dissolved. Leave the jelly to cool completely, then remove the lemon and orange rind.
3 Divide the berries among eight ¹/₂ cup (125 ml/4 fl oz) wine glasses and gently pour the jelly over the top. Refrigerate for 6 hours or overnight, or until fully set. Remove from the fridge 15 minutes before serving.

NUTRITION PER SERVE
Protein 3 g; Fat 0 g; Carbohydrate 37 g;
Dietary Fibre 1 g; Cholesterol 0 mg;
965 kJ (230 cal)

Sprinkle the gelatine over the Champagne and then leave to go spongy.

Leave the jelly to cool completely before removing the lemon and orange rind.

Put the berries in the wine glasses and then pour jelly over the top.

BAKED CHEESECAKE

Preparation time: 30 minutes +
   20 minutes refrigeration + chilling
Total cooking time: 55 minutes
Serves 8

250 g (8 oz) butternut cookies
1 teaspoon mixed spice
100 g (3¹/₂ oz) butter, melted
500 g (1 lb) cream cheese,
   softened
²/₃ cup (160 g/5¹/₂ oz) caster sugar
4 eggs
1 teaspoon vanilla essence
1 tablespoon orange juice
1 tablespoon finely grated orange
   rind

TOPPING
1 cup (250 g/8 oz) sour cream
¹/₂ teaspoon vanilla essence
3 teaspoons orange juice
1 tablespoon caster sugar
freshly grated nutmeg

1 Lightly grease the base of a 20 cm (8 inch) springform tin. Finely crush the biscuits in a food processor for 30 seconds, or put them in a plastic bag and roll with a rolling pin. Transfer to a bowl and add the mixed spice and butter. Stir until all the crumbs are moistened, then spoon into the tin and press firmly into the base and side. Chill for 20 minutes, or until firm.
2 Preheat the oven to 180°C (350°F/ Gas 4). Beat the cream cheese until smooth. Add the sugar and beat until smooth. Add the eggs, one at a time, beating well after each addition. Mix in the vanilla, orange juice and rind.
3 Pour the mixture into the crumb case and bake for 45 minutes, or until just firm. To make the topping, combine the sour cream, vanilla, orange juice and sugar in a bowl. Spread over the hot cheesecake, sprinkle with nutmeg and return to the oven for 7 minutes. Cool, then refrigerate until firm.

NUTRITION PER SERVE
Protein 10 g; Fat 50 g; Carbohydrate 45 g; Dietary Fibre 0.5 g; Cholesterol 230 mg; 2885 kJ (690 cal)

Press the biscuit mixture into a springform tin with the back of a spoon.

Add the eggs one at a time to the cream cheese mixture and beat well.

When the filling is smooth, mix in the vanilla, orange juice and rind.

TIRAMISU

Preparation time: 30 minutes +
  2 hours refrigeration
Total cooking time: Nil
Serves 6

3 cups (750 ml/24 fl oz) strong black
  coffee, cooled
3 tablespoons Marsala or
  coffee-flavoured liqueur
2 eggs, separated
3 tablespoons caster sugar
250 g (8 oz) mascarpone
1 cup (250 ml/8 fl oz) cream, whipped
16 large sponge fingers
2 tablespoons dark cocoa powder

1 Mix together the coffee and Marsala in a bowl and set aside. Using electric beaters, beat the egg yolks and sugar in a bowl for 3 minutes, or until thick and pale. Add the mascarpone and mix until just combined. Transfer to a large bowl and fold in the cream.
2 Beat the egg whites until soft peaks form. Fold quickly and lightly into the cream mixture.
3 Dip half the biscuits into the coffee mixture, then drain off any excess coffee and arrange in the base of a 2.5 litre ceramic dish. Spread half the cream mixture over the biscuits.
4 Dip the remaining biscuits into the remaining coffee mixture and repeat the layers. Smooth the surface and dust liberally with the cocoa powder. Refrigerate for at least 2 hours, or until firm.

NUTRITION PER SERVE
Protein 7.5 g; Fat 24 g; Carbohydrate 28 g;
Dietary Fibre 1 g; Cholesterol 180 mg;
1545 kJ (370 cal)

STORAGE: Tiramisu is best made a day in advance to let the flavours develop. Refrigerate until ready to serve.

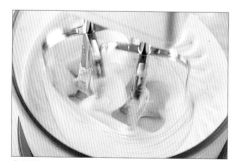
Add the mascarpone to the egg yolks and sugar and mix until just combined.

Fold the beaten egg whites gently into the cream mixture with a metal spoon.

Dip half the biscuits in the coffee mixture, drain, and arrange in the serving dish.

235

APPLE AND PEAR SORBET

Preparation time: 10 minutes +
  freezing
Total cooking time: 10 minutes
Serves 4–6

4 large green apples, peeled, cored
  and chopped
4 pears, peeled, cored and chopped
1 strip of lemon rind
1 cinnamon stick
1/4 cup (60 m/2 fl ozl) lemon juice
4 tablespoons caster sugar
2 tablespoons Calvados or poire
  William liqueur (optional)

1 Place the apple and pear in a large deep saucepan with the lemon rind, cinnamon stick and enough water to just cover the fruit. Cover and poach the fruit gently over medium–low heat for 6–8 minutes, or until tender. Remove the lemon rind and cinnamon stick. Place the fruit in a food processor and blend with the lemon juice until smooth.
2 Place the sugar in a saucepan with 80 ml (2^3/4 fl oz) water, bring to the boil and simmer for 1 minute. Add the fruit purée and the liqueur and combine well.
3 Pour into a shallow metal tray and freeze for 2 hours, or until the mixture is frozen around the edges. Transfer to a food processor or bowl and blend or beat until smooth. Pour back into the tray and return to the freezer. Repeat this process three times. For the final freezing, place in an airtight container—cover the surface with a piece of greaseproof paper and cover with a lid. Serve in small glasses or bowls.

NUTRITION PER SERVE (6)
Fat 0.5 g; Protein 1 g; Carbohydrate 42 g;
Dietary Fibre 4.5 g; Cholesterol 0 mg;
730 kJ (175 Cal)

HINT: Pour an extra nip of Calvados over the sorbet to serve.

Check if the fruit is tender by poking with the tip of a sharp knife.

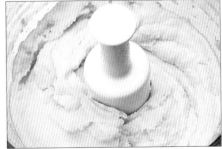

Blend the partially frozen mixture in a food processor until smooth.

STRAWBERRY TRIFLE

Preparation time: 20 minutes +
  4 hours refrigeration
Total cooking time: Nil
Serves 8

2 x 85 g (3 oz) packets red jelly
  crystals
1 cup (250 ml/8 fl oz) brandy or rum
1 cup (250 ml/8 fl oz) milk
2 x 250 g (8 oz) packets thin sponge
  finger biscuits
500 g (1 lb) strawberries, sliced

750 ml (24 fl oz) carton custard
1¼ cups (315 ml/10 fl oz) cream,
  whipped

1 Mix the jelly crystals with 1¾ cups
(440 ml/14 fl oz) of boiling water and
stir to dissolve. Pour into a shallow
tin and refrigerate until the jelly has
just set but is not firm.
2 Combine the brandy and milk in a
dish. Dip half the biscuits in the
brandy mixture then place in a single
layer in a 3-litre glass or ceramic dish.
Spoon half the jelly over the biscuits.
Scatter with half the strawberries and

then half of the custard.
3 Dip the remaining sponge fingers in
the brandy mixture and place evenly
over the custard, followed by the
remaining jelly and custard. Spread the
whipped cream evenly over the
custard and top with the remaining
strawberries. Cover and refrigerate for
4 hours before serving.

NUTRITION PER SERVE
Protein 13 g; Fat 24 g; Carbohydrate 75 g;
Dietary Fibre 2 g; Cholesterol 165 mg;
2570 kJ (615 cal)

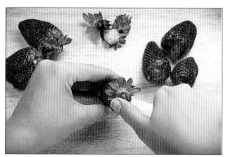

Using a small sharp knife, hull the strawberries
and cut into slices.

Spoon half the jelly over the biscuits before
scattering on half the strawberries.

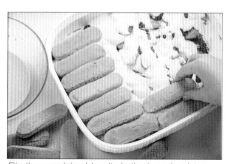

Dip the remaining biscuits in the brandy mixture
and layer evenly over the custard.

CREAMY LIME TART

Preparation time: 30 minutes +
  20 minutes refrigeration
Total cooking time: 1 hour
Serves 12

1¼ cups (155 g/5 oz) plain flour
½ cup (95 g/3 oz) ground almonds
90 g (3 oz) butter, chopped

FILLING
6 egg yolks
½ cup (125 g/4 oz) caster sugar
100 g (3½ oz) butter, melted
⅓ cup (80 ml/2¾ fl oz) lime juice
2 teaspoons finely grated lime rind
2 teaspoons gelatine
½ cup (125 ml/4 fl oz) cream,
  whipped
½ cup (125 g/4 oz) sugar
rind of 4 limes, finely shredded

1 Preheat the oven to 180°C (350°F/ Gas 4). Sift the flour into a large bowl and add the almonds and butter. Rub in the butter until fine and crumbly. Add 1–2 tablespoons cold water and mix to a firm dough, adding more if necessary. Turn out onto a lightly floured surface and roll out to fit a 23 cm (9 inch) fluted flan tin. Trim the edge and refrigerate for 20 minutes.
2 Line with baking paper and beads or dried beans or rice and bake for 20 minutes. Remove the paper and beads and bake the pastry shell for a further 20 minutes, or until lightly golden. Cool completely.
3 To make the filling, put the egg yolks, sugar, butter, lime juice and rind in a heatproof bowl. Whisk together to dissolve the sugar. Place the bowl over a pan of simmering water and stir constantly for 15 minutes, or until thickened. Leave to cool slightly.

4 Put the gelatine and 1 tablespoon water in a small bowl. Leave until spongy, then stir until dissolved. Stir into the lime curd. Cool to room temperature, stirring occasionally.
5 Fold the cream through the lime curd and pour into the pastry case. Refrigerate for 2–3 hours until set, removing 15 minutes before serving. Put the sugar in a small pan with 3 tablespoons water. Stir without boiling until the sugar has completely dissolved. Bring to the boil, add the lime rind and simmer for 3 minutes. Remove the rind and dry on a rack then use to decorate the tart.

NUTRITION PER SERVE
Protein 4 g; Fat 21 g; Carbohydrate 32 g; Dietary Fibre 1 g; Cholesterol 144 mg; 1391 kJ (332 cal)

Blind bake the pastry case, filled with baking paper and baking beads or dried beans.

Mix the gelatine with the water and then stir into the lime curd.

To make the glazed lime rind, simmer the lime for 3 minutes in sugar syrup, then drain on a rack.

GINGER AND LYCHEE JELLY

Preparation time: 10 minutes +
  4 hours setting
Total cooking time: 5 minutes
Serves 6

500 g(1 lb) can lychees
2 cups (500 ml/16 fl oz) clear apple
  juice (no added sugar)
1/3 cup (80 ml/2³/₄ fl oz) strained lime
  juice
2 tablespoons caster sugar
3 x 3 cm (1 x 1 inch) piece fresh
  ginger, peeled and thinly sliced
4 sheets gelatine
fresh mint, to garnish

1 Drain the syrup from the lychees and reserve 1 cup (250 ml/8 fl oz) of the syrup. Place the reserved syrup, apple juice, lime juice, sugar and ginger in a saucepan. Bring to the boil, then simmer for 5 minutes. Strain into a heatproof bowl.
2 Place the gelatine sheets in a large bowl of cold water and soak for 2 minutes, or until they soften. Squeeze out the excess water, then add to the syrup. Stir until dissolved. Leave to cool.
3 Pour 2 tablespoons of jelly into each of six 150 ml (5 fl oz) wine glasses, and divide the lychees among the wine glasses. Refrigerate until the jelly has set. Spoon the remaining jelly over the fruit and refrigerate until set. Garnish with mint leaves.

NUTRITION PER SERVE
Fat 0 g; Protein 1 g; Carbohydrate 31 g;
Dietary Fibre 0.5 g; Cholesterol 0 mg;
530 kJ (125 Cal)

After soaking, squeeze the sheets of gelatine to remove any excess water.

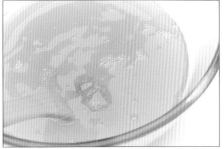

Stir the gelatine sheets into the hot liquid until they have dissolved.

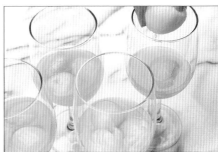

Divide the lychees among the wine glasses, gently dropping them into the jelly.

PAVLOVA

Preparation time: 15 minutes
Total cooking time: 40 minutes
Serves 8

6 egg whites
1¹/₂ cups (375 g/12 oz) caster sugar
1 cup (250 ml/8 fl oz) cream, whipped
125 g (4 oz) strawberries, halved
2 kiwi fruit, peeled and sliced
1 banana, sliced
pulp of 2 passionfruit

1 Preheat the oven to 150°C (300°F/ Gas 2). Line a tray with baking paper and mark with a 22 cm (9 inch) circle. Beat the egg whites until soft peaks form. Gradually beat in the sugar, then beat for several minutes, or until thick and glossy.
2 Spoon the meringue mixture onto the circle on the tray. Smooth the edge and top with a flat-bladed knife.
3 Bake for 40 minutes, or until pale and crisp. Turn off the oven and leave the meringue inside to cool, with the door propped ajar. Just before serving,

spread with cream and top with strawberries, kiwi fruit, banana and passionfruit pulp.

NUTRITION PER SERVE
Protein 3 g; Fat 14 g; Carbohydrate 52 g; Dietary Fibre 1 g; Cholesterol 40 mg; 901 kJ (215 cal)

STORAGE: Pavlova can be made 1 day in advance and stored in an airtight container. Top with cream and fruit just before serving.

Beat the egg whites to soft peaks, then gradually beat in the sugar.

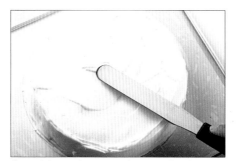

Spread the meringue onto the paper-lined tray, using the circle as a guide.

Just before serving, spread the cooled meringue with the whipped cream.

FRUIT KEBABS WITH CARDAMOM SYRUP

Preparation time: 15 minutes + 1 hour marinating
Total cooking time: 5 minutes
Makes 8 kebabs

¹/₄ small pineapple, peeled
1 peach
1 banana, peeled
16 strawberries

CARDAMOM SYRUP
2 tablespoons honey
30 g (1 oz) butter, melted
¹/₂ teaspoon ground cardamom
1 tablespoon rum or brandy
1 tablespoon soft brown sugar

1 Cut the pineapple into bite-sized pieces. Cut the peach into 8 wedges and slice the banana. Thread all the fruit pieces onto skewers and place in a shallow dish.
2 To make the cardamom syrup, mix together the honey, butter, cardamom, rum and sugar and pour over the kebabs, brushing to coat. Cover and leave the kebabs at room temperature for 1 hour.
3 Cook the kebabs on a hot, lightly oiled barbecue flatplate for 5 minutes. Brush with the syrup during cooking. Serve drizzled with the remaining syrup, topped with ice cream.

NUTRITION PER KEBAB
Protein 1 g; Fat 2 g; Carbohydrate 16 g;
Dietary Fibre 2 g; Cholesterol 6 mg;
376 kJ (90 cal)

Cut the fruit into bite-sized pieces and thread onto the skewers.

Mix together the honey, butter, cardamom, rum and sugar to make the syrup.

Cook the kebabs on a hot barbecue, brushing with the syrup during cooking.

GINGER PEAR CHEESECAKE

Preparation time: 25 minutes + 3 hours refrigeration
Total cooking time: Nil
Serves 8

250 g (8 oz) gingersnap biscuits
2 tablespoons caster sugar
125 g (4 oz) butter, melted

FILLING
1 tablespoon gelatine
375 g (12 oz) cream cheese
1/3 cup (90 g/3 oz) caster sugar

1 tablespoon lemon juice
1 cup (250 ml/8 fl oz) cream, whipped
425 g (14 oz) can pear halves, drained and sliced
2 tablespoons chopped glacé ginger

1 Brush a 20 cm (8 inch) springform tin with melted butter or oil. Chop the biscuits to crumbs in a food processor. Transfer to a bowl, add the sugar and butter and mix well. Press firmly into the tin and refrigerate for 20 minutes.
2 To make the filling, put the gelatine in a small bowl with 3 tablespoons water. Leave until spongy, then stir until dissolved. Beat the cream cheese until softened. Add the caster sugar and beat for 3 minutes. Add the lemon juice and beat until combined. Add a little of this mixture to the gelatine and mix well, then add all the gelatine to the filling mixture. Fold in the whipped cream.
3 Arrange a layer of pear slices on the biscuit crust, then pour over half the filling. Top with another layer of pears and the remaining filling. Refrigerate for 3 hours or until set. Decorate with chopped glacé ginger.

NUTRITION PER SERVE
Protein 6 g; Fat 42 g; Carbohydrate 43 g; Dietary Fibre 1 g; Cholesterol 128 mg; 2372 kJ (567 cal)

Chop the biscuits to crumbs in a food processor (or put in a bag and crush with a rolling pin).

Beat the cream cheese and sugar together and then add the lemon juice.

Arrange layers of pear slices and then the cream cheese filling.

CHOCOLATE MOUSSE FLAN

Preparation time: 35 minutes
Total cooking time: 5 minutes
Serves 10

250 g (8 oz) plain chocolate biscuits,
    finely crushed
125 g (4 oz) butter, melted

FILLING
200 g (6½ oz) dark cooking
    chocolate, chopped
2 tablespoons cream
2 egg yolks
2 teaspoons gelatine
²/₃ cup cream (170 ml/5½ fl oz),
    extra, whipped
2 egg whites

TOPPING
1½ teaspoons instant coffee
1 cup (250 ml/8 fl oz) cream
1 tablespoon caster sugar
cocoa powder, for dusting

1 Brush a 28 cm (11 inch) round
fluted flan tin with melted butter or oil.
Line the base with paper. Mix the
biscuit crumbs and butter and press
into the tin. Refrigerate until firm.
2 To make the filling, put the
chocolate and cream in a small pan.
Stir over low heat until smooth. Cool
slightly, then stir in the yolks. Sprinkle
the gelatine over 1 tablespoon water in
a small bowl and leave until spongy,
then stir. Cool slightly and stir into the
filling. Fold in the whipped cream.
3 Beat the egg whites until soft peaks
form. Fold into the filling and spread
over the biscuit base. Refrigerate until
set. Just before serving, remove from
the tin and spread with the topping.
4 To make the topping, dissolve the
coffee in 3 teaspoons water. Stir in the
cream and sugar. Beat until soft peaks
form, then spread over the flan. Dust
with sifted cocoa powder to serve.

NUTRITION PER SERVE
Protein 6 g; Fat 37 g; Carbohydrate 32 g;
Dietary Fibre 1 g; Cholesterol 158 mg;
1983 kJ (474 cal)

Mix together the biscuit crumbs and melted butter
and press into the tin.

Add the egg yolks to the cooled chocolate and
cream mixture.

Beat the egg whites until soft peaks form and
then fold into the filling.

Just before you are ready to serve, spread the
topping over the flan.

243

COCONUT LIME ICE CREAM

Preparation time: 10 minutes +
  30 minutes freezing
Total cooking time: Nil
Serves 4

1/4 cup (30 g/1 oz) desiccated
  coconut
1 1/2 tablespoons grated lime rind
1/3 cup (80 ml/2 3/4 fl oz) lime
  juice
4 tablespoons coconut milk
  powder
1 litre good-quality vanilla ice cream,
  softened
coconut macaroon biscuits,
  to serve

1 Put the coconut, lime rind, lime juice and coconut milk powder in a bowl and mix together well.
2 Add to the ice cream and fold through with a large metal spoon until evenly incorporated. Work quickly so that the ice cream does not melt. Return the ice cream to the freezer and freeze for 30 minutes to firm. Serve in glasses with coconut macaroons.

NUTRITION PER SERVE
Protein 5 g; Fat 19.5 g; Carbohydrate 19 g;
Dietary Fibre 1.5 g; Cholesterol 30 mg;
1230 kJ (293 cal)

Mix together the desiccated coconut, lime rind, lime juice and coconut milk powder.

Add the coconut mixture to the ice cream and fold in with a large metal spoon.

POACHED DRIED FRUIT WITH WHOLE SPICES

Preparation time: 10 minutes +
  2 hours soaking
Total cooking time: 30 minutes
Serves 8

1 orange
1 lemon
1 cup (250 ml/8 fl oz) apple juice
6 whole cardamom pods, lightly
  crushed
6 whole cloves
1 cinnamon stick
1/2 vanilla bean

375 g (12 oz) packet dried fruit salad
1/2 cup (125 g/4 oz) sugar
3 tablespoons soft brown sugar
1 tablespoon brandy

1 Peel 3 large strips of orange rind, avoiding too much white pith. Peel the lemon rind into thick strips. Cut half the rind into thin strips.
2 Put the apple juice, whole spices and thick strips of rind in a large pan with 3 cups (750 ml/24 fl oz) water and bring to the boil. Add the dried fruit. Remove from the heat and set aside for 2 hours.
3 Return to the heat, add the combined sugars and thin strips of rind and cover. Cook over low heat for 5 minutes, or until soft. Remove the fruit with a slotted spoon. Simmer the juice for another 5 minutes, or until reduced and thickened slightly. Add the brandy. Serve the fruit warm or cold, drizzled with juice.

NUTRITION PER SERVE
Protein 1 g; Fat 0.5 g; Carbohydrate 58 g;
Dietary Fibre 3 g; Cholesterol 0 mg;
994 kJ (237 cal)

STORAGE: This will keep well for at least a week.

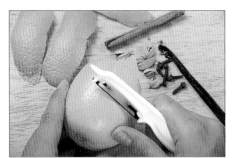

Use a vegetable peeler to remove 3 strips of the orange rind.

Put the apple juice, whole spices and thick strips of rind in a pan with water.

Remove the dried fruit from the poaching syrup with a slotted spoon.

SPICED APPLE SLICE

Preparation time: 25 minutes +
  30 minutes refrigeration
Total cooking time: 55 minutes
Serves 8

750 g (1½ lb) green apples
⅓ cup (90 g/3 oz) sugar
½ teaspoon ground cloves
2 tablespoons lemon juice
1 cup (125 g/4 oz) plain flour
1 cup (125 g/4 oz) self-raising flour
1 teaspoon ground cloves, extra
½ teaspoon ground cinnamon
150 g (5 oz) butter
½ cup (125 g/4 oz) caster sugar
1 teaspoon vanilla essence
1 egg, lightly beaten
1 tablespoon milk
1 tablespoon caster sugar, extra
1 teaspoon ground cinnamon, extra

1 Brush a 20 x 30 cm (8 x 12 inch) shallow tin with oil. Line the base with paper and grease the paper. Preheat the oven to 180°C (350°F/Gas 4). Peel, core and slice the apples and put in a pan with the sugar, cloves and juice. Stir over heat to warm. Cover and simmer, stirring often, for 20 minutes or until soft. Remove from the heat, drain and cool.

2 Sift the flours with the extra cloves and cinnamon. Beat the butter and sugar until light and creamy. Add the vanilla and egg and beat thoroughly. Fold in the flour in batches, mixing after each addition. If the mixture is too dry, add a little milk. Knead gently on a lightly floured surface until smooth. Divide in half, cover with plastic wrap and chill for 30 minutes.

3 Roll out one portion of pastry to fit the tin base. Spread with apple filling. Place the second pastry sheet on top of the filling and press down gently.

4 Brush the top with milk and sprinkle with the extra sugar and cinnamon. Bake for 30 minutes or until golden brown. Leave for 15 minutes, then turn onto a wire rack to cool.

NUTRITION PER SERVE
Protein 5 g; Fat 17 g; Carbohydrate 64 g;
Dietary Fibre 3 g; Cholesterol 72 mg;
1772 kJ (423 cal)

Peel, core and slice the apples and put in a pan with the sugar, cloves and apple juice.

Beat the butter and sugar, then add the vanilla essence and egg.

Line the tray with one of the pastry sheets and spread the filling on top.

Brush the top of the slice with milk and then sprinkle with sugar and cinnamon.

CHOCOLATE MINT ICE CREAM

Preparation time: 25 minutes + freezing
Total cooking time: 10 minutes
Serves 6

1 cup (250 ml/8 fl oz) cream
3 tablespoons chopped fresh mint
100 g (3½ oz) dark chocolate, broken
60 g (2 oz) milk chocolate, broken
2 eggs, lightly beaten
1 tablespoon caster sugar

1 Place the cream and mint in a small pan. Stir over low heat until the cream is almost boiling. Cool slightly. Add the chocolate to the cream. Stir over low heat until the chocolate has melted and the mixture is smooth.
2 Whisk the eggs and sugar in a small bowl until creamy. Gradually add the warm chocolate mixture through a strainer. Discard the mint. Whisk until well combined and then cool.
3 Freeze the mixture in an ice-cream machine according to the manufacturer's instructions. Alternatively, freeze in a metal container until just firm around the edges. Remove from the freezer and beat for 1 minute. Return to the freezer and freeze overnight.

NUTRITION PER SERVE
Protein 5 g; Fat 27 g; Carbohydrate 21 g;
Dietary Fibre 0 g; Cholesterol 118 mg;
1413 kJ (338 cal)

STORAGE: Ice cream can be stored in the freezer for up to 3 weeks.

Bring the cream to boiling point then allow to cool a little and add the chocolate.

Add the warm chocolate mixture slowly, through a strainer, discarding the mint.

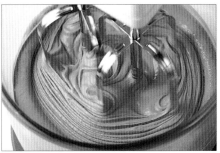
If you don't have an ice-cream machine, freeze the mixture and then beat.

POACHED APPLES WITH CLOVES, MINT AND BASIL

Preparation time: 15 minutes
Total cooking time: 30 minutes
Serves 4

4 large or 6 small green apples
2 tablespoons lemon juice
1/2 cup (125 g/4 oz) sugar
4 whole cloves
4 fresh mint sprigs
6 fresh basil leaves

1 Peel and core the apples and cut into quarters. Put the lemon juice, sugar, cloves and mint in a pan with 625 ml (21 fl oz) water. Stir over low heat without boiling until the sugar dissolves. Bring to the boil.
2 Add the apple to the pan. Cook over low heat, partially covered, for 10 minutes or until the apple is soft but not breaking up. Add the basil. Remove from the heat and set aside until cold.
3 Carefully remove the apple segments from the syrup and place in a bowl. Pour the syrup through a sieve onto the apple. Serve chilled with cream or yoghurt.

NUTRITION PER SERVE
Protein 0.5 g; Fat 0 g; Carbohydrate 51 g; Dietary Fibre 3 g; Cholesterol 0 mg; 834 kJ (199 cal)

STORAGE: Store for up to 4 days in an airtight container in the fridge.

Peel and core the apples and then cut each apple into quarters.

Bring the lemon juice, sugar, cloves, mint and water to the boil and add the apple.

Put the apple in a bowl and then pour the syrup over the top through a sieve.

GRILLED ORANGES WITH CARAMEL MINT BUTTER

Preparation time: 20 minutes
Total cooking time: 20 minutes
Serves 4

6 oranges
1/3 cup (90 g/3 oz) sugar
3 tablespoons cream
45 g (1 1/2 oz) unsalted butter, chopped
2 teaspoons grated orange rind
2 tablespoons finely chopped fresh mint

1 Peel the oranges in a circular motion, cutting only deeply enough to remove all the white membrane. Cut the oranges into thin slices.
2 Place the sugar and 3 tablespoons water in a small pan. Cook over very low heat without boiling until the sugar has dissolved (shake occasionally but do not stir). Increase the heat and bring the syrup to the boil. Cook until deep golden. Remove from the heat and gradually add the cream (the mixture will become lumpy). Return to the heat and stir until the caramel dissolves.
3 Add the butter, orange rind and mint to the pan and whisk until blended. Transfer to a bowl and chill.
4 Preheat the grill. Arrange the orange slices slightly overlapping in a 23 cm (9 inch) round shallow ovenproof dish. Dot with the caramel butter and grill until the butter has melted and the oranges are hot.

NUTRITION PER SERVE
Protein 2 g; Fat 16 g; Carbohydrate 36 g; Dietary Fibre 4 g; Cholesterol 49 mg; 1215 kJ (290 cal)

Peel the oranges, removing the white pith, and then slice thinly.

Cook the sugar and water until the mixture becomes a deep caramel colour.

Add the butter, orange rind and mint to the pan and whisk to blend.

Arrange the orange slices, slightly overlapping, in the dish.

Fruit Ice Blocks

An ideal way to finish off a barbecue, especially if there are hungry children invited, is with a colourful array of fruit ice blocks. You can buy ice block moulds (like ice trays but with separate handles for freezing in the moulds) at supermarkets. All these fruit ice blocks will keep in the freezer for up to 3 weeks (although the mango and raspberry blocks are best eaten the day they are made), but they taste so good it is pretty certain they won't last that long.

PINEAPPLE AND MINT ICE BLOCKS

Purée 500 g (1 lb) fresh pineapple flesh and 10 fresh mint leaves in a blender or food processor until smooth. Sweeten to taste with 1–2 teaspoons caster sugar. Pour the pineapple purée into 6 plastic ice block moulds. Freeze for 30 minutes, add the ice block sticks and return to the freezer. Freeze for a further 2½–3 hours, or until the ice blocks are frozen solid. Makes 6

PEACH AND YOGHURT ICE BLOCKS

Peel and remove the seeds from 6 ripe peaches and purée the flesh in a blender or food processor. Add 2 tablespoons plain yoghurt and mix well. Sweeten to taste with 1–2 teaspoons caster sugar. Pour the mixture into 6 plastic ice block moulds and freeze for 30 minutes. Add the ice block sticks and refreeze for 2½–3 hours, or until the ice blocks are frozen solid. Makes 6

GINGER AND LYCHEE ICE BLOCKS

Combine $1/3$ cup (90 g/3 oz) sugar and 1 cup (250 ml/
8 fl oz) water in a small saucepan. Bring to the boil and stir
over medium heat until the sugar dissolves. Boil for
5 minutes, then remove from the heat and add 1 tablespoon
chopped fresh ginger. Set aside for 10 minutes. Strain into a
bowl, add 1 tablespoon lime juice, cover and chill until cold.
Pour into 4 plastic ice block moulds and freeze for 1 hour.
Add 6 seeded and chopped lychees, add the ice block sticks
and freeze for $2^{1}/_{2}$–3 hours, or until frozen solid. Makes 4

BERRY ICE BLOCKS

Purée 300 g (10 oz) mixed berries in a blender until smooth
(reserving a few berries for decoration if you want). Push
the mixture through a sieve and add 2 teaspoons lemon
juice. Sweeten to taste with icing sugar. Pour the mixture
into 4 or 6 plastic ice block moulds, dropping any reserved
berries into the mixture, and freeze for 30 minutes. Add the
ice block sticks and refreeze for $2^{1}/_{2}$–3 hours, or until the
mixture is frozen solid. Makes 4–6

MANGO AND RASPBERRY ICE BLOCKS

Peel 2 large mangoes and purée the flesh in a blender or
food processor until smooth. Add $1/4$ cup (60 ml/2 fl oz)
orange juice, mix well and pour into 4 or 6 plastic ice block
moulds. Randomly add 4–6 raspberries into each mould as
you fill them. Freeze for 30 minutes, add the ice block sticks
and freeze for a further $2^{1}/_{2}$–3 hours, or until frozen solid.
Makes 4–6

WATERMELON AND KIWI FRUIT
ICE BLOCKS

Purée 300 g (10 oz) seeded watermelon pieces in a food
processor or blender until smooth. Sweeten to taste with
1–2 teaspoons caster sugar. Peel and slice 2 kiwi fruit and
place the slices decoratively on the inside wall of 6 plastic
ice block moulds. Pour the watermelon purée into the
moulds and freeze for 30 minutes. Add the ice block sticks
and freeze for a further $2^{1}/_{2}$–3 hours, or until frozen solid.
Makes 6

Ice blocks, from left: Pineapple and Mint; Peach and Yoghurt; Ginger and Lychee; Berry; Mango and Raspberry, Watermelon and Kiwi Fruit

Index

USEFUL INFORMATION

The recipes in this book were developed using a tablespoon measure of 20 ml. In some other countries the tablespoon is 15 ml. For most recipes this difference will not be noticeable but, for recipes using baking powder, gelatine, bicarbonate of soda, small amounts of flour and cornflour, we suggest that, if you are using the smaller tablespoon, you add an extra teaspoon for each tablespoon.

The recipes in this book are written using convenient cup measurements. You can buy special measuring cups in the supermarket or use an ordinary household cup: first you need to check it holds 250 ml (8 fl oz) by filling it with water and measuring the water (pour it into a measuring jug or a carton that you know holds 250 ml). This cup can then be used for both liquid and dry cup measurements.

Liquid cup measures

$^1/_4$ cup	60 ml	2 fluid oz
$^1/_3$ cup	80 ml	$2^3/_4$ fluid oz
$^1/_2$ cup	125 ml	4 fluid oz
$^3/_4$ cup	180 ml	6 fluid oz
1 cup	250 ml	8 fluid oz

Spoon measures

$^1/_4$ teaspoon	1.25 ml
$^1/_2$ teaspoon	2.5 ml
1 teaspoon	5 ml
1 tablespoon	20 ml

Nutritional Information

The nutritional information given for each recipe does not include any garnishes or accompaniments, such as rice or pasta, unless they are included in specific quantities in the ingredients list. The nutritional values are approximations and can be affected by biological and seasonal variations in foods, the unknown composition of some manufactured foods and uncertainty in the dietary database. Nutrient data given are derived primarily from the NUTTAB95 database produced by the Australian and New Zealand Food Authority.

Oven Temperatures

You may find cooking times vary depending on the oven you are using. For fan-forced ovens, as a general rule, set oven temperature to 20°C lower than indicated in the recipe.

Note: Those who might be at risk from the effects of salmonella food poisoning (the elderly, pregnant women, young children and those suffering from immune deficiency diseases) should consult their GP with any concerns about eating raw eggs.

Alternative names (UK/US)

bicarbonate of soda	—	baking soda
besan flour	—	chickpea flour
capsicum	—	red or green bell pepper
chickpeas	—	garbanzo beans
cornflour	—	cornstarch
fresh coriander	—	cilantro
single cream	—	cream
aubergine	—	eggplant
flat-leaf parsley	—	Italian parsley
hazelnut	—	filbert
minced beef	—	ground beef
plain flour	—	all-purpose flour
polenta	—	cornmeal
prawn	—	shrimp
Roma tomato	—	plum or egg tomato
sambal oelek	—	chilli paste
mangetout	—	snow pea
spring onion	—	scallion
thick cream	—	heavy cream
tomato purée	—	tomato paste
courgette	—	zucchini

Weight

10 g	$^1/_4$ oz	220 g	7 oz	425 g	14 oz
30 g	1 oz	250 g	8 oz	475 g	15 oz
60 g	2 oz	275 g	9 oz	500 g	1 lb
90 g	3 oz	300 g	10 oz	600 g	$1^1/_4$ lb
125 g	4 oz	330 g	11 oz	650 g	1 lb 5 oz
150 g	5 oz	375 g	12 oz	750 g	$1^1/_2$ lb
185 g	6 oz	400 g	13 oz	1 kg	2 lb

Published by Murdoch Books® , GPO BOX 1203, Sydney, NSW 1045, AUSTRALIA
Ferry House, 51–57 Lacy Road, London SW15 1PR, UK

Editor: Jane Price **Designer:** Annette Fitzgerald **Chief Executive:** Mark Smith

National Library of Australia Cataloguing-in-Publication Data. The complete barbecue cookbook. Includes index. ISBN 174045 041 8 1 74045 098 1 (pbk) Barbecue Cookery 641.5784 Printed by Toppan Printing Hong Kong Co. Ltd. PRINTED IN CHINA.

Reprinted 2001